Farewel

Free Love

Keeping the ownership dream alive during global and personal crises

By Tony Linnett

Portrait of Free Love, oil on canvas, painted by Sara Miller

i

For Jennie Linnett, my lifelong love, inspiration and best friend. May this book bring her comfort and joy when I am no longer able to laugh with her.

I would like to thank the following for their generous help:

Cover illustration: Shamar Bennett Skepple
Cover design: Jennie Linnett and Vanessa Burton
Proof reading: Emma Turtle, Peter and Siobhan Linnett, and Michael Purves

First published May 2023

ISBN 9798391651871

Also by the author:

A Year of Free Love
Another Year of Free Love

Contents

Foreword by Bob Champion   iv
Author's note   v

PART I
1   Epiphany   1
2   Black Type   6
3   Getting Ready to Roll   11
4   Storm Clouds Gather   23
5   Lockdown   37
6   Green Shoots   56
7   Back in Business   68
8   Blown Off Course   92
9   The Ecstasy and the Agony   103
10   Yorkshire Pudding   121
11   Fade to Grey   137
12   When the Going Gets Soft   148
13   End Game   170
14   Promised Land   191
PART II
1   Here We Go Again   204
2   Road Trip   236
3   Here Comes the Summer   249
4   False Step   260
5   Bolt from the Blue   274
6   A Leap in the Dark   283
7   The End of the Affair   302
8   Last Word   318

Foreword

Farewell to Free Love is an honest, informative and thoroughly enjoyable account of a journey in shared racehorse ownership during some of the most challenging times our sport has faced in living memory. Add to that the author's shocking, out of the blue diagnosis – something I can relate to only too well – and the simple task of gaining enjoyment from owning a cheaply bought sprinter must have felt impossible at times.

Nevertheless, Tony Linnett describes in vivid and entertaining detail how the racing show managed to keep itself on the road during a global pandemic. This enthralling book captures the essence of racing, and the value of friendship in a sport where there are plenty of lows along with exhilarating highs.

This is a great read for the racing fan, with so many familiar names and places mentioned along the way. However, it is its lively and optimistic tone will also be appreciated by the uninitiated.

Bob Champion CBE
Grand National winning jockey
President of the Bob Champion Cancer Trust

Author's note

This is not a book about the pandemic. It is a story about the highs and lows of shared racehorse ownership on a budget. It was always my intention to write a third and final instalment following the publication of two earlier books. It is merely an unhappy coincidence that the backdrop to events was the Covid-19 catastrophe, and an equally catastrophic health diagnosis for myself.

However, in some strange way I'm glad I've recorded my horse racing experiences during such troubled times. As I tackled the final proofing stage, I was struck by the surreal nature of what I had written: racing behind closed doors, masks and social distancing, temperature checks and vaccination passports at the entry gate, owner zones, incomprehensible tiers, and the rule of six. Did these things really happen? They seem to belong to another time and place.

Farewell to Free Love describes the final leg of an exhilarating ownership journey. More than anything, it captures my enthusiasm for the sport and my love of the thoroughbred racehorse; more accurately my love for a particular thoroughbred racehorse.

Finally, I have a plea for anyone reading this book who loves their racing and dreams of getting into ownership one day. Do it! Pick a model you can afford and just do it. It's almost impossible to describe the intensity of the racehorse ownership experience with its intoxicating peaks and heart-breaking troughs, but it's what I've tried to do in this book. I leave it to you, the reader, to judge if I've succeeded in some modest way.

Tony Linnett
February 2023

In aid of the Bob Champion Cancer Trust

PART I

1 Epiphany

Monday 6th January 2020

I enjoy my trips to the recycling centre. That might be over-egging it, but I've come to embrace the little ritual involved with every visit. I used to display mild impatience when stopped at the entrance by the staff who check that cars have a valid local resident sticker, and the occupants know where to dump their rubbish.

'Morning. I've got a load of old wood.'

'That goes with the wood. Bay five mate.'

After a while the irritation of being told that the cardboard goes in the cardboard bay, and the metal in the metal bay, dissipated and my encounters became more nuanced and playful.

'I've got an old wooden fence panel and some garden waste.'

After a pause to sum up this more complex situation, I would receive my instructions.

'Right. The wooden panel with the wood in bay five, and the garden waste with the garden waste in bay eight mate'

Today's visit was to get rid of the tree that had twinkled in the corner of the lounge for the last fortnight. I'm a bit set in my ways when it comes to Christmas. I'm not a fan of lights and decorations going up in November and, even worse, coming down the day after Boxing Day. It's a bit of a household tradition that the tree is taken down on the feast of the Epiphany, celebrated the day after twelfth night.

I mused on the passing of another year as I hurled the sorry

1

looking Nordic Spruce into its final resting place. It had been some year as far as the Free Love story was concerned. Our filly, along with the flat turf season, was in a period of hibernation. The Racing Post was all about Cheltenham. Would Envoi Allen run in the Champion Hurdle? Should the festival be extended to five days? We were clearly in the heart of winter, but the memory of Free Love's dazzling early summer form was still fresh in my mind and her return to full training was tantalisingly near.

After her thirteenth and final race of the season at Southwell in mid-November, we decided to repeat last year's trick of giving our sprinting superstar a little break. She was put out to grass and was happily mooching around a field at Castle View Stud near Oakham. Some folk fly to the other side of the world for their winter breaks. In Free Love's case, it was less than five minutes in a horsebox from her home at Mick Appleby's Langham yard to where she would spend her ten-week holiday.

The plan was to bring her back into training at the beginning of February and, like last year, be fit and ready for an early season campaign. Last April, Free Love roared into life with two emphatic wins from her first two starts. By the end of the season, her three victories and three placed efforts meant that there was no need to top up our racing account. I didn't anticipate asking the boys for another £500 payment until the beginning of March.

It was still a hand-to-mouth ownership experience, and the plan was to send Free Love to the July sales unless everyone agreed to carry on. We all wanted to have another full season, almost certainly our final one, but it all depended on Free Love recapturing the early season verve she had shown in the spring. If she threw in some weak efforts at the start of the campaign which saw her official rating slip into the low seventies, and we were faced with shelling out over two grand a month to keep the show on the road, I would have to accept that the majority vote would be for selling up.

On the way back from the dump I turned over the options. Our filly had been a real success story. What we thought might be one season of fun in small races at lowly courses, had turned into four wins in a 25-race career that spanned two seasons. Free Love had taken us to Sandown, Haydock, Doncaster and York, and her current rating of 83 suggested that more visits to grade one tracks were on the cards.

Despite her successes - last season's £25k prize money haul put Free Love in the top 10% of equine earners for the year - the five owners who made up the North South Syndicate had ploughed over eight grand each into their dream of racehorse ownership since that bright autumn morning in October 2017 when lot 1383 ambled into the sales ring at Tattersalls, and we agreed a sum of 10,000 guineas for the bay daughter of Peace And Love.

The original budget was £6,000 each. That was bust by August of our first season, by which time Free Love had run seven times without getting her head in front and had a modest official rating of 63. An unsuccessful final campaign could cost us another four or five grand each before we sold up for buttons in the autumn, so it was prudent to have the July sale as a finishing point if things didn't go our way in 2020.

The truth is, I didn't want the ride to stop. I was sure that we couldn't afford to breed from Free Love ourselves and the long-term plan was to enter her for next December's breeding stock sale where a small stud would hopefully purchase her as a broodmare. With her modest pedigree and decent but far from spectacular racing record, we wouldn't make a fortune, but we'd get some of our money back.

More importantly, I could track Free Love's offspring. I could still be involved in a vicarious way. It was the idea of selling our filly to somebody who would continue to race her that elicited pangs of dread. I couldn't bear that.

When I arrived home from the dump, my wife Jennie had already finished packing away the nativity figures, card holders, lights and other yuletide paraphernalia into several large plastic boxes that live under the eaves of our loft conversion. The lounge looked spacious and bare, and I experienced a momentary tinge of sadness, redolent of my childhood. I remembered how it used to feel when something that had been so eagerly anticipated was gone, and its return seemed so impossibly distant.

My misty-eyed sentimentality was short-lived as there were plenty of jobs to be done. Until a couple of years ago, one of them would have been to prepare a barnstorming assembly for the first day of the spring term which quite often fell on the feast of the Epiphany, or close to it.

It was always a challenge to find something new and fresh to say about the start of a new year. I did nearly two decades as a primary school head and, by the time I retired, I had long since resolved never to talk about New Year resolutions ever again in my first assembly back after the Christmas break. It was a depressing experience reminding young Josh or Jason that their resolution to 'be good', which they had so freely volunteered only a few hours earlier, hadn't been sustained during a bad-tempered football match during the first morning break of the new calendar year.

I felt on safer ground with the Epiphany, which commemorates the visit of the Wise Men to the infant Jesus in Bethlehem. At least it meant I had a story to tell. Narrative works with young children. It trumps highbrow philosophy any day of the week.

The real challenge was to help young primary school children understand the meaning of the word 'epiphany'. Telling them it's a moment of sudden revelation or realisation was bound to produce blank stares. Difficult words and sentences usually needed rephrasing or explaining in simpler language. Throw in a bit of skilful questioning, and I might be able to get the sea of young faces before me to understand how the child of a humble carpenter revealed himself as a special person through the gifts offered by three mysterious visitors from the East.

But sometimes it's best to root the teaching in everyday experience. As I pushed the plastic boxes under the eaves it occurred to me that if I was still in the business of presenting primary school assemblies, maybe I would have plumped to illustrate the meaning of 'epiphany' through the exploits of Free Love. Perhaps I'd ask the front row of puzzled five-year-olds what they thought Free Love revealed herself to be when she won the *Class 3 Download The Marathonbet App Handicap* at Windsor last July and in doing so achieved a BHA rating of 90.

Maybe a few hands would go up and I might even get a tentative answer. 'Did she show herself as being black type material, Mr Linnett?' It was just a thought.

2 Black Type

Saturday 25th January 2020

Black type. We just needed one tiny piece, achieved, perhaps, in a pattern race backwater. Italy, Belgium or even somewhere remote in Scandinavia. It wouldn't really matter where we pinched it - and with a filly rated in the mid-eighties, it would be something close to theft - so long as the sales catalogue showed a scrap of bold print on the top line:

"**Free Love (GB) won** 4 races at 2 and 3 years and placed 12 times including third in the Premio Spaghetti Carbonara, Capannelle **L**".

When I fell in love with racing as a green teenager in the mid-1970s, I didn't know the significance of black type. It was just another piece of racing jargon bandied about by the likes of Julian Wilson and Jimmy Lindley during the BBC's arcane coverage of Royal Ascot or Glorious Goodwood. 'With her pedigree, connections will be keen to get some black type for this filly, and today might be her chance,' would be a typical observation as the horses milled behind the stalls before the start of a prestigious race.

Sure, I knew there were various categories of races, and all horses had to start somewhere. They usually started in contests confined to youngsters, or for animals who had yet to manage a win of any description. After three runs they were eligible for handicaps. It didn't take me long to get to grips with all of that.

It took me a bit longer to twig that better class races, which include the ones known even to those who pride themselves on their ignorance of horseracing – the 2,000 Guineas, the Epsom Derby and so on – are part of the European Pattern Race system which was introduced in 1971. All the major horseracing jurisdictions managed to agree an annual calendar or 'pattern' of top races, which avoided own goals such as running the French Derby on the same weekend as the Epsom showcase.

By the age of eighteen I understood the set up, and I knew that a horse achieved black type by being placed in one of the top races which was listed in the pattern race schedule. But what that meant remained a mystery to me for some years to come.

It was only much later that I became aware that the likes of Tattersalls and Goffs, two of the biggest equine auction houses on the planet, printed pedigrees in their sales catalogues that showed a win or place at pattern race level in bold type. For a filly, securing that third-placed position in even the humblest listed race, was a significant boost to their value as a potential broodmare.

But it wasn't the financial value that was important. For me, it was as much about the kudos of owning a filly who had achieved black type. Our small ownership group started off with a cheap yearling who won a little race at Catterick towards the end of her two-year-old career which allowed us to keep the dream alive for a little longer. Free Love's first season yielded one win and a few places from twelve runs. But she was improving and started her winter rest with an official rating of 74. By the following July, she had won three of her first five races and her mark had soared to 90 thanks to a tenacious victory in a useful class 3 handicap at Windsor.

Perhaps we should have gone all out for black type after that win. Listed races restricted to fillies and mares are often quite weakly contested, and horses rated in the high eighties to low nineties frequently crop up in the first three home. They rarely win, but that didn't matter. Scrambling into third place meant a fragment of bold print on the pedigree page which would attract the interest - and cash - of plenty of breeders.

If you want an illustration of the value of listed race form and how lucrative it can be in the sales ring, look no further than Free Love's old galloping companion, Gypsy Spirit. When our filly was with Tom Clover and being readied for her racecourse debut, some of her last pieces of work on the Newmarket gallops were done upsides a cheaply bought Gregorian filly secured by Tom the day after he had helped us to buy Free Love.

I was later to discover that Tom's wife to be, Jackie Jarvis, took a shine to the bay filly whose pedigree was ordinary looking even by Tattersalls Book 3 standards. They purchased the yearling for 6,000 guineas. She won on debut at Windsor but failed to get her head in front on the next 18 occasions. However, 13 of those were in listed races where she was placed five times over distances ranging from six furlongs to a mile. Her black type roll of honour is made up of heroic near misses at Dusseldorf, Chantilly, Maisons-Laffitte, Ayr and Ripon. She did all that without exceeding an official rating of 95, a mark within touching distance for Free Love.

Gypsy Spirit amassed over £73k in prize money and, when she went through the ring at the Tattersalls broodmare sale in December 2019, the auctioneer's hammer finally fell when the electronic display board registered 160,000 guineas.

It wasn't too late for Free Love to join the party and I hadn't given up on the prospect of listed race glory even if the other boys thought our chance had gone. If you looked, it was easy enough to unearth evidence of modestly rated fillies making the frame in weak pattern races restricted to their own gender. I did some trawling and found out that Futoon (84) was runner-up in the Lansdown Stakes at Bath in 2017. Two years before that it was Holly Shiftwell's (83) turn to gate-crash the black type party when she too was runner-up. What my digging seemed to prove was that although fillies rated in the mid-eighties rarely win listed races - excepting those who are lightly raced and on a serious upward curve – they regularly pop up in the first three, and sometimes they are just useful, genuine handicappers. Why shouldn't one of them be Free Love?

I turned my attention away from listed race research to look at what was going on in the real world. The Racing Post headline confirmed that all roads lead to Cheltenham. The annual jumping festival was only seven weeks away and several big race contenders were putting their reputations on the line in the trials taking place at the Gloucestershire course that afternoon.

That's what I love about racing. There's always something exciting on the horizon, the next great event is never far away. The racing year has a wonderful pattern of its own. Cheltenham finishes, and once Aintree is out of the way, full attention turns to the start of the flat turf season. By early June, the first four British Classics have been run and we've found out if any of those promising juveniles have grown up to be winners of the Guineas, Oaks or Derby.

In the height of summer, championship races for all ages over a variety of distances take place at Royal Ascot, Glorious Goodwood and York. Spectacular displays from two-year-olds prompt excited talk of next year's Classics. And by the time the St Leger and Arc de Triomphe have been run, we're deep into autumn, the National Hunt season has begun in earnest, and all roads lead to Cheltenham.

I've often thought that the best time to die would be immediately after Royal Ascot. It's just a whimsical thought I've had from time to time. I'm not sure I've ever asked a fellow racing enthusiast for their thoughts on the subject. 'From a purely horseracing perspective, at what point of the year would you choose to die?'

It's hardly a good icebreaker at a party either, or a subject of conversation to lift the spirits of a sombre gathering in the pub following a disastrous afternoon of punting at York (and there have been a few of those). 'Now,' might be the unhesitating response in such circumstances. But there's a certain logic in choosing the end of June, just after Ascot, when lots of things have been decided but far too early to be thinking about next year's Classics, never mind the Cheltenham Festival.

I suppose my flippant thoughts about death and the racing calendar are about seeing things through. We all want the satisfaction of completion. In the short-term it might be a project at work or in the home. It could be modest in scope or terrifyingly ambitious. For many, playing a longer game, it's seeing their children grow up into happy, independent adults. Who wants to leave this world with significant unfinished business?

I wouldn't describe the non-acquisition of black type for Free Love as significant unfinished business. In truth, it fitted more snugly into the terrifyingly ambitious bracket. Whether we went for it or not during the coming season wasn't that important. What really mattered was the chance to have one final roll of the dice with our little filly. Another dozen runs would do. Maybe there would be a win and, for one last time, I'd experience that surge of adrenalin when Free Love started what looked like a winning run, quickly followed by the wave of exhilaration that comes when your horse crosses the winning line ahead of all the others.

I was mesmerised by the whole experience and couldn't wait for Free Love's return to the gallops at Langham, and for spring to herald the beginning of a new flat season.

3 Getting Ready to Roll

Wednesday 29th January 2020

I received a couple of nice photos of Free Love from the Mackleys at Castle View Stud. I had hoped to make a visit during our filly's winter break but wasn't sure how visitors would be received. When you go as an owner to a racing stable it's usually possible to make sure that the visit coincides with a piece of exercise. It might only be a canter, but you see your horse in action and have a chance afterwards to pat a warm, moist slab of neck muscle as they are held by the work rider who tells you with great confidence that 'she went really well.'

It's a close-up, visceral experience. There are opportunities for pictures and a chat with your trainer who listens patiently while you babble on about the hopes you have for the coming season. I love it. It's one of the great joys of ownership.

I couldn't see how I would get the same buzz from visiting Free Love in her winter quarters. I imagined a bemused Anne Mackley pointing to a distant corner of a field and saying, 'She's the one in the brown rug standing next to the big tree.'

Instead of trying to arrange a visit during the short, dark days of mid-winter, I asked the Mackleys if they could take a couple of pictures of Free Love and WhatsApp them to me so I could share them with the others. The filly looked in decent shape. She had been on a pre-training regime for the last fortnight in readiness for her return to Mick Appleby's yard. I'm not sure what that entailed. Perhaps a bit more exercise and a little more feed. Whatever it was, she looked good on it, staring brightly into camera, her vibrant skin condition captured in the winter sun.

Free Love was due back at Langham on Monday, giving Mick the same amount of time as he had last year to prepare the filly for an early season campaign. While I wouldn't describe our sprinter as small, she's neat and doesn't carry much condition. She's always been an enthusiastic worker as well, so it was reasonable to assume that she might be more ready than most to give her best when the season was young. Two wins before the end of April 2019 seemed to confirm that view.

It would be harder this time, though. When Free Love reappeared last spring, it turned out that she had improved and was clearly a well-handicapped horse. She scooted up on debut at Nottingham off a mark of 74 and followed up in a six-runner handicap at the same course three weeks later defying a 7lbs rise in the ratings.

In about ten weeks she would be back in action trying to overcome a mark of 83, but that didn't look too dauting to me. After all, she won at Windsor off 86, but during a tough autumn campaign which featured unplaced efforts in good company, sometimes on unsuitably soft ground, the handicapper took pity and our filly's rating slid downwards, pound by pound, to a resting place of 83.

Nevertheless, there was good reason to be optimistic about our third season, which would almost certainly be our last. If Free Love improved just 5lbs for her winter break and moved back into the high eighties, valuable handicaps were back on the agenda. So was black type.

Thursday 30th January 2020

I pinged the pictures of Free Love to the others which prompted an excited conversation about plans for a stable visit. The more mundane matter of funding also needed attention. I decided it was time to send everyone a brief financial update:

Gents

Hope you are all well. This is just a quick reminder of what we agreed about the money needed to get us through to the July horses in training sale which is the next milestone in our journey.

I attach a summary of where we are. Basically, we each need to put £1,500 into the account but this can be done in three stages with the first £500 payment due on or before 1st March.

It looks like Wednesday 25th March is shaping up for the stable visit, which should be within two or three weeks of FL's seasonal debut providing her preparation goes smoothly. I think it's just Trevor who's yet to say whether he can make it

I won't contact Mick until the beginning of March when I'll just touch base to make sure all is going according to plan. At that point I'll let him know about the intended visit on the 25th.

I think that's all. Here's hoping for another successful season with our flying filly.

Regards Tony

If Free Love completely bombed-out in her first few races and her handicap mark spiralled downwards toward 70, a July fire sale would be inevitable. However, it was something that I was keen to avoid. A lowly rated, out of form filly who had just missed the breeding season which finishes in the first week of July, wouldn't be the most enticing proposition for buyers at the Tattersalls horses in training sale. We'd be lucky to get £5k. There would also be the disappointment of our ownership journey ending in such an abrupt and anticlimactic way.

It would be far better to continue to the end of the season and sell the filly to somebody who was looking for a broodmare for their small stud. Whatever Free Love did in 2020, she'd still have four wins to her name and a respectable highest rating of 90. Those achievements couldn't be taken away from her whatever she did this year.

Monday 3rd February 2020

I returned from a fabulous break in Trieste to discover that everyone was happy with the financial arrangements. It was Jennie's birthday last week and our trip to northern Italy was a repeat of the surprise visit we made as a family for her 60th last year.

This time around it was just the two of us, joined by fellow Free Lover Peter Smith and his wife Melanie. I've lost count of the number of great holidays and short breaks we've had with my old university pal, Pete, and his fun-loving partner, Melanie. They're always up for a trip to somewhere different and Ryan Air's ridiculously low fares sealed the deal for Pete who can be painfully careful with his money. Had I suggested Chernobyl and the price was right, Pete would be there.

We had another motive for a return visit to Trieste. When last there, I noticed that Venice was only a two-hour jaunt on the train. One of the attractions of going back so soon was the opportunity to make a daytrip to a city regarded as one of the wonders of the modern world.

Pete and Melanie had been before, so we left them to explore Trieste in the rain while Jennie and I headed towards the drier weather of Venice. It wasn't Jennie's first visit, but she was in her teens the last time she had walked through the intricate and bewildering maze of streets traversing the city's canals.

I was genuinely excited at the prospect of seeing Venice in the flesh. It must be one of the most photographed and painted locations on the planet, but none of those images was a preparation for the sight that confronted me when we walked out of the Stazione di Venezia Santa Lucia. The Grand Canal was barely twenty yards in front of me, and across the water a pewter sky hung above the imposing pale green cupola of the San Simeone Piccolo. A handful of small water taxis and gondoliers glided languorously on the lifeless water. I had walked into a Canaletto painting.

I adored Venice. For lunch we had a glass of Refosco and a snack in a small bar full of gregarious and animated locals. Afterwards we strolled through the city, crossing small bridges at every turn, seemingly lost until we stumbled onto a large piazza, home to the magnificent, gilded domes of Saint Mark's Basilica.

The square, like the rest of the city, was only moderately busy, but it was obvious that even in the depths of winter it attracted visitors from all over the world. With a new virus spreading rapidly in Wuhan, the Chinese contingent seemed down in numbers, but there was still a smattering of mask-wearing tourists who had gone ahead with their plans despite growing problems at home.

We did all the things that tourists are meant to do. We paid to explore the interior of the Basilica, wandered around the Doge's Palace, gawped at the Bridge of Sighs, and wearily traipsed over the Ponte di Rialto on our way back to the railway station. Wherever we walked, we seemed to be part of a small stream of humanity ebbing and flowing over narrow streets and tiny bridges. If this was quiet, I shuddered to think what Venice must be like in the summer. Somewhere to avoid, I imagine.

Thursday 6th February 2020

It was Sidney Banks Memorial Hurdle day at Huntingdon and an opportunity to go racing with Trevor. The race, named after a local trainer, has an impressive roll of honour. Grand Canyon was the winner of the inaugural contest in 1976, and perhaps the best horse to capture the prize. The front-running New Zealand-bred gelding broke track records for fun and was twice victorious in the prestigious Colonial Cup, one of America's top jumping prizes.

It was the usual chat as we drove up a fairly quiet M11. Trevor is the busiest member of the North South Syndicate and the hardest one to pin down. He's a few years younger than the rest of us and being the vicar of Christ Church Bexleyheath is a full-on, full-time job. I was really pleased he was able to make it as it was a chance to catch up with what was going on in our lives, in between talking horses.

Trevor was optimistic about the coming season and was keen to make a stable visit next month by which time Free Love would be back in fast work. Wednesday 25th March was looking like the firm favourite. That was the corresponding date of last year's trip to Langham which took place exactly a fortnight before Free Love made her winning reappearance at Nottingham. I'm not superstitious, but there was a pleasing symmetry about our filly's preparations. We'd be quite happy for history to repeat itself.

Huntingdon experienced the type of bright February afternoon that made you jump the gun and think that spring was within touching distance. Nicky Henderson's Shishkin sauntered away with the feature race prompting feverish speculation that not only was the Supreme Novices Hurdle at Cheltenham within his grasp, but maybe greatness as well.

On the way home, the early evening news on Radio Four was the usual indigestible diet of Brexit, Donald Trump's impeachment, and China's efforts to halt the coronavirus outbreak, which only recently had been declared a global emergency by the World Health Organization.

At least we had the prospect of a stable visit and a new flat season to look forward to. Racing was famously described as a 'magnificent triviality' by the renowned journalist, Hugh McIlvanney. In turn, he modestly attributed the quote to Timeform's Phil Bull. Whoever coined the phrase was spot on. We all need a bit of escapism, a chance to dwell in another world, if only briefly. Roll on next month,

I thought to myself, as we sailed over the Queen Elizabeth II Bridge on the way home to Dartford. The good times were near at hand.

Saturday 15th February 2020

Spring clearly wasn't in touching distance. It was the filthiest of mornings when I clambered onto a sparsely occupied train at Crayford. Up until an hour beforehand, I was certain that I wouldn't be making the journey to Ascot. The rain had fallen steadily all night and I was sure that the early morning inspection would lead to the inevitable abandonment of the meeting.

As soon as the unexpected go ahead was given, I exchanged messages with my old racing pal, Ronan, and agreed a meeting time. He was driving up from Bristol. The warmth of the car was an obvious choice given the atrocious weather and his intention to stay dry.

The weather didn't relent, and Ronan and I made only the briefest of visits to the parade ring for one or two races. We forced ourselves to steal a glance at Cyrname, the highest-rated chaser in the UK and favourite for the feature race, the Grade 1 *Betfair Ascot Chase*.

Cyrname had been beaten out of sight by his stablemate, Clan Des Obeaux, in the King George on Boxing Day, and I was among those who regarded his lofty rating with some suspicion. True, the Kempton showpiece was over three miles, but he was beaten a long way and the handicapper's official assessment of his ability seemed to rest on one piece of outstanding form at Ascot.

Back at the Berkshire track and down in trip, I had no quibble with Cyrname's prohibitively short price. He was long odds-on to dispose of his three rivals, and the large crowd which had braved the driving rain to see him in action expected nothing less than an exhibition round of jumping and a facile victory.

We all know there's no such thing as a certainty in racing -

excepting the arrival of the monthly training invoice. When the race started, Cyrname was immediately taken to the front by Harry Cobden, which is often how the horse is ridden. But with three to jump it was obvious that he was toiling in the stamina-sapping ground. Two out, he was headed and beaten, looking destined for no better than third place. With the race at his mercy, Gary Moore's Traffic Fluide crashed out at the last, handing the spoils to the appropriately named Riders Onthe Storm (sic). An exhausted Cyrname barely took off at the final obstacle where he also fell heavily.

While Traffic Fluide struggled to his feet and cantered away unharmed, all eyes were on Cyrname who lay motionless on the landing side of the final fence. The screens were quickly erected and racegoers either stood in the rain or pressed their faces to the glass windows of the grandstand, hoping for a miracle.

It didn't look good. It was an exhausted, juddering fall. I've seen plenty of horses stay down for minutes when winded by a late nose-dive at a fence or hurdle, but Cyrname hit the ground awkwardly, sprawling sideways on his neck. It didn't look good at all.

You always hope in these situations that, no matter how horrific it looked, the horse might just be winded, and a huge appreciative roar will be heard when the animal staggers to his feet, weary but unharmed. I think most of the racegoers were resigned to the worst when at last some figures appeared and started rolling up the screens. But instead of being greeted by the sight of a wretched empty patch of turf, there stood a bedraggled but unscathed Cyrname. He got the biggest roar of the day.

It was another reminder of why I have gravitated towards flat racing over the years. I don't think my nerves would be up to owning a jumper. I'd watch every race through the cracks of my fingers. I know fatal accidents can happen during contests on the level – they can even happen when cantering on the gallops or ambling around a field – but it's much less likely on the flat.

We spent most of the afternoon tucked away on the unoccupied top floor of the King Edward stand, where we found a neglected table and a pair of comfortable leather armchairs that became our base for the day. One of my rare forays away from our camp was to seek out Rupert Mackeson.

I knew Rupert as the gent who sold racing books and prints at the likes of Epsom and Sandown. I don't think I've ever passed a word with him during my occasional and fleeting visits to his stall. From time to time, I would admire an expensive print and promise myself to buy it if I won a small fortune that afternoon. Sadly, I was never required to rush back to Rupert to fulfil my pledge.

I was taken by surprise when Sir Rupert (a hereditary title courtesy of the baronetcy bestowed on his father, Sir Harry, for his work in politics) contacted me via Facebook Messenger. It was a harmless enough enquiry about my wellbeing but, as I had recently self-published *A Year of Free Love,* I thought it might be something to do with the book. I had already made up my mind that I wanted to talk to Rupert about the possibility of him selling my publication via his mobile shop, so his communication was timely. I made him aware that I would be at Ascot and hoped to speak to him about the matter if he was planning to attend.

There was no reply, which I took to mean that Rupert wouldn't send his dog out in the appalling weekend weather, let alone contemplate setting up a book stall. When I went in search of him on the ground floor of the enormous grandstand, I didn't have high hopes of finding him. Yet there he was, sat surrounded by tables of racing books.

'Hello Rupert. It's Tony Linnett. I sent you a message about my book,' I opened cheerfully. Rupert looked blankly at me, offering no response.

'You got in touch with me on Facebook Messenger,' I continued doggedly. There was a pause but no sign that Rupert had any idea what I was talking about. A flicker of enlightenment was followed by a bald statement of fact.

'My Facebook account has been hacked.'

We ended up swapping email addresses and I promised to send him some details about the book. He could then make up his mind if he wanted to stock and sell it. Rather foolishly, I didn't bring a copy with me to Ascot, but my oversight might have been a blessing in disguise. I'm not sure what soggy state it would have been in by the time I handed it over to Rupert.

The incessant rain and swirling wind didn't stop me and Ronan from enjoying our day at the races. We even managed to find a winner or two, which always helps. It was a shame that the hideous conditions prevented us from taking advantage of Ascot's magnificent facilities. It wasn't a day for strolling down to the pre-parade ring and having a leisurely drink or two in some of the racecourse's many bars. That, we agreed, would have to wait for the summer when Free Love was back in action.

4 Storm Clouds Gather

Wednesday 26th February 2020

The front page of the Racing Post led with a couple of upbeat items. In one, readers were informed of an exclusive interview with Richard Thompson, owner of big Cheltenham Festival hopes Envoi Allen and A Plus Tard. In the other, a beaming James Frank held aloft the employee of the year trophy, presented to him at the Godolphin Stud and Staff Awards night. But below these two rosy stories lurked a headline of a completely different hue. 'coronavirus on racing's radar with Cheltenham 13 days away.'

Like everyone else, I had been following the progress of the outbreak. At first, Wuhan seemed a long way away, as did the prospect of the virus having much of an impact on life at home. That all changed when clusters of cases were detected in the Lombardy and Veneto regions of Northern Italy on February 21st, with the first deaths reported a day later. That was a shade over three weeks since we were in Venice.

Grim pictures of Italian hospitals struggling to cope with huge influxes of patients became a regular feature of the evening news. A growing awareness of the spread of the virus had entered our living rooms, and soon it would be the virus itself that was here, according to the epidemiologists tracking its inexorable advance.

The RP article stated that the British Horseracing Authority, Racecourse Association and Horsemen's Group had already met to consider the implications of the growing health crisis on the sport. The Italian government had put in place emergency measures designed to halt the spread of the disease and these included restrictions on large gatherings. The impact on sport was already evident. Last Sunday's women's Six Nations rugby international between Italy and Scotland had been cancelled at short notice.

Cheltenham was less than a fortnight away and around a quarter of a million racegoers were expected to attend jump racing's four-day jamboree. The virus wasn't present in the UK yet, but what was, until recently, something that was taking place in distant lands was now in our backyard.

I can't say that I was unduly worried about what might happen next, but that says more about me than anything else. My optimism often gets the better of me. I rarely let experience triumph over hope. We'd all be fine. I was sure that everything would soon blow over. In any event, as far as the UK was concerned, it wasn't even here yet.

Monday 2nd March 2020
We were met with glorious sunshine when we arrived at Chartwell House in Kent, the family home of Sir Winston Churchill. It was one of those days which defies neat categorization. The snowdrops and crocuses were in bloom, but the trees on the estate's gently rolling hills were weeks away from bursting into hazy, green foliage. It was either late winter or early spring, depending on your mood.

Jennie was working a seven-day fortnight for her charity which recruits, trains and deploys volunteers who visit and befriend senior citizens in South London. They all live on their own and are appreciative of the contact that Link Age Southwark provides. It was one of her days off and we decided on a trip to Chartwell, a local place of historic interest that neither of us could remember visiting before, although I have a vague recollection of going there as a child.

If I had been previously, all vestiges of memory had been expunged. I didn't recognise a single brick of the building. Nothing was familiar, including the emphasis on hygiene and social distancing. The latter term was beginning to be heard more and more in the context of strategies employed to combat the spread of coronavirus.

We were required to book a timed ticket to the house in advance to ensure that numbers inside were limited. It made for an uncrowded and fascinating tour. There's no doubt that Churchill was a remarkable man, revered for his leadership during the Second World War. He was also a prolific and talented writer as well as an accomplished artist.

The final room attempted the inevitable reassessment of the man and drew the visitor's attention to the controversy surrounding the bombing of Dresden, and the questionable nature of Churchill's views on imperialism and race. I have no doubt that Sir Winston will be seen as an increasingly divisive figure as the years and decades pass.

But whichever way the final judgement goes, if indeed a definitive one can ever be made, we can surely agree that anyone who gets involved in racehorses can't be all bad. Churchill owned a few and his best was the grey mare, Colonist II, who was a prolific winner. She can include the Jockey Club Cup and Ribblesdale Stakes among her notable victories.

Our former Prime Minister was also responsible for keeping racing going during the war. In spring 1941, he advised the Home Secretary, Herbert Morrison, that if the war threatened to suspend horseracing and have a negative impact on the bloodstock industry, the whole matter should be thrashed out in Cabinet first. Should I expect Boris Johnson to follow suit?

I was thinking of Churchill the racehorse owner when we wandered into the gift shop and café at the end of our visit. Over a coffee, I quickly glanced at my messages and saw an email from Rupert Mackeson. I had sent Rupert a copy of my modest self-published book, *A Year of Free Love,* soon after bumping into him at

Ascot.

I understood that Sir Rupert could be a little tricky and there is no doubt that he has led a colourful life. I'm wary of the reliability of any online encyclopaedia and it could be that some of the more outrageous aspects of Rupert's life have been exaggerated or embellished. However, in a 2018 interview with Star Sports, we got it from the horse's mouth.

Sir Rupert Mackeson was educated at Harrow where he was a contemporary of Julian Wilson and John McCririck, two legendary television racing commentators who are no longer with us. After Harrow came a four-year stint in the Royal Horse Guards during which time our hero rode in point-to-points and had some success as an amateur jockey.

Next was a spell in the city where Rupert ended up running a bank with strong ties to the Mafia. Fearing for his own safety, Mackeson fled to Rhodesia (now Zimbabwe), which was then under the control of Ian Smith's white-minority government. He earned the disapproval of the UK government through his smuggling activities and, at one point, the Rhodesian authorities arrested him and threw him into a prison camp, where he is alleged to have started a riot. When the UK attempted to extradite him from Rhodesia, the fiery baronet punched his guard on the nose while on board a plane, forcing the flight to be abandoned. He was eventually transported back to the UK, but the judge presiding over the case ruled that it was an illegal extradition and had him freed.

That's not half of the story. Sir Rupert went on to write racing books under the *nom de plume* Rupert Collens. One of them was about the cloning of a Derby winner. He also worked for the Racing Post and, during a long association with the turf, he has mixed with the likes of Lester Piggott and Dick Francis. Nowadays, he concentrates on his art gallery in Weston-super-Mare and the mobile book shop he sets up at southern racecourses.

I was aware of his rather forthright manner as I looked him up after our Ascot encounter and discovered an article in a 2001 edition of The Guardian. When quizzed about his Harrovian contemporary, Julian Wilson, Sir Rupert gave this blunt assessment: 'I'm known to dislike Wilson, whom I regard as a pompous little prick. His sense of humour is zero.' It's not the type of quip you'd expect from man who, at first glance, looks mildly eccentric but harmlessly avuncular.

I opened the email hoping for a sugar-coated book review without really expecting one. I was right to have kept my feet on the ground. Apparently, Rupert was 'pissed off' with the conclusion of the book. I thought finishing on a high with Free Love's first win was a satisfying ending to the story, but my fellow author disagreed.

Good morning Tony,
You are an interesting man/writer. However, most writers need good editors.
You lose the plot after Free Love's first win. The informed reader like me wants the total story until the horses in training sale. Suddenly, you changed from a switched-on, financially aware, and well-reasoned man to writing like a silly 12-year-old girl. Fine, everyone wants to win races, but you went over the top for one egg and spoon race at a gaff.
Rupert.

There was more. He advised making up some errata slips which could be placed in the back of the book to explain what happened after Free Love's win at Catterick. I think he envisaged the text of the slip saying something like, 'Sorry the ending of this book is so crap. I don't know what came over me.' I wasn't keen on that but thanked him nevertheless for his help. I replied observing that if feedback is truly the breakfast of champions, he had provided a full-English. I also took encouragement from the fact that I might have forged a career writing for *Jackie* or *Bunty,* had both magazines not gone out of publication 20 years ago.

Jennie thought the exchange of emails was hilarious but felt Rupert had a point. When pressed she said that the end of the book could be viewed as a bit dewy-eyed. It was something for me to ponder as we drove home after our grand day out. Dewy-eyed about Free Love? Guilty as charged, I suppose.

Saturday 7th March 2020

Media interest in the virus continued to intensify. Infections started to appear in the UK and, although the numbers looked small, they were scrutinized in forensic detail by the press. Public health figures expressed the view that the widespread transmission of what had now become known as Covid-19 was highly likely. Although the new, more scientific name for this particular coronavirus lacked the type of descriptive imagery conjured up by the likes of Swine Flu, Covid-19 seemed a better choice than 'Chinese Flu' which was favoured by Donald Trump and spat out with venom during his public addresses.

On March 5th, the first UK death from Covid-19 was registered. A Berkshire woman in her seventies was the victim. Later that day, an eighty-year-old man from Milton Keynes also succumbed to the disease.

I spent the afternoon at the Valley with another 18,000 misguided optimists who witnessed Charlton slump to a 0-1 home defeat against fellow strugglers, Middlesbrough. After the match, I hopped on a train and made my way to Sidcup Rugby Club where an informal reunion of my secondary school year group had been organised. The proposed format was simple: sink a few beers while watching England's Six Nations encounter with Wales, have a few more beers after the final whistle, then go for a curry if anybody had the stamina to carry on.

I continued afterwards with two old schoolmates, Colin Aslett and Ralph Raison, ending up in the Old Black Horse for a nightcap after our evening curry at The Mogul. Some of our chat was about the old school friends who had failed to turn up for the reunion. In a sad number of cases their absence was due to their no longer being with us.

Our relaxed chat meandered towards closing time, but we couldn't depart without touching on current events. It wasn't a cheery conversation. The situation in Italy and Spain looked to be deteriorating, and Ireland was already preparing for the worst despite incredibly low rates of infection and no fatalities to date. At least we could agree that we faced an uncertain future. On that note, we drained our glasses and said our farewells.

Saturday 14th March 2020
It had been quite a week. Our youngest, Joe, turned 18 on Monday. Cheltenham started with a defiant fanfare on Tuesday and ended on Friday mired in controversy. There were plenty who thought it should have been abandoned halfway through, or maybe not taken place at all given what was going on elsewhere. However, the horseracing authorities worked with the British Government on this one and the decision was made to go ahead, something that was to be conveniently forgotten by those who wanted to portray racing as a sport for selfish toffs who put their own interests above those of public health.

The FA jumped the gun and announced that all grassroots football was suspended. I spent Wednesday morning cancelling the arrangements for Old St Mary's FC's weekend fixtures, a club I help run with fellow North South Syndicate member, Pete Smith. On Friday, Ireland's Taoiseach, Leo Varadkar, announced the closure of all schools until 29th March. The announcement came one day after the World Health Organization formally declared that the coronavirus outbreak was a pandemic. To cap it all, the Irish government looked set to order bars and public houses to close, piling pressure on Boris Johnson to be more decisive and draconian in his approach.

It felt as if this evening's charity boxing event at the Troxy was the last hurrah, to borrow the Racing Post headline employed to describe Al Boum Photo's thrilling Cheltenham Gold Cup victory on Friday.

My eldest son, Matthew, was taking part in an evening of amateur boxing for which he'd been training hard for a couple of months. He hitched up with White Collar Boxing, an outfit that provides a training programme for those who have never stepped inside a ring before. The target is a proper bout of three two-minute rounds against an opponent of similar size and ability.

The Troxy is a magnificent Art Deco building on the Commercial Road near Limehouse Docklands Light Railway station. Built in the 1930s as an enormous cinema, it went through the doldrums that many buildings of its type have suffered, before triumphantly re-emerging as a music and events venue in 2006. Its interior décor is sumptuous and was only matched by the evening attire of the young graphic designers, advertising agents and teachers who had come to support their friends' pugilistic escapades.

The seats in the lower arena had been removed and replaced with tables laid out in cabaret style. We had ringside seats which were occupied by a huge contingent of Matthew fans including his girlfriend, Anna, whose anxiety about the possibility of serious injury had reduced her to tears. By contrast, Matt's siblings, Celia and Joe, were on their feet screaming and whooping when, after a seemingly interminable wait, the fighters were introduced for the main event.

Anna's nerves had not been helped by the sight of knock-outs and stoppages in previous bouts, and a bit of her trepidation rubbed off on me. What, if after all the hard work, Matt got clobbered early on and it was "game over" inside thirty seconds? I was less worried about injury and more concerned about how deflating it would be for him. I didn't care who won, I just wanted Matt to go the distance and come away from the ring feeling good about what he had achieved.

When the bell sounded for round one, I was transformed. Of course I bloody cared who won. Me, Jennie, Celia and Joe were on our feet shrieking at the top of our voices along with half the football club and their partners.

During the first few seconds, Matt's opponent lunged at him looking for an early kill. 'Please God, anything but that,' I thought to myself as Matt backed away, looking slightly startled by the aggressive start from the blue corner. My unease was short-lived. Our boy was soon jabbing away, keeping his adversary at distance while landing some telling blows in between.

Matt had obviously been well schooled, and his boxing was a model of technical correctness. In the second round, his opponent was forced to take a standing count, and when the scantily clad young lady paraded around the ring holding up the number three board to denote the final round was on its way, we knew that all Matt had to do was keep jabbing and stay out of trouble. He was already streets ahead.

I won't forget those last few seconds in a hurry. I just remember screaming, 'Keep jabbing Matt! Stay your distance! Stay out of trouble! Keep jabbing!' The final bell sounded and there wasn't a soul in the Troxy who could dispute the outcome. When the referee did the inevitable and raised Matt's arm to signify his victory, the place erupted - or at least our little corner of it did - and Anna's tears turned to expressions of joy instead of dread.

It was an exhilarating night, but a foreboding one. The promoters were aware that it was touch and go whether the event would be able to go ahead, and I imagine it survived by the skin of its teeth. It felt like a farewell party. At the end of the night everyone departed with hugs, kisses and victorious backslapping. Jennie and I joined friends for a nightcap in a trendy local pub while the youngsters headed to Stoke Newington for the after-fight party held in a club near Matt's flat. Joe was able to tag along without the need of fake ID. His provisional driving licence confirmed that he had turned eighteen less than a week ago.

All felt good with the world, but we knew that dramatic change was on the way. Crowds of punters at amateur boxing nights and late drinks in loud and busy city centre pubs were surely heading for a period of suspension. The inevitability of that prospect lingered over last orders in the Limehouse Craft Beer Co. where we finished the evening before jumping into an Uber to Dartford.

Wednesday 18th March 2020

The bad news was coming thick and fast and, if it wasn't bad, it was perplexing. On Monday, the Prime Minister advised everyone in the UK against non-essential travel and contact with others. He also suggested people should avoid pubs, clubs and theatres, and work from home if possible. But what the hell did that mean? I'm sure pub owners were delighted at being allowed to stay open and trade but less enthusiastic about the government's advice for punters to give them a wide berth.

We were exactly one week away from our visit to Langham to watch Free Love complete some fast work ahead of her seasonal debut, which we hoped would be in mid-April. It would be a chance to talk to Mick Appleby about a suitable target for the filly's reappearance. I'd been looking forward to the day since the beginning of the new year.

The plans were now in tatters. The Racing Post headlines charted the swift demise of the racing calendar. On Sunday, the front page announced that racing in Britain now stood alone as the only major sport allowing paying customers to attend. Not unreasonably, the British Horseracing Authority (BHA) insisted that it was business as usual until there was an official change in government policy. A ban on large gatherings looked imminent and racing's rulers gave assurances that they would continue working with government officials and comply with any restrictions put in place.

We didn't have to wait long for the next move. A day later, Monday's headline confirmed that all British racing would take place behind closed doors, most likely within the next 48 hours. Only those working in the industry would be allowed to attend. These arrangements would be maintained until the end of March, but no decision had been made about the future of Aintree's Grand National meeting which was due to commence on 2nd April.

No prizes for guessing what Tuesday's Racing Post front page screamed. **Grand National Cancelled.** Boris Johnson's announcement that emergency services would no longer support any type of mass gathering was the final nail in the coffin. Racing looked dead and buried.

This morning's headline confirmed that reports of racing's temporary death had not been exaggerated. **Racing Shuts Down** was the blunt introduction to Peter Scargill's article which stated, 'Racing in Britain will not take place until May at the earliest after a dramatic escalation in response to the coronavirus pandemic from the BHA, with chief executive Nick Rust admitting the authority is unsure when action will resume.'

The RP was full of sombre analysis and tales of woe. Trainers were concerned about the viability of businesses, as were racecourses. Shares in leading bookmakers continued to tumble as they did in all other sectors. Our own trainer was quoted as supporting the initial six-week shut down but warned about the consequences if the period of inactivity went beyond that length.

I was devastated. Next week's visit to Langham - if it was allowed to go ahead - would be an opportunity to see Free Love in the flesh, but that was about all. Asking Mick about how near our filly was to race fitness would be pointless. There were no races to enter. The calendar had been suspended and a new one would need to be created whenever racing returned. We were in limbo. There was nothing to do other than to wait patiently for developments – and keep paying the bills.

Thursday 19th March 2020
By now we were all used to bad news arriving on a regular basis. There was little point in adopting an upbeat, positive approach to life, wondering what each new day would bring. It was always the same. More bad news. I received an email from the stable which confirmed yet another inevitability:

Dear Owners,

In view of the latest directives from the Government we appreciate your help by not visiting the yard until further notice – it is important that we keep our staff as healthy as we can.

You will all be aware that racing is cancelled until the 30th April. Our all-weather horses will be freshened up as they normally would at the end of the season. Our turf horses, in the main, have just come into work and it is our intention to train them as normal with a view to being ready to hit the ground running as soon as racing resumes.

Louise will be here as normal on Wednesday, Thursday and Saturdays – she will video horses working and send to you on request, and also be available for queries and questions.

32

Trying to be positive, racing has resumed today in Hong Kong after a 6-week break. As the spread of the virus here seems to be following a similar pattern to China, we are hopeful that this initial period will not be extended – should it be, we will re-evaluate the position.

The fee increase, of which you were all informed, will now not be implemented until 1ˢᵗ May 2020.

As ever we thank you for your continued support, especially through this tricky time. It is much appreciated.

Mick & Team

So that was that. I couldn't even turn up and pat Free Love on her pretty head. I replied and said that we'd like Mick's member of staff, Louise, to send video clips of Free Love on the gallops. It was better than nothing.

Friday 20th March 2020

I made some calculations and emailed the others to put them in the picture:

Gents,

I attach some figures based on no racing until the end of June. I have included estimates for monthly insurance, vet's visits and farrier fees in the £1750 monthly figure.

We didn't get the rub of the green with our winter grazing arrangements. The daily rate was £19 but for the last ten days we were charged a £30 a day pre-training rate in readiness for Free Love's return to full training and the prospect of an early April seasonal reappearance. If the coronavirus shut down had come six weeks earlier, we could have left Free Love in a field at Castle View Stud on a grazing rate.

We now face the prospect of running down our cash without seeing a racecourse. Worse still, we couldn't even cut our losses and sell up as sales are being cancelled and I imagine bloodstock values are plummeting. Who wants to buy a racehorse when there's no racing?

I know this is all based on worst outcomes, and I suppose we could be back to racing behind closed doors in May. However, it raises the question about how long we can afford to go on. If we want to bail out in July, we need to be realistic about what Free Love would fetch. If we want to continue until the end of the season in October, we'd need to commit a further £2k each. Maybe a bit more if we finally start racing and are unsuccessful. A bit less if we pick up some prize money.

I know there are all sorts of unknowns. Things are changing daily, but we need to look ahead and at least consider what we are all prepared to pay to keep Free Love.

. Finally, there are always cashflow issues with these calculations. We haven't enough money in the bank to pay the next training bill, so I'm going to put my first £500 in on 1 April. If one of you can do the same that would be very helpful.

Hope you are keeping well and your spirits aren't flagging too much!
Regards Tony

Later that day the government announced the closure of all public venues. Restaurants, pubs, cinemas and theatres were instructed to shut their doors. Schools had been closed two days earlier and it was obvious that we were on course for the type of lockdown that our European neighbours had been forced to introduce earlier in the month. We seemed to be three weeks behind the unfortunate pacesetters. You only had to look at events in France, Italy and Spain to predict what would happen next in the UK. If only backing horses was as simple.

5 Lockdown

Monday 23rd March 2020

The odds-on favourite hosed up. The government announced a stay-at-home order that would last for at least three weeks. An emergency coronavirus bill was rushed through the House of Commons in the afternoon, and by early evening our dishevelled leader was delivering his address to the nation, shown live on the main terrestrial television channels.

I'm not a fan of Boris Johnson, but at least he sounded coherent on this occasion. Mind you, like a class 6 handicapper, he was improving from a low base. The central message made sense. If we didn't do anything, our health service would be overwhelmed. The PM insisted that there wasn't a country on the planet that could cope with the virus if rapid community transmission was facilitated by carrying on with business as usual.

I looked at my Google calendar. The coming week was littered with eagerly anticipated events that wouldn't take place. A trip to the Kent seaside to catch up with a friend and play a round of golf would have to be rearranged. Wednesday's stable visit was postponed until who knows when. To cap it all, around 40 family members and friends had to be told that the house party on Friday to celebrate Joe's eighteenth was now cancelled. It felt as if the world was grinding to a halt, or at least my little corner of it was.

Wednesday 25th March 2020

Although the stable visit was off, I received a glimpse of life at Langham courtesy of a couple of video clips and pictures sent by Louise via WhatsApp. It looked to be a beautiful day in County Rutland. Free Love was captured doing a gentle solo canter on Mick's all-weather gallop. You could hear the filly breathing through flared nostrils as she met the rising ground, hooves pounding rhythmically on the synthetic surface. It was only eight seconds in duration, and the amount of time that Free Love was close enough to Louise's phone to hear and see her clearly was less than half of that. But it was something, and something is better than nothing.

The video was accompanied by three pictures of Free Love posing on her own and one with her regular pilot, Theo Ladd. Louise had even persuaded Theo to do a short report to camera. He stated that the filly was fresh and well and was looking fantastic in her coat. He was pleased with the way she was moving. Warming to the task, Theo concluded his little interview by saying it was a shame about the interruption to racing as the filly was on track for a mid-April reappearance, an event which now joined a growing list of postponements.

Of course, such optimistic reports are commonplace in racing. You're unlikely to be told that your pride and joy moved like a crab, appeared listless and uninterested, and might be better off pulling a milk cart around the villages of Rutland. But Mick and the team have always been straight with us and if Free Love was a bit backward and nowhere near race fitness, we would have been told. In any event, young Theo was entitled to be just as biased as the filly's owners. He had ridden her in 15 of her last 18 races and was on board for all Free Love's four victories. He had developed a real bond with our little sprinter and, like us, he couldn't wait to be back in action.

Apart from the cheering bulletin from Louise, it wasn't a good day for racing. After an extended flirtation with conducting the sport behind closed doors, Ireland threw in the towel and shut down all sporting activities until 19th April at the earliest. The new flat season was one day old when the decision was made.

The Racing Post decided to lead with that story rather than the cancellation of the North South Syndicate's stable visit to Langham. By 5.30pm the trade paper had another scoop on its hands. Its editor, Tom Kerr, posted a letter to readers on the website. The opening two paragraphs said it all:

Dear Reader,

It is with great sadness I must announce that following Thursday's edition the Racing Post will be temporarily suspending publication. Unfortunately, with racing in Britain and Ireland halted, betting shops closed, and our governments urging everyone to stay at home as much as possible to slow the spread of the coronavirus, we have been left with no other choice.

Recent events have had an unfathomable impact on our world. We have seen harrowing pictures of overcrowded hospitals and overwhelmed medical professionals in other countries, and in Britain and Ireland we are bracing ourselves for similar scenes, while hoping the extensive measures announced thus far will forestall them.

Tom's letter went on to express the wish that things would return to normal as soon as possible and, once we were through the worst of this growing global health crisis, racing would return as would the Racing Post. After Thursday, the paper would exist in digital format only, available to existing subscribers. The website and app would continue to publish content of some description.

I wondered what I'd get for my thirty quid a month subscription. There were only so many features and fillers that could be used to pad out each daily edition. Racecards from the States would begin to appear, no doubt. Sky Sports Racing was covering the likes of Gulfstream Park, Tampa Bay Downs and Santa Anita. In the absence of anything else, I took a passing interest in what was happening on the other side of the pond, but it looked alien. It was all about early pace and there was nothing elegant about tired horses slogging through dirt surfaces encouraged by jockeys with unwieldy whip actions.

I pondered on the plight of all those people employed by the Post. I was lucky enough to have visited the paper's smart new Southbank headquarters last October. The Vivo building is the type of brash and confident construction that has sprung up close to the Thames over the last decade or two. The Racing Post occupied the top floor which was a hive of activity when I was given my little tour. Most of its employees were now without work and only the recent announcement of the government's Job Retention Scheme prevented a spate of redundancies.

I felt obliged to keep paying my monthly subscription. From where else was the RP getting any income to keep its skeleton staff going? If I had been made redundant or furloughed on reduced pay and was struggling to make ends meet, I might have looked at where savings could be made. But I was one of the lucky ones. I was retired and had a regular pension coming in. Jennie was still working part-time so we were ok. Comfortable is the word that people use. That can mean anything from being able to pay the bills to having enough cash for half a dozen lavish holidays a year. In our case it meant being able to give our third and final offspring a bit of help when he went to university in September. And own 20% of Free Love.

Sunday 5th April 2020

It was the hottest day of the year so far. The mercury climbed to 24 degrees, and everyone was grateful for a spell of weather that meant long walks were possible during a period when there was little else to do with your spare time. Jennie and I opted for a slightly longer yomp today, cutting across Dartford Heath before making our way up Birchwood Road towards the entrance of the woods surrounding the golf course.

I've played Birchwood Park quite a few times. It's an insanely busy public course. Its proximity to the junction of the M25 and M20 motorways makes it a popular target for keen golfers who fancy the idea of sloping off work on Friday to start to the weekend early. Unfortunately, in the height of summer it's an idea shared by scores of like-minded skivers. That idyllic round of golf, made all the more enticing by knowing that you really should be at work, can often become a frustrating and interminable five-hour slog.

It wasn't like that today. We walked along the bridle path running through the woods at the highest part of the course, and when we emerged at the back of the eighth green to pick up the footpath that meanders along the edge of the fairway leading back to the carpark and entrance, I viewed Birchwood as I've never seen it before. It was deserted. The course was in immaculate condition, immersed in the most wonderful spring sunshine, but it was eerie standing on the elevated ninth tee, which afforded a panoramic view of large parts of the course, and being unable to see another soul.

We returned home, passing a shut and forlorn looking Horse and Groom pub where we would have surely stopped for a quick drink in normal circumstances. We encountered plenty of other walkers on the way back but the usual indifference towards each other was now replaced with circumspection and a desire to avoid eye contact. Some chose to cross the road, attempting to avoid any awkwardness.

I wasn't coping particularly well with this new world order. My daughter, Celia, was out of work within days of the lockdown being announced. She organises locations and sets for television and film productions. The industry immediately shut down and, as Celia didn't qualify for any financial help because of her largely self-employed status, she had to rely on her modest savings and the much-maligned Universal Credit to keep her head above water.

Our oldest, Matt, was working from home on full pay. For the time being he was ok, although I detected a bit of cabin fever which was hardly surprising as his smart, but not overly spacious rented flat in Stoke Newington lacked a garden or billiard room, either of which would have made life more tolerable. As for Joe, the closure of schools was quickly followed by an acceptance that public exams would not be able to go ahead in May and June. His university place would be determined by teacher assessments instead of exam results. Funnily enough, he was initially upset by the cancellation of his exams just six weeks before he was due to take them. He soon got over it.

People's individual circumstances varied enormously. Infection rates were rising sharply, as were fatalities, and there was no doubt that health workers and carers were under enormous pressure. Some working in other fields reported that they too had never been busier. The supermarkets were certainly doing well.

One of my former primary school headteacher colleagues was run ragged keeping his school open during the Easter holidays to cater for the children of key workers. He was amazed by the number of his parents who felt that their office jobs amounted to an essential service. When he wasn't sorting out staff to look after the relatively small number of pupils who were attending school, he was making sure that his teachers were uploading activities onto the school website and other digital platforms in an attempt to keep the learning going for the children who were confined to their homes, which was the overwhelming majority.

Jennie's charity was flat out trying to come up with imaginative ways of maintaining contact with the elderly folk it supports at a time when home visits were out of the question. She had to endure endless Zoom meetings as Link Age Southwark grappled with the development of new protocols. She certainly wasn't short of things to do.

It wasn't so bad for me. I was at the editing and proofing stage for my second book. It can be a time-consuming task but there was no excuse for rushing the job or cutting corners given the hours and days that now stretched out before me. I could have gone on forever agonising over word choices and the redrafting of clunky sentences. I almost had too much time to think about these decisions.

I knew I was lucky. We were able to spill out into our neat garden when the weather was good, where we could eat and drink alfresco under the shade of the willow tree which was a central feature of our little patch of Dartford greenery.

There were plenty of people worse off than us. That was true before the pandemic, and maybe even more so now. I wasn't ungrateful for what I had, but I was down about the things I couldn't do. Nearly everything I enjoyed was now on the prohibited list. Seeing family and friends, going racing, watching Charlton play, having a meal out, supping a pint, swimming, golf, and the occasional cultural experience such as a visit to a theatre, cinema or art gallery, were all swept aside as soon as the national lockdown came into force.

But it was Free Love's predicament that was the most frustrating of the lot. There was no indication of when racing would return. How could there be? There was no telling when normal life would resume, and racing was just a tiny part of the fabric.

Thursday 9th April 2020
I received another video clip of Free Love working at Langham. It was another solo canter, perhaps a little brisker than the last one, but it was hard to tell from the eight-second footage I viewed on my mobile phone.

I suppose it was difficult for our trainer to be sure about what to do with Free Love and all the other horses who were being prepared for the new turf season, since it was impossible to tell when they

41

would be able to race. We all hoped it would be by the beginning of May, but nothing was decided.

The Racing Post led with a story about tentative plans to organise the return of racing on a regional basis. A small number of 'hubs' could be created utilising racecourses with hotels on site. Key staff, including jockeys, might be able to base themselves at one of the tracks for a few weeks, effectively placing themselves in quarantine. It all seemed a bit fanciful to me, but there was no harm in racing's rulers engaging in a bit of blue-sky-thinking. At least it was evidence of some urgent activity aimed at getting the show back on the road.

The rest of the 10-page slimline edition of the digital paper contained a feature by Tom Kerr on how other jurisdictions had managed racing during the pandemic. Page 5 was devoted to the successful spell down under of young British jockey, Tom Marquand. He had been taken to heart by the locals who gave him the matey soubriquet 'Aussie Tom', which must have been quite flattering for a mere Pommie.

I was reading an interesting article on page seven about the restrictions to racing imposed during the First and Second World Wars, when what sounded like an air raid alarm jolted me back into the real world. At first, I couldn't work out where the noise was coming from or what it meant. I was fairly sure that I wasn't supposed to put on a hardhat and crawl under the table, but for a few seconds I was genuinely disorientated.

It was my phone. I grabbed it and swiped it into action. The fug cleared when I saw the GoodSAM Responder logo reminding me that I had signed up as an NHS volunteer. The Royal Voluntary Service was co-ordinating the mobilisation of an army of helpers who would be needed to collect prescriptions for the housebound, do shopping for those who were self-isolating, and so on. I had the time to help, so I put my hand up along with around 600,000 others which was more than double the original target.

This was it, my first piece of active duty. I looked at the map on my phone which showed the household in need was around the corner in Havelock Road, less than 200 yards from me. Details of the mission confirmed that I needed to pick up a prescription from a pharmacy in Greenhithe. It seemed odd. Greenhithe is three miles away, but I didn't question why somebody living in Dartford would use a chemist so far from home as I jumped in the car and sped away on my first Covid-busting task.

The day hinted at farce as soon as I arrived at Greenhithe. It had just turned 1pm and the pharmacy was empty. I was told it was their lunch break and I would need to return at 2pm and join the queue. I explained that I was an NHS volunteer and I had driven from Dartford, but it was to no avail. I was informed that pharmacies were under enormous pressure, and it was essential that the staff took a decent break. There could be no exceptions.

To cut a long and tedious story short, I returned bang on 2pm and was greeted by a queue of around twenty glum-looking punters, standing dutifully at two-metre intervals. My volunteer status afforded me no privileges, no fast-track benefits. It took nearly two hours to get to the counter at which point the pharmacist (who was looking well-fed and rested) told me that there was no record of the prescription.

He suggested I call the patient to check their details. I'm glad I did. There had been an error, a simple misspelling of her surname, but I also discovered that she lived in Havelock Drive, Greenhithe and not Havelock Road around the corner from me. I had been a phone call away from turning up at the wrong address to force an unwanted prescription on a bemused local resident, four hours after setting off on my act of compassion. And I'd worked through my lunch break.

Thursday 16th April 2020

The glorious weather continued to provide an incongruous backdrop to the growing national crisis. Last weekend, as Jennie and I prepared the lamb for our alfresco Easter Sunday lunch, and Joe fired up the barbecue, we were well aware that the politicians and scientists were getting their figures ready for the daily briefing which had become part of the nation's television diet.

The figures hadn't been great for a while. Daily UK deaths attributable to Covid exceeded a thousand for the first time on 7th April and fatalities had remained high subsequently, except for weekend figures which were always lower due to irritating lags in reporting.

If the data offered little scope for optimism, today's front page of the RP afforded none. **BHA extends racing's shut down – with no date set for return.** The article went on to say that chief executive, Nick Rust, was adamant that racing was set to resume as soon as it was safe to do so. However, the 1st May target had been ditched with no alternative put forward. There was more speculative talk of regional hubs, but nothing concrete, nothing to raise realistic hopes of racing returning any time soon.

It made the sight of this morning's video clip of Free Love cantering up the all-weather gallop at Langham a demoralising experience. It was a faster piece of work and the filly looked to be moving well. A second clip showed the string walking back towards the stables. As they passed Mick Appleby, who was stationed at his usual spot towards the top of the gallop, Theo said something about 'power' or at least that's what it sounded like. 'Power?' enquired Mick, struggling to hear Free Love's work rider above the noise of traffic speeding along the A606 on the other side of the tall hedgerow. 'There's some power there,' Theo confirmed as he made his way back towards base.

It was all very encouraging, and in normal circumstances I'd have been delighted and even excited. But with racing in a permanent state of limbo the immediate future looked set to be made up of weekly video clips and monthly training bills. That was as close as we'd get to some meaningful action.

Wednesday 22nd April 2020

I should have been at Epsom for the course's first meeting of the season, where I had hoped to meet with Rupert Mackeson. He had suggested that I bring a quantity of books (preferably accompanied with errata slips) and take part in some sort of low-key book signing event. Given his unflinching criticism of *A Year of Free Love,* I was a little surprised that the offer was still on the table. Maybe Rupert's bark was worse than his bite.

There had been noises coming from those involved with organising the resumption of racing, but there was nothing definite. Preserving the big races was seen as a priority, even if it meant holding them at times of the year that were different to the established pattern.

Whenever the show returned it was obvious that prize money was going to be reduced. No racing meant no betting revenue, a share of which is returned to the sport. And when the resumption came it would surely be behind closed doors to begin with, meaning that racecourses would not be able to bolster prize money pots. Without crowds, their income would be derived solely from the sale of media rights. For smaller courses, the absence of paying customers would be a disaster.

I decided to give my two pennies' worth on the subject and yesterday emailed a letter to the Racing Post's editor, which I was surprised to see appear in a news item posted on today's website - another indication of how the publication was underwhelmed with content during the absence of racing in the UK.

Dear Tom,

Ideas about how the flat racing season will be salvaged are coming thick and fast from respected industry sources. Everyone seems to agree that preserving the Classics as well as a raft of important Group races is essential. Of course, we all want to see the top horses in action, but to suggest that it is somehow imperative for the breed strikes me as a strange claim.

What is imperative is that the well-being of the whole sport is maintained. A narrow focus on big owners and big Newmarket yards, will result in small trainers and owners being forced out of racing, perhaps for good.

I'll state my vested interest now. I part-own a cheaply bought sprinter with four friends. We fulfilled our lifelong ambition of owning a racehorse when we bought Free Love as a yearling in 2017. I've even written a book about the experience.

....Unless we strike a balance when racing returns, small owners face the prospect of being squeezed out of the game through limited opportunities and reduced prize money.

....The democratisation of racehorse ownership, built up by racing clubs and syndicates during the last two decades, is under real threat if we become obsessed with the preservation of the Pattern Race calendar which, after all, primarily benefits the likes of Godolphin and other wealthy owners.

If we really are 'all in this together' we need to make sure that all of racing's stakeholders are given a fair chance to survive.

Tony Linnett, Part-owner and author

My diatribe made me feel a bit better. At its heart was the belief that prize money should be redistributed from the rich to the not so rich. Who would have thought racehorse owners like me would be at the forefront of the next revolution?

My fellow North South Syndicate member and old school mate,

Patrick, drily observed that although the letter contained some good points, he particularly admired my continuing ability to shoehorn a reference to *A Year of Free Love* into any and every communication. I don't think he was insinuating that I was ruthlessly profiteering from the pandemic, but you never can tell with Patrick.

Saturday 25th April 2020

It was Free Love's birthday. Although officially a four-year-old for racing purposes from 1st January onwards, today was her foaling date, her real birthday. It was now two-and-a-half years since Pete and I made the short journey from Dartford to Newmarket to attend the Tattersalls yearling sales where, with the help of Tom and Jackie Clover, we bought lot 1383, a bay filly by Equiano out of Peace And Love. Nobody thought that our modest purchase would still be racing at four. The fact that we were still in the game and ready to embark on another season was entirely down to Free Love's wonderfully genuine temperament and natural speed, which had yielded four wins and over £30k in prize money.

This morning's video clip showed Free Love doing a fast piece of work upsides one of Mick's stable stars, Danzeno. Both horses were moving comfortably within themselves so you couldn't read anything into the fact that our filly's galloping companion was a former Group 3 winner who had finished a close third in last year's Wokingham handicap at Royal Ascot off a mark of 102. Danzeno was currently rated 106 and there was our little filly breezing along with him, unfazed by the exalted company she was keeping. But you couldn't read anything into it.

I pinged the video to the others via our WhatsApp group with an excited message. 'How about this gents! Free Love working well with Danzeno! What do you think of that?' The others didn't think much of it at all judging by the silence that ensued. They probably didn't have the heart to tell me that you couldn't read anything into it.

Wednesday 29th April 2020

Another video of some fast work, again with Danzeno. This was a proper gallop and Louise's twelve-second clip showed the two horses flying up the hill, neck and neck, under an overcast Langham sky.

Free Love looked as if she was nearly ready to roll, which made it all the more exasperating that I still had no idea when that would be. I wanted to be at the stables, to see and smell the horses, to stand at the top of the all-weather strip, to be close up as Free Love powered up the incline, flashing past at a speed nudging 40 miles an hour. It's always faster, more physical, and arresting when you're there in the flesh.

I wanted to be back on a racecourse. My visit to Huntingdon with Trevor in February felt like a distant memory from another life. As for Windsor last July, did that really happen? But my impatience appeared muted when compared with the irritation displayed by a pair of high-profile trainers who broke rank and demanded a more pro-active response to the crisis from the BHA.

Mark Johnson and Ralph Beckett became two of the main players in an unwelcome brouhaha when their emails to the BHA Chair, Annamarie Phelps, critical of Nick Rust's leadership, were leaked to the press. They both felt that the BHA's chief executive was more interested in managing public perception and appeasing government, when he should be taking the lead and forging ahead with plans to get racing started again.

Beckett and Johnson may have felt that they had been unfairly thrust into the limelight when all they were asking for was a more confident and independent approach to the thorny issue of when and how to resume the sport. However, it came across as misguided at best, arrogant at worst.

Their intervention received short shrift from the Racing Post's editor-in-chief, Alan Byrne, who decided to pick up his pen and write a leading article in Monday's paper. Mr Byrne, who has a very long association with the Post, leaves the day-to-day editorial decisions to Tom Kerr, and rarely gets involved these days in producing copy himself. He must have felt strongly about the matter in order to roll up his sleeves and compose a detailed comment on the controversy.

It was an incisive piece of analysis. The grandee of racing journalism made it clear that everyone involved with the sport, including his own newspaper, was desperate for it to return. He went on to state that it would be a spectacular own goal if racing presented itself as some sort of special case, immune from the social responsibilities which had severely affected every aspect of our daily lives.

Fatalities had exceeded 20,000 and infection rates were still high. Shops and many businesses remained shut and gatherings between households were still prohibited. Until the government decided that the time was right to ease restrictions, racing, along with other sports, would have to sit tight, as far as Alan was concerned. That didn't mean the sport's rulers should recline idly in their High Holborn offices twiddling their thumbs waiting for the telephone to ring. They must continue to work closely with other sports and central government, Mr Byrne concluded, and make sure that when racing returned it had everybody's support, including that of the general public.

I couldn't disagree with any of that. Free Love looked ready to race, but I told myself that I'd just have to be patient; something easier said than done. Tomorrow would be a year to the day that our filly's season really took off when she won again at Nottingham, making it two victories from her first two starts. Twelve months later, we were still on the launch pad waiting for lift-off. It was all so wretchedly frustrating, but Alan was correct. We needed to hang on in there and wait until the time was right for the sport to shake itself down and start all over again.

Saturday 2nd May 2020
Patience came with a price tag. The initial plan was to put in enough cash to get us through to the July horses in training sales. If Free Love's early races provided sufficient encouragement and she bagged a bit of prize money, we had the option of carrying on until the end of the season in October. It was the usual hand-to-mouth existence that had characterised our little partnership since its inception.

This morning's video captured Free Love doing another impressive piece of work, again with Danzeno, but when I contacted the others, I ditched the wide-eyed enthusiasm about the gallop and asked for money instead. It was time for everyone to put another £500 each into the pot.

One of the perverse positives of the current situation was cheaper monthly training bills. As Free Love wasn't racing, there were no additional costs to meet beyond basic keep fees and the odd small invoice from the vet or farrier. If we were in action, race entries, transport costs and riding fees were all added to the bill. To run at Nottingham, one of the racecourses nearest to Mick's yard, would cost the North South Syndicate around £300. If we wanted to go further afield, maybe to York, make that £450.

Perhaps we'd hit on a winning formula. If the whole of the flat racing season were cancelled, we'd save approximately five grand on costs associated with getting Free Love to the racecourse. Instead, we could sit in our locked-down homes and watch endless ten-second video clips of Free Love cantering and galloping. All this for the giveaway price of two grand a month.

If you thought about it too much it would drive you crazy, and I was thinking about it a lot. At least today's Post offered a crumb of comfort. Concrete plans were revealed for racing's return. The provisional schedule aimed at a restart in the penultimate weekend in May, when some of the key Classic trials such as the Craven and Greenham Stakes would be run. A week later was the slot identified for the Dante and Musidora, with the 1,000 and 2,000 Guineas earmarked for the first weekend in June. Other big races, usually run in April and early May, were also to be saved.

On the negative side, all the talk was of preserving the Pattern Race schedule. The focus was on big, prestigious races which invariably fall to big owners. I'm not saying that cheap horses and small owners can't gate-crash the party, but it's not something that you see that often, and when it happens, it's big news.

Tuesday 5th May 2020

The talk about preserving the Classics and the tragedy facing racing if the superstars of Ballydoyle and Godolphin were forced to go to stud following a truncated career was beginning to irritate. What about the little guys? If it was distressing that we might not be able to reschedule every group and listed race that should have been run in April and May, it was absolutely catastrophic for owners of horses rated below 70 - of which there were thousands - if grassroots opportunities were thin on the ground when we got going again.

There had also been grim warnings about prize money levels. Last year's levy yield of £97 million was a few quid up on the forecast, which was a help. But other income streams would vanish for a sport that had to conduct its business behind closed doors.

I felt compelled to invoke the spirit of Citizen Tone and was soon at the computer composing a lengthy message which I intended to send to the BHA's Brant Dunshea, who was leading the Resumption of Racing Group. In the end I also decided to burden Charlie Liverton, the chief executive for the Racehorse Owners Association (ROA), with my missive. They must have both winced when they opened the email and saw the length of my gripe.

Good afternoon, Brant,

I hope this message finds you in good health. I know you, and everyone involved with the Resumption of Racing Group, are exceptionally busy so I apologise in advance for the length of my message.

From what I have read, the group appears to be working hard to put together a package that will allow racing to take place in the very near future, initially behind closed doors. I am a racing enthusiast, part-owner and author who appreciates everything that is being done to make this possible.

My key concern is about prize money. I'll come straight to the point. I believe the only equitable and sustainable way forward in the short term, is to significantly reduce the prize money for Group races and redistribute it to support prize money levels for lower class races.

If you read no further, that's it in a nutshell.

I should have stopped here, but I didn't. I banged on and on about trainers going bust and even threw in some melodramatic language about small owners being 'sacrificed on the altar of the Pattern Race Programme'. God knows what I was thinking when I wrote that embarrassing tosh. It sounded like something from an evangelical sermon. Maybe it was an indication of an increasingly tenuous grip on reality. We were in the middle of a global health crisis, and I was reserving my fire and brimstone for the plight of horseracing. I couldn't help it though. I was obsessed with the sport and smitten with Free Love. Keep calm and carry on with the lockdown? What a depressing thought.

6 Green Shoots

Thursday 7th May 2020

It was another fabulous morning. I decided to scarify the lawn before the sun was high and it became too hot to rake by hand. It wasn't a large patch to work, the addition of small, paved areas over the years causing it to shrink in size to a rectangle of no more than eight by six yards.

I like sorting out the lawn. I'm not a gardener by any stretch of the imagination, but I get a lot of pleasure from cutting the grass and tidying the edges. Once in a blue moon, I get ideas above my station and throw on some lawn feed. But the real satisfaction is derived from sitting in the shade admiring my handiwork while sipping a cold beer. A gin and tonic works just as well.

I'm not saying that words like 'manicured' spring to mind when you look at my plot of grass, and I'm sure neither the clerk of the course at Ascot nor the head groundsman at Lord's would rush to offer me a job, but it only takes a little bit of attention to make our garden a pleasant place to relax in. Jennie provides the colour and finesse with the plants and shrubs in the borders, and the tomatoes, courgettes and herbs in the two little vegetable patches she's created at the back in front of the shed. It's a traditional division of labour. I do all the cutting, lopping and destroying while Jennie does all the things that are of any real value.

I finished the scarifying before noon and sat under the parasol with a cup of tea to admire the fruits of my labour. It was a bit early for anything stronger. It was a chance to glance at the BBC news app to catch the morning headlines. They were predictably about the pandemic, although the prospect of the PM making an important announcement on Sunday raised hopes that some sort of good news was on the way.

A check of my emails revealed a message from the ROA's Charlie Liverton. I had sent him a note to thank him for all his efforts on behalf of owners. It accompanied my interminable gripe and was now taken aback by the swiftness of his reply.

Good evening Tony,
Many thanks for your note and kind words.
We are working hard to ensure a fair distribution of prize money once racing resumes and I can assure you that the distribution model has changed significantly with regards to the value of class 1 races with more of a focus on class 4 to 6 races. The intention is to produce, wherever possible, a fixture list in the coming few days with race values shortly thereafter.
My thanks again for your note and I hope you are safe and well.
Best wishes, Charlie.

My original message of thanks was sincere. Judging by the regular communications pushed out by the ROA, and from coverage in the Racing Post, Charlie and the team were actively fighting the corner for all owners. We still had no idea when racing would start again and at what point owners would be allowed to see their horses run, but the news about the proposed interim prize money arrangements was good for grassroots racing. It was an indication that racing's rulers were not viewing the sport's resumption through the narrow lens of the Pattern Race schedule.

Sunday 10th May 2020
It had been an encouraging last few days. Infection rates and fatalities appeared to be on a downward trajectory, suggesting we may have passed the peak. Boris Johnson was expected to present his road map to recovery when he addressed the nation this evening and the public eagerly awaited confirmation that things would start returning to something like normal. Being able to see family and

friends again would be a welcome start.

News about the return of racing gathered pace. Shortly after I received Charlie Liverton's encouraging reply about protecting grassroots racing, the Post reported that the sport would return with an action-packed schedule of handicaps following the release of the proposed programme for the first seven days of racing.

Of the 104 races spread across the first week, nearly three-quarters would be handicaps with the emphasis placed on lower grade contests. There would also be a dozen two-year-old races, which made sense. If it was agony not knowing when our experienced sprinter would get back on the track, it must have been a purgatorial wait for the owners of young horses who had been prepared for months to make their eagerly awaited racecourse debuts. They needed plenty of opportunities when the show got back on the road.

No return date had been set, but the Resumption of Racing Group would sit tomorrow following the PM's update this evening. The sport was ready to go. It just needed the green light from Westminster.

Later that night I tuned into the PM's address along with just about everyone else in the country. To be fair to Boris, he didn't look too bad considering he was in an intensive care unit only a month ago. Perhaps the nursing staff's care extended to the loan of a comb. Our leader looked passably groomed for a change.

I'm not a fan. I didn't vote for him, but I had no desire to see his government, or any other government for that matter, flounder in a time of great national need, and I was irritated by those who couldn't put party politics aside while we grappled with a pandemic that had the capacity to take lives, destroy livelihoods and pull society apart.

The Prime Minister's address didn't inspire me, as was clearly the intention. It looked as if Johnson thought that this was his moment of Churchillian destiny as he leaned forward, jabbing the air with clenched fists, nodding vigorously for emphasis, and employing the type of language that alarmed rather than galvanised.

There was truth in his statement that, 'There are millions of people who are both fearful of this terrible disease and of what this long period of enforced inactivity will do to their livelihoods.' Ironically, it was the language of Johnson and his ministers that was partly responsible for the fear. Covid was typically referred to as 'this deadly virus' or 'this vicious enemy.' It was the rhetoric of war.

It was becoming apparent that the virus was mainly claiming the lives of the old and the infirm. There were fatalities amongst younger people, but they were rare and nearly always associated with a significant underlying health problem. However, what was known to be factually correct about the virus was at odds with public perception. Last week's Ipsos Mori poll revealed that nearly 60% of those aged 18-34 felt genuinely threatened by the virus. If the government's aim was to create a heightened sense of fear to ensure that its citizens complied with the national lockdown, it had succeeded. Shutting down society had proved to be the easy bit. More of a challenge was navigating a route out of the labyrinth of restrictions to open it up again.

Johnson huffed and puffed through his thirteen-minute address which included the type of inane graphics with which we were all becoming wearily familiar. He talked about five Covid alert levels and up popped a vertical bar divided into five coloured sections each containing a number. If you had any difficulty counting past five, this was the chart for you. Level one was 'no infection present' but my attention drifted away before we got to five, which I assumed was Armageddon.

Then we came to the important bits. The PM made it clear that this was a rough sketch rather than a detailed map, but he flagged up some signposts and key dates. It wasn't three steps to heaven, but it was a start.

Step one was to be implemented with immediate effect. Those who were unable to work from home were encouraged to return to their jobs. This covered activities such as construction and manufacturing. More exercise was also sanctioned, so long as it was with members of your own household. From 1st June, step two kicked in and schools were expected to open again but in a phased way. Only selected year groups would return to begin with. Step three was scheduled for the beginning of July, and it would herald the re-opening of some aspects of the hospitality industry. I instinctively thought of pubs.

There was no specific mention of sport, but I jumped to the conclusion that if restrictions were being gradually eased, professional sport would be looking to pick up where it left off, even if everything took place behind closed doors without a single spectator in sight. It's funny, but if you had told me six weeks ago that racing would remain dormant for over two months and when it returned owners wouldn't be allowed to go, I would have fallen into a deep, self-pitying depression. Now I was relieved, and maybe even a little excited, about the prospect of a return on those terms.

Saturday 16th May 2020
May was heading for the record books, and it had nothing to do with infection rates. The extraordinary weather continued to accompany the health crisis. Day after day, the sun shone with reassuring relentlessness as people conducted isolated lives, unable to share their homes and gardens with family and friends.

I was out and about a lot. I didn't see the point of doing massive weekly shops when I had time on my hands and enjoyed the opportunity to walk to my local Lidl or Sainsbury's every day for a bit of exercise. Things had calmed down a bit, and the queues subsided as people felt less inclined to buy a month's supply of toilet rolls and tinned soup every time they ventured out of their Covid bunkers to visit a supermarket.

There was good news for golfers as well. On Tuesday, pairs were allowed to start playing again, providing they were in the same household. Me and Joe were on the first tee at Dartford faster than Free Love can cover five furlongs on quick going. I played badly, even by my low standards, but my God, did we enjoy ourselves.

On the same day that Joe and I reacquainted ourselves with the challenges of Dartford's short but deceptively difficult golf course, the government announced that professional sport would not resume in any guise, even behind closed doors, until 1st June at the earliest.

Racing was quick to respond and on Thursday revised plans were unveiled which included staging the 1,000 and 2,000 Guineas on the first weekend in June. The Derby and Oaks were pencilled in for the opening weekend of July. Royal Ascot would remain in its usual mid-June slot.

It all seemed feasible. In terms of the pattern of the pandemic, we were about three weeks behind our hardest hit western European neighbours. French racing had roared back into action on Monday with a star-studded card at Longchamp which featured the seasonal debuts of the country's leading three-year-old colt, Victor Ludorum, and last year's Arc third, Sottsass. Both managed to fluff their lines but it was great to see quality horses back in action on a date that was exactly three weeks short of the day targeted for the resumption of racing in the UK.

This morning's video from Louise showed Free Love doing a fast piece of work upsides one of Mick's newer acquisitions, Sampers Seven. Once again, our filly appeared to travel strongly giving the impression that if there was a race for her tomorrow, she'd be ready.

I had to look up her galloping companion and discovered that she had raced four times in Ireland, winning once, a five-furlong 14-runner maiden at Dundalk. Rated 67, the three-year-old daughter of Anjaan looked just the sort of animal to thrive in Mick Appleby's care. There was no information about how much money changed hands when Sampers Seven left the ownership of Mr N Hartery, but she now belonged to the Value Racing Club, whose members looked sure to have plenty of fun with their newly acquired sprinter.

We were surely close to getting on a racecourse again. If there was a suitable opportunity for Free Love during the first week of the programme, she might be only three weeks away from making a belated return. It was time to do a few calculations about how much it would cost the syndicate to go right through to the end of the turf season.

Gents,

I bet you've missed these updates! Hope everyone is well and doesn't feel too queasy after reading this.

I'll come straight to the point, we need to put in £2,500 each, in 5 x £500 payments, to get us through to the sales in early November. As usual, that's an absolute worst-case scenario.

We have £24.17 left in our Weatherbys account. Mick's core training bill, based on the £40 a day fee he currently charges (should have gone up to £42 on 1 April) means a monthly invoice of around £1,550 inclusive of VAT. Insurance and farrier bills come to £170 a month combined, and the vet's average is about £50 a month, but it varies greatly. So, it's about £1,800 a month when we're not racing.

It costs approximately £400 to run, slightly less if we stay at a local track. Two runs a month means a bill of around £2,600, one run is £2,200. I'm taking £2,400 as our average. Our total outgoings until the sales should be

May £1,800, June, July, August, September & October £2,400 per month giving a grand total of £13,800.

Our 5 x £2,500 contributions represent a shortfall of around £1,300 but we are due a £800 VAT reimbursement in about three weeks and £300 sponsorship money from Tattersalls as soon as Free Love makes her seasonal reappearance. We'll also be due around £2k additional VAT (quarters May-July & August - October) if Free Love wins no prize money and it's all outgoings and no income. That's why we won't need to make a sixth contribution on the 31 October.

Of course, it could be like last year and Free Love wins early making subsequent payments unnecessary, but on the basis that we're not successful, everyone would need to transfer £500 into the account on 31 May, 30 June, 31 July, 31 August and 30 September.

The only other option is to sell in July. Tattersalls intend to go ahead with their horses in training sale on 8-10 July, entries for which close next Monday, 18 May. Having got this far, that doesn't seem the best route to take but we all must agree on what we should do.

Regards Tony

I don't know how many emails of this type I've sent to Pete, Patrick, Trevor and Mick. It would have been so much easier if, as we edged towards the end of each flat turf season, we all shook hands and agreed to go again the following year. That would require a five grand commitment from each owner, which would be fine if money was no object. But I could never take it for granted that all five of us would give the nod to continue. And that included me.

After Free Love won her first race at Catterick in September 2018, just a month before she was due to be sold at the sales, the mathematical calculations began. Was it viable to keep the filly for a bit longer? How much would we need if we wanted to extend the partnership until Ascot's March sales? How much more to the

Tattersalls horses in training sale in July? If we made it to there, I could recalculate what it would cost to keep Free Love in training until the end of the season.

And so it would go on. Every few months I'd provide a comprehensive breakdown of how much cash was needed for us to limp on to the next milestone, always assuming the worst regarding prize money. It's a bit like going racing as a punter. You agree your betting budget for the day and write off the whole amount. Anything you win is a bonus.

Whenever I presented the figures to the other boys, they were based on Free Love failing to win a bean which would mean a downward slide in her official rating and an accompanying fall in her residual value. There was no point saying that if Free Love won a race we would only need to put in another x-amount each. The deal had always been to wave goodbye to the lot as soon as the bank transfers were made.

Tuesday 26th May 2020

The return of racing was less than a week away. Well, that's what the front page of yesterday's Racing Post suggested. Brant Dunshea, the BHA's chief regulatory officer and the man at the helm of the Resumption of Racing Group, was quoted as being 'incredibly confident' that horseracing would be back on 1st June.

Dunshea based his optimism on what appeared to be Oliver Dowden's acceptance that racing was well placed to make an early start as it was a non-contact sport conducted in the great outdoors. The minister for the Department of Digital, Culture, Media and Sport indicated that while football, rugby and the like would have to wait a little longer, horseracing was on course for the beginning of June.

I read the rest of the article to see if there were any clues about when owners would be allowed on racecourses, but that wasn't a priority. It was all about making a start. Top Newmarket handler, William Haggas, backed the protocols developed by the BHA designed to make the resumption safe and socially responsible. Only staff working in the industry whose attendance was essential would be allowed on course. Temperature checks, jockeys having to wear masks and strict social distancing were all parts of the package. It was clearly one step at a time, although Haggas went on to express the hope that we could edge back to normality once racing had demonstrated that it was safe, and the national picture continued to justify the further easing of restrictions.

Not long after yesterday's announcement about the 1st June restart, an updated fixture list was released, and it contained several five-furlong handicaps that were definitely within Free Love's range. The following morning, I fired off an email brimming with optimism.

Gents,

First of all, we need to send Trevor a 'get well soon' message. Like an inexperienced novice hurdler, he took a false step and tumbled down his stairs on Sunday morning. It required a visit to A&E and although nothing is broken, he'll be on crutches for a bit and his knee will probably require surgery at some point. Hope you're not in too much pain Trevor.

Back to racing, I attach a filtered version of the fixture list released by the BHA yesterday evening. I've only included races for 3yo+ at class 4 and above.

The BHA recognises that owners may be frustrated in the early days of resumption. For example, the 69-88 race at Haydock may end up with twelve horses all rated 85 and above meaning we don't get in.

Looking on the more positive side, if we repeat last season's trick and bolt up on debut, the race to have a good look at is the listed Land O'Burns Stakes at Ayr on 22 June, restricted to fillies and mares. Past runnings are littered with winners and placed horses rated in the high 80s and low 90s. It was a race on our agenda until we blew out at York last May.

We're getting closer. I think it's behind closed doors in June with owners allowed to attend by July, at the latest. I reckon the public will be back by August even if there are ticket restrictions put in place to manage crowd sizes. What price that treble?

Finally, don't forget, your next £500 is due into the account by Monday. Regards, Tony

Everyone was keen on Haydock. Our trainer asked if we were interested in the class 4 handicap at Kempton in the first week back, which was for horses rated 71-85. We declined. The scars of Free Love's horrific career debut, made at the tight, right-handed Sunbury track, ran deep. In my mind's eye, I could still see our bemused filly falling out of the stalls before getting further and further behind to the consternation of her owners. We couldn't go back to Kempton. A straight five-furlongs on turf and decent ground were the prerequisites.

But the black type dream was still alive. Nobody came back to dismiss the idea. Maybe they thought it was another one of my unrealistically optimistic plans, but they didn't rubbish it. They opted for the usual silence instead.

You've got to keep hoping in this game. If you spent too long dissecting the reality of racehorse ownership, you'd give up before starting. An impressive win on seasonal debut would lift our filly's rating into the high 80s and that's sometimes good enough to sneak into the frame in a weak listed sprint confined to fillies and mares. No, I hadn't given up on stealing a bit of black type.

As for owners and the paying public returning, we'd have to wait and see. Infections, hospitalisations and fatalities were all going in the right direction. Falling figures and the continuation of stunning weather made me feel that we had turned a corner. Maybe we were in the home straight, which could be a short two-furlong dash like Lingfield, or perhaps something akin to Newmarket's punishing mile and a quarter slog to the line. It was a hard one to call.

7 Back in Business
(Doncaster, 26th June 2020)

Monday 1st June 2020

May finished in a blaze of sunshine and controversy. It became the sunniest and driest calendar month on record in the UK. The implications for farming and the country's water supply were concerning, but not everyone wore a furrowed brow. We've always felt that Free Love is a better horse on quickish ground, so at least the members of the North South Syndicate had smiles on their faces.

The controversy was provided by the Prime Minister's chief advisor, Dominic Cummings, who broke lockdown rules with a trip to visit his parents in Durham which also involved a detour to Barnard Castle. It's fair to say that Cummings is a divisive figure; you either loathe or hate him. For some, his actions had completely undermined the national lockdown. I liked to think that his influence didn't extend that far and found the whole episode quite absurd, especially the farrago of dates, personal circumstances and justifications presented to a baying press corps in the garden of Number 10, Downing Street. I was just grateful that he had nothing to do with the resumption of racing.

That project was in safer hands. Yesterday's Racing Post carried features on how Newcastle racecourse planned to stage the sport behind closed doors. An aerial photograph was annotated to show where the Social Distancing Officer would be located. Presumably, he or she would need to tackle miscreants from a distance of two metres to avoid a breach of their own rules. Perhaps a loudhailer was part of their uniform. And a long stick.

Further inspection of the photograph revealed mask and hand sanitiser symbols dotted around buildings, concourses and paddocks. The entry point for horses and staff contained information about the temperature checks, health questionnaires, and online Covid training modules that all personnel needed to negotiate before being allowed in. If a horsebox driver failed any of the tests, they'd be asked to make a three-point turn and head for home, taking their equine companion with them.

The measures were extraordinarily stringent, especially compared with what was required for my daily trips to the supermarket. But racing couldn't afford to put a foot wrong. It was back in action before the likes of football, whose millions of fans were desperate to see the return of their favourite sport. Every base had been covered, there was even an agreement to limit field sizes to a maximum of 12 to reduce the chances of an accident which would require the involvement of emergency services.

In the afternoon I tuned into the television coverage of Newcastle. The new flat season kicked-off with a seven-furlong class 6 handicap for horses rated 0-65. Who won it might become an obscure quiz question in years to come. Roger Fell's seven-year-old gelding, Zodiakos, was steered to victory by James Sullivan at odds of 22/1. In doing so, the hardy son of Kodiac chalked up his eighth career win from 50 visits to the racecourse. He netted a first prize of £2,781.67 which, after the usual deductions, would be enough to cover the total cost of keeping him in training for one month.

Despite the low-key start to the new season, it wasn't a bad card. Art Power confirmed the promise he had shown in the York mud in October by sauntering away with a warm looking six-furlong novice event. He appeared to be a sprinter going places. John Gosden's beautifully bred three-year-old filly, Frankly Darling, was the facile winner of a maiden race which prompted excitable talk about the Epsom Oaks.

But it wasn't all good news. In fact, it could have been a disastrous start to life behind closed doors. The eighth event of a bumper ten-race card was a decent mile-and-a-half handicap. With two furlongs to run, the well-backed December Second was making his challenge when he clipped heels with something in front and crashed to the ground. Financial Conduct was a little off the pace, but there was no time for his rider to take evasive action. Jim Crowley was shot out of the saddle as his mount stumbled badly trying to avoid the prone December Second.

It all happened at the stage of the race when the horses were travelling at their fastest. Unlike jump racing, where some of the falls appear to take place in slow motion as horses slither to a halt on soft ground when over-jumping a fence or hurdle, this was high-speed crash stuff. It looked terrifying.

You always hope for the best when these horror shows take place on the flat. They don't happen very often and when they do the horses can be quickly on their feet, galloping loose, showing that no great harm has been done. For the jockeys propelled into the ground at 40 miles an hour, a broken collar bone is seen as a bit of a let-off.

It was a miracle that neither PJ Macdonald nor Jim Crowley was injured. Racing was spared the headlines of two jockeys taken to hospital in ambulances that could be better deployed elsewhere during a time of national crisis. By contrast, there was no miraculous escape for December Second, who was sadly fatally injured in the fall.

It's what I worry about every time Free Love ambles compliantly into her starting stall. During those anxious seconds before the starter's flag falls and the gates burst open, I can't help thinking about the worst that could happen. Every owner wants their horse to come back safely. On this occasion it was former England footballer, David Platt, who suffered the anguish of knowing that the box reserved for December Second at Philip Kirby's North Yorkshire yard would be empty this evening.

Wednesday 3rd June 2020

I decided to make an impromptu visit to Langham. Last week, the government announced that up to six people could meet outside or in a private garden from the beginning of June, providing social distancing and sensible levels of hygiene were observed. It felt like a giant step towards the return of civilised society.

When I found out yesterday via Mick's Facebook page that socially distanced visits to the stables were now permitted on an appointment basis, I was on to Louise like a shot. She confirmed that I could come but would need to stay at the top of the yard and not walk around the barns. To observe social distancing, owners were also asked to drive their own cars to the top of the gallop rather than cadge a lift in Mick's ancient Range Rover.

As sharing cars with anyone outside your own household was prohibited, with the police having powers to order drivers and their passengers to turn around and head home, I didn't even bother to let the others know about my plan. It was intended to be a brief solo raid.

It seemed fitting that as soon as the country was given the go ahead for a little bit of outdoor socialising, the record-breaking period of sunshine came to an end, and it was cool and overcast when I arrived at the stables just before 10am. I parked up and walked tentatively towards the wooden gate at the entrance to the yard.

Everything looked normal enough. Horses who had been exercising in earlier lots were being washed and groomed. Some were having a few minutes on the circular walker to warm down and get rid of any fizz produced by their fast work upsides other horses. The yard was a picture of busy routine, a little world unaffected by the wearisome restrictions affecting everybody's lives.

Louise was soon there to greet me, but now in the awkward way we were all getting used to. To ensure we were at least two metres apart, I remained on my side of the gate, holding up a hand to gesture that I realised I should come no closer. Fortunately, there was no need for a prolonged, distanced conversation as I was told to jump in my car and head for the top of the gallop where I'd find Mick. Free Love was due to work with the next lot.

I didn't find Mick surrounded by owners. In fact, he was on his own. Louise joined us to take the videos she had been sending to everyone since stable visits had been prohibited in March. As I had our trainer to myself, it was a chance to pick his brains about Free Love's four-year-old campaign.

Our filly's galloping companion was Sampers Seven, Mick's newly acquired three-year-old filly who had won a maiden race at Dundalk. Mick liked her.

'This is a fast filly,' was his sparing description as the pair charged up the hill. 'I think she's a lot better than 67,' he continued as the two flying fillies flashed past us.

I thought to myself that we must be quite handy as well, as Free Love cruised upsides Sampers Seven, effortlessly matching strides with the new apple of Mick's eye. Not that I was jealous, but it looked to my uneducated and partisan eye that we had worked the fractionally better of the two.

I didn't venture this opinion with Mick but asked him some general questions about possible races instead. He had already entered Free Love for next week's Haydock race, but a quick check on his phone revealed that there were plenty of hopefuls already registered, and there was still more than an hour to closure.

Everybody wanted a run and with field sizes restricted to 12, it was hard work finding a suitable race to get into, never mind one that provided a decent winning opportunity. Monday's opening card at Newcastle illustrated the dilemma. Every runner in the 0-85 sprint six-furlong handicap, won by the wittily named Brian The Snail (a son of Zebedee), was contested by horses rated 83-85. It was the same for the other handicaps. You needed to be no more than three pounds off top-weight to get in. As Free Love was currently rated 83 and the Haydock sprint was for horses rated 0-88, our chances of getting a run looked less than 50-50.

I turned away from the depressing subject of Haydock and asked Mick some general questions before heading back to my allotted position by the gate outside the yard. Free Love was ready to run. Mick felt she was more forward than when she made her seasonal debut last year, but I suppose that wasn't surprising given that she was put back into training at the start of February with the aim of reappearing in mid-April. For the last few weeks, she'd been all dressed up with nowhere to go. While I had the chance, I couldn't resist asking Mick about black type.

'The filly looks to be in good shape,' was my opening gambit. Mick agreed without adding much more. 'I know towards the end of last season she had a few reverses on bad ground and from bad draws,' I continued doggedly. 'But if she can improve 5-7lbs back up to a mark in the high eighties, we were thinking that it might be worth having a pop at pinching a bit of black type.'

'Yes, that's possible I suppose,' was Mick's undemonstrative endorsement. I took it as positive affirmation of the plan. After all, he could have dismissed it out of hand telling me that I was mad and should leave the ambitious dreaming to the owners of Sampers bloody Seven. Even worse, he could have met my suggestion with resolute silence.

Back at the yard, Theo's girlfriend, Erika Parkinson, was washing down Free Love. Theo had shot off early to Yarmouth where he had a couple of rides for the stable and Erika had been entrusted with riding our filly.

As I leant on the gate, about 15 yards away from Erika and Free Love, an extraordinary thing happened. I was trying to grab some photos on my phone when the filly stood stock still, sideways on, before turning her head to stare in my direction. I know it's fanciful, and plenty of experienced horse people would dismiss as absurd the notion that I should take my filly's pose as a sign of recognition, but I swear she fixed me with a gaze that seemed to say, 'I know you. You're the big one with the glasses who's always there when I run as fast as I can. I haven't seen you for ages!'

Erika called over to me suggesting I could come a little closer if I wanted to take some pictures. I accepted the offer and, after grabbing a few snaps which I intended to send to the others, I gave Free Love a couple of reassuring pats. It had been over six months since I'd seen my girl in the flesh. God! How I had missed the feel and smell of the warm sweat on her neck.

When I arrived home in Dartford, I checked the status of the Haydock race before posting the photos on our WhatsApp group and composing a report about my spontaneous visit to Langham.

Gents,
Hope you are all keeping well. Following the WhatsApp update, I thought I'd give you a slightly more detailed account of my impromptu visit to Mick's yard this morning.
Free Love looked in great shape. I had a quick chat with Erika afterwards (Theo had to leave early for Yarmouth) who told me that Free Love always 'works all over' whoever she is paired with. In this case it was Sampers Seven, a sprinter who Mick really rates. One to back next week when she makes her

debut for the yard!

I had a chance for a good chat with Mick. We talked about the difficulties about getting into races and our Haydock entry proved the point. There are more than 20 horses rated higher than us and we're only five pounds off top-weight. Rather irritatingly, the Newmarket race on Sunday which wasn't considered because it's a 0-95 race, has attracted only 11 runners with the lowest two rated 83 and 82.

I also asked Mick if he felt that having a cut at pinching some black type in a weak listed race for fillies and mares was realistic if Free Love got back to a mark of around 90 which she achieved at Windsor. Mick thought it was feasible which brings another target into view.

The Land O'Burns Stakes run at Ayr on 22nd June is a five-furlong listed race for fillies and mares. It's usually not the strongest and might be worth a look.

Maybe we need a Zoom meeting after we know what's happening at Haydock. If we get in, the filly's performance will tell us where we go next. I have a feeling that, like last year, her best form may come when she's fresh and has summer going conditions. If that's the case, maybe we should consider striking while the iron is hot.

Regards, Tony

Not for the first time, I was dreaming of an unlikely triumph and had got the bit between my teeth as far as the *Land O'Burns Stakes* was concerned. There is no doubt that a bit of black type would significantly increase Free Love's value. As to what that was, during these strange and challenging times, I had only the vaguest idea. But if she was worth £12-15k now, her price tag would be more like £20-25k if she scrambled into third place at Ayr.

But it wasn't about the money. It was more about the glory. Having framed photographs on my lounge wall that proudly proclaimed I had once been associated with a filly who won four races and had been third in the **Listed Land O'Burn Stakes** was the ambition. Until it was proved beyond all doubt that Free Love wasn't capable of such a feat, I'd keep the dream alive.

Sunday 7th June 2020

It was 17 degrees, cloudy, and by 4.30pm it was raining which meant that fellow joint owner, Pete Smith, had to pull on a waterproof to capture the historic moment on his mobile phone. We were in the Smiths' back garden having Sunday lunch, socialising with people from outside our own household for the first time in nearly three months.

Pete and Melanie were fastidious with the arrangements. Every dish was duplicated. There were separate bowls for the Linnetts and Smiths, each with a serving spoon that was forbidden to cross over to the other household. Only Pete and Melanie were allowed to pour the wine, which kept them busy all afternoon.

I think Jennie and I would have been a bit more slapdash had we been hosting - I was rather dubious about the risks of infection from touching surfaces compared to the obvious dangers of coughing and spluttering - but it was a small price to pay in exchange for meeting up with close friends again.

There had been high prices paid elsewhere. A couple of days ago the UK Covid death toll hit 40,000. It was therefore a relief to see the rate of fatalities in decline and today's figure of 61 gave hope that maybe we were over the worst.

It had been a strange three months since the middle of March when the government started putting measures in place to halt the spread of the virus. We'd all got used to changes to our routines and the type of deprivations that were frustrating and upsetting rather than life-threatening. However, I had no doubt that, for a significant minority, the ongoing restrictions must have been miserable.

I felt particularly sorry for youngsters working in the hospitality and retail industries. There were plenty on zero-hours contracts who looked to have slipped through the Chancellor's safety net. Many of them were consigned to impoverished lives in home environments far removed from the lockdown idylls described by some broadsheet journalists.

I am sure Alison Pearson is lovely, but her article in a recent of edition of The Telegraph was typical of some of the dewy-eyed thinking doing the rounds amongst the middle classes. Here's a slice of it.

'Our whole attitude to consumerism has changed. Psychologists reckon it takes 21 days to create a new habit. Well, lockdown afforded us that time. Unable to 'just pop to the supermarket' or to secure the self-isolation Holy Grail – an online shopping delivery – we learnt how to shop less often. Millions began to use greengrocers and butchers. I came to rely on a nearby farm shop and my family competed to turn their fresh, locally sourced ingredients into delicious meals. Weaned off ready meals and posh nibbles, we discovered it was possible to eat better than before and for a third of my weekly Waitrose spend.

Millions? And where are all those nearby farm shops? I didn't see one the last time I wandered through the Tree Estate in Dartford. Gosh, and saving money by shopping somewhere other than Waitrose. The thought had never occurred to me. At least Alison refrained from extolling the virtues of working (on full salary) from home. She didn't marvel at the opportunities to build yurts with Jack and Esme in the back garden as part of their bohemian home schooling. She left that type of tosh to The Guardian.

We tried hard to steer the Sunday lunch conversation away from the pandemic, but as it was never out of the news and the government's response to it dominated every breathing minute of our lives, the topic was always crouching at the door, ready to enter.

Trying to keep things in a lighter vein, I swapped a few horseracing snippets with Pete. We were both impressed with Kameko's victory in the first Classic of the season, and disappointed that Free Love missed the cut for Haydock on Tuesday. All 12 runners were rated 85-88, a direct result of the extraordinary times in which we found ourselves. We also noted, to our collective chagrin, that this afternoon's 0-95 sprint which closed the card at Newmarket was down to nine runners. We didn't even think about entering as we were sure it would attract the same high levels of interest that all these handicaps were drawing and, with an official rating of 83, Free Love would have no chance of getting in.

But these were minor irritations. The rain cleared, the wine flowed, and we talked about plans for the summer. The chance to meet up with family and friends again lifted everybody's spirits.

Monday 15th June 2020

We somehow managed to arrange a Zoom meeting last week to discuss our options for Free Love. It took about 30 WhatsApp messages to establish a time and date that all five could make. Even then it was nearly scuppered by Patrick who sent a text message on Wednesday to inform everyone that he was having technical difficulties and couldn't access the meeting. In a second message, sent ten minutes later, he owned up to being a day early.

The following day, the owners' Zoom conference went ahead dodging Trevor's funeral commitments, Pete's French lessons (adult education class, just to be clear), Mick's church activities, and Patrick's calendar problems.

We all agreed that Free Love needed a run and there was palpable frustration with the current situation. Having endured a suspension of racing for the first two months of the season, we now had to put up with a further month's delay as we scrabbled around trying to get into a race, any race. We'd ask Mick to make an entry for another handicap at Haydock, this time for horses rated 0-90. That was on the 24th but it seemed unlikely that we'd get in. Two days later there was a 0-85 class 4 contest at Doncaster which seemed ideal. It was a straight, flat five furlongs and the ground was likely to be decent. We'd surely make the cut for that one.

We also had a chat about the *Land O'Burns* Stakes and decided it was worth an entry. The others felt we could only justify the expense of sending Free Love to Ayr if she had a realistic chance of making the frame. Finishing a respectable fifth would cost us over a grand in entry fees and travel, and might even result in a small, unhelpful rise to our rating.

After our virtual meeting, I wasted no time getting in touch with Mick. I remembered his text over a year ago following Free Love's impressive win at Nottingham on her seasonal debut. He threw out the possibility of a speculative entry for the listed *Lansdown Stud Stakes* at Bath. His text had started with the words, 'You might think I'm mad but…'

It was my turn now. My text about the *Land O'Burns* read:

Morning Mick.

I know you think we're mad, but we wouldn't mind throwing a few quid away making an entry for the listed fillies' race at Ayr which closes tomorrow. After the initial rush, some of these races are cutting up. If it looked like half a dozen runners and a realistic shot at black type it might be worth considering. What do you think?

Mick simply replied that that it was worth an entry to size up the opposition. I left it at that. He would also enter for Haydock, and the Doncaster race was on the agenda as well. One way or another,

Free Love would be on a racecourse again before the end of the month.

Tuesday 16th June 2020

While every racing enthusiast worth their salt was immersed in the form for the Queen Anne Stakes, the curtain raiser for Royal Ascot behind closed doors, I was on the BHA website anxiously checking the entries for next Monday's *Land O'Burn Stakes*.

It wasn't terrible. When the race closed at noon, there were 16 entries with only five rated 90 or above. Topping the list on a mark of 100 was Queen's Gift who had run respectably on seasonal debut when fifth in the Group 3 Palace House Stakes at Newmarket on 2,000 Guineas day. Que Amoro (98) took the eye. She was a runaway winner of the big apprentice handicap that Free Love contested at York on Ebor day last summer. She went on to finish a close second in a listed sprint at Ayr in September, giving the impression that there was plenty more improvement to come.

Sure, Free Love had a bit to find if she was to be competitive, but there was a gaggle of fillies in the mid-eighties who were making up the numbers. I didn't think we had much to fear from the likes of Ishvara, Dandy's Beano and Yolo Again. As for Merry Banter, a run-of-the-mill, six-year-old handicapper currently rated 82, and never been higher than 85 in her life, it was reassuring to know that I wasn't the only one foolish enough to tilt at windmills.

The little group of higher rated fillies held the key. If they all ran, it would almost certainly be a wasted journey. We needed two of them to come out, preferably three. If that were the case and we were left in a field of seven or eight runners, it would be worth a go.

I watched the televised coverage of Ascot and found the experience for the sofa spectator to be surprisingly good. I'm aware of the noise generated by a big crowd when watching on the box, but it only kicks in during the final two-furlongs and it's often drowned by the commentator, whose frenzied words skilfully bring the race to a crescendo.

It's not like football where the ebb and flow of the game is matched by the roars of triumph, howls of derision, and moans of despair throughout its loud and tribal 90 minutes. I wondered what football would be like when it returned without crowds. Charlton were due to resume their League One relegation battle on Saturday away at fellow strugglers Hull City. I could buy a live stream of the game for a tenner. Out of a mixture of loyalty and curiosity, I had to give it a go.

Saturday 20th June 2020
It was the final day of a memorable Royal Ascot. The lack of crowds and the strange, distanced interviews with masked riders couldn't detract from the pleasure of watching top-class thoroughbreds in action. There were plenty of performances to quicken the pulse, but Stradivarius completing a Gold Cup hat-trick was surely the pick.

Over the extreme distance of two-and-a-half miles, and on softened ground that encouraged bookmakers to push out the champion stayer to a tempting price of even money, Stradivarius was imperious in victory. It's only every now and then that you see a performance of this kind at the highest level. It's not rare for horses to record impressive, facile victories when they simply outclass inferior opposition. But to come there at the furlong pole pulling double, before sprinting ten lengths clear in Europe's premier staying flat race, was a feat to savour. 'The best stayer in the world! Three Gold Cups!' was Simon Holt's exuberant and throaty commentary as Stradivarius galloped into the history books in breath-taking fashion.

Free Love was at the other end of the spectrum. Although her current mark of 83 put her in the top 15% of all 13,000 horses in training who had an official rating on the flat (something I worked out in one of my many anorak moments), she was 42lbs shy of the great stayer's classification, which was raised to 125 after his Ascot Gold Cup romp. It was a reminder of the level of ability needed to make an impression at the highest level of the sport.

There was also the issue of stamina that kept the two horses apart. Stradivarius could cope with trips from one-and-a-half to two-and-a-half miles, and there was even talk of a tilt at the Prix de l'Arc de Triomphe. Free Love could manage the minimum trip of five furlongs and her two attempts at six suggested that anything slightly further was out of reach.

These were sobering thoughts as I checked how many declarations had already been made for Monday's listed race at Ayr over my first cup of tea of the morning. By 8.30am there were already half a dozen. An hour later Mick sent a text saying the figure now stood at ten. I gave him a quick call and we both agreed to leave it.

The decision to give the race a swerve was made easier by the tough stance adopted by Scotland's first minister in her attempt to control the virus north of the border. It wasn't difficult to feel that Nicola Sturgeon's approach served two purposes, the second of which was always to do something a little bit different to whatever the PM announced at Westminster. If Johnson set out details of an 18-point recovery plan, I swear that Sturgeon would unveil her devolved government's 19-point plan an hour or two later.

With a beady eye fixed firmly on Scottish independence, everything that Sturgeon announced was designed to appear more stringent, more coherent, and more competent than anything that came out of the mouth of Boris Johnson which, let's face it, wasn't too hard.

A consequence of Sturgeon's draconian strategy was to make it difficult for us to run in the *Land O'Burns* Stakes even if we wanted to. Horses and stable staff weren't permitted to stay overnight which meant that the 632-mile round trip from Langham to Ayr would have to be undertaken in one hit. It was an inhumane and unreasonable stipulation which made it even harder to justify running. The BHA might as well have added an additional race condition: *A listed race over five furlongs for fillies and mares, three-year-olds and upwards. Sassenachs not welcome.*

Mick told me that he'd already given the transport arrangements some thought. If Free Love went to Ayr, the horsebox would have to leave the yard at about 4am, aiming to arrive at the racecourse around noon. The race was at 4.15pm which would mean a 5.30pm departure, arriving back at Langham at around 2am. I couldn't inflict that on Mick's staff, never mind the horse. By the time we finished our chat, the declarations had crept up to 12 making the decision not to run even easier.

There was always Doncaster, and I finished my brief chat with Mick on an upbeat note. We'd surely get into Friday's 0-85 handicap at the South Yorkshire track. I had no regrets about taking a flyer with our listed race entry, but that was behind us. It was all eyes on the *Sky Sports Racing Sky 415 Handicap*. The race title lacked the poetry of the *Land O'Burns Stakes*, but at least we'd get in.

The Doncaster race closed at noon. The bad news was another bumper entry of 41 sprinters. The good news was that we were in. There were 11 horses rated above us and three shared our filly's mark of 83. Free Love was therefore in the top 14 which was the new, slightly increased maximum field size. At last! What had been eagerly anticipated since our filly went for her winter break in mid-November, was finally about to happen.

That afternoon I paid my £10 and watched Charlton grab three valuable points away at Hull, courtesy of a scrappy far-post header by centre-half and captain, Jason Pearce. I took winning ugly in South Yorkshire as a good omen, but the match experience was an odd one. You had to admire the competitiveness of the players who were used to performing in front of noisy crowds. They seemed to cope well with their new, surreal surroundings. It was harder for the fans, who would have preferred to be there singing, shouting and getting fully involved with the tense relegation battle. It was a strange and muted experience.

Wednesday 24th June 2020

Free Love was declared for Doncaster on Friday. The race was over-subscribed and, as sometimes happens, it was divided into two contests of 12 and 11 runners. Our filly was in the first division, which looked the tougher of the two, and was set to concede a pound to Merry Banter.

Merry bloody Banter! I watched the *Land O'Burns Stakes* on Monday in which Que Amoro was an emphatic winner. I was sure that Free Love wouldn't have been able to live with her, but my eyes were drawn to the 82-rated Merry Banter who showed her usual early dash and only surrendered the lead approaching the final furlong. But instead of dropping back through the field like a stone sinking in water, she hung on tenaciously for third place, half a length in front of the similarly moderately rated and fully exposed Fool For You (87).

That could have been us. That may have been our chance and we were unable to grasp it. Instead, we were heading for Doncaster on Friday where we would be required to give weight to the black type thief, otherwise known as Merry Banter.

Shortly after the declarations became available, Louise sent a video of Free Love doing her last piece of brisk work with Sampers Seven ahead of Friday's race. Our filly looked in great shape breezing upsides her talented galloping companion.

Since I visited the yard at the beginning of the month, Sampers Seven had been backed from 11/1 to 6/1 on her debut for the stable at Wolverhampton. Greed got the better of me and my win only bet was sunk when Mick's flying filly was gunned down in the final furlong and had to settle for second place. I consoled myself with the knowledge that had I gone each way she would have finished fourth. This is an immutable law of punting that will be recognised by all weary followers of racing. A clause of the same law prevented me from backing the filly when she hosed up by three lengths at Chelmsford eight days later, proving Mick to be spot on about the leniency of the filly's mark of 67.

I was casually looking at Friday's opposition when my phone buzzed. It was Mick Appleby. My first instinct was to think that bad news was on its way. The filly had trod on a stone and was lame. Or maybe she was a bit sore after this morning's gallop. There was always the bad trachea scope rabbit to pull out of the hat. It could be anything - other than news that Free Love had produced such a sparkling piece of work that Mick felt compelled to re-mortgage his stable and put the biggest bet of his life on the flying filly at Doncaster on Friday.

I greeted our trainer in the most buoyant way I could muster, bearing in mind I was bracing myself for a fall. To my surprise, Free Love was fine, a picture of good health. She was fit and ready to race, but the prospect of fast ground worried Mick. He didn't want the filly to come back sore from her first visit to the racecourse for seven months, which would mean more time on the sidelines.

We were desperate for a run. We were also convinced that Free Love was better on a sound surface. It was like a road at Yarmouth when she first showed a glimmer of ability as a juvenile. It was also quick, summer ground at Windsor in July when she posted the highest rated performance of her career.

I explained all this to Mick but took his point. Most trainers don't want their horses to run on firm ground unless they are sure that the animal will stand up to it. At the very least, they have a duty to express their reservations to owners. It's also prudent. Who wants an unreasonable owner shouting down the phone demanding to know why you risked the apple of their eye on dangerously firm going when it was 'obvious' that the precious creature would be jarred up by the traumatic experience?

The going description for Doncaster was currently good to firm with no rain forecast until Friday. I wasn't unduly concerned about conditions. It was Town Moor's belated seasonal debut, and I was sure there would be a lush covering of grass on a track that would have been watered if the clerk of the course thought the going was edging anywhere near dangerously firm.

We agreed to keep an eye on going updates but, unless there was a dramatic change, we'd run. I relayed a summary of the conversation to the others, and they were happy to go ahead. We weren't being reckless. In fact, we were sure the good to firm conditions would be ideal. More than anything, we wanted to see Free Love back on a racecourse.

Although attendance at behind closed doors racing remained restricted to essential workers, the return of owners looked to be nearing. Yesterday, the PM set out the next phase of changes to lockdown measures which would allow people to see more of their family and friends and help businesses to get back to work.

From Saturday 4th July, the Prime Minister announced that hairdressers would be able to open, which was surely good news for our unkempt leader. Of more interest to me was the news that pubs and restaurants could reopen, providing they adhered to 'Covid secure' guidelines. From the same date, staycations in England would be allowed, with campsites given the green light to open their doors to holidaymakers.

There was other stuff about cinemas, museums and places of worship. It meant I could attend mass again, provided I was prepared to jump through several safety hoops. I had mixed feelings about that. I'd become accustomed to a more informal experience, watching live streamed services in my dressing gown from the comfort of my sofa, a mug of tea and a plate of toast on my lap, a top-up during the homily if needed.

The main thrust of the government's proposals - apart from making me feel guilty about my newly acquired church going habits - was all about opening up society a little bit more, easing everyone back into a way of life that looked more normal. That surely meant owners returning to racecourses soon, maybe with small crowds not long afterwards.

Friday 26th June 2020
The WhatsApp group had been buzzing for the last two days. Despite not being allowed to be at Doncaster and having to settle for watching the race on Sky Sports Racing or by placing a small bet via a home computer or smartphone to give access to a live stream of the great event, levels of excitement were high and rising.

All agreed that National Anthem was the one to beat. He was making a quick reappearance after making all the running in a class 3 handicap at Ayr on the same day that the *Land O'Burns Stakes* was run. That made it four wins from eight attempts for the lightly raced five-year-old who surely had more improvement to come.

By 9.30am the field was down to nine. Jumira Bridge, Restless Rose and my old friend Merry bloody Banter were all declared nonrunners. It wouldn't surprise me if it was the last we saw of Merry Banter. She had thieved her bit of black type, which was mission accomplished. She was probably heading for the breeding sheds before any subsequent failures on the racecourse dulled the lustre of her Ayr achievement. With seven wins from 46 races and a career high mark of 89 secured by her listed race heroics, the hardy six-year-old mare surely had a decent chance of producing offspring who could run a bit. Good luck to her.

The mood in the North South Syndicate camp was generally positive. Mick Corringham was hopeful for a place but felt that our filly faced a stiff task on her belated reappearance and would need a personal best to win. Trevor predicted a less ambitious top five finish while hoping we made the first three. Patrick wasn't a contributor to the frenzied WhatsApp debate, which was not particularly unusual. He was probably sat at his walnut writing bureau penning a measured treatise about our prospects. As for Pete, who could usually be relied upon to pour buckets of cold water over my enthusiasm for Free Love's chances, he restricted himself to noting that our filly's price had drifted from an overnight 8/1 to 20/1 which was still freely available less than an hour before the off.

The betting didn't bother me. None of us could be described as serious punters. I had a tenner each way at 20/1 and I doubt if any of the other boys risked much more. It's not the weight of money required to spark a price collapse.

Ignoring the insultingly big price offered by the bookmakers about Free Love, I concentrated on the facts instead. Towards the end of last season, our filly faced some stiff tasks, sometimes from bad draws or on unsuitable going. It saw her official rating ease from 90 to today's mark of 83. You could argue that she was well handicapped, especially as conditions looked in her favour. Doncaster's flat five furlongs on quickish ground looked made for her. The high draw didn't look ideal but in a such a small field it could hardly be used as an excuse. It was a niggling concern, nevertheless.

As noon approached, the televised action switched from the studio to Doncaster racecourse. The *Sky Sports Racing Sky 415 Handicap (Division I)* was due off at 12.15pm, the first contest on the type of elongated ten-race card to which we were now accustomed.

I really thought we could win, and idly daydreamed about Free Love streaking clear inside the final furlong to push her official rating back into the high eighties and black type territory. But as the moment of truth neared, confidence drained from my blood. Free Love was the only filly in the field. All eight opponents were experienced geldings, seasoned sprinting warriors. National Anthem looked a beast of a horse as he strode around the paddock with an insouciant swagger. He dwarfed Free Love, as if to underline the size of her imminent task.

The public latched onto Abel Handy as their 6/4 favourite. The son of Arcano had won the Group 3 Cornwallis Stakes as a two-year-old which earned him an official rating of 105. Although he didn't build on that heady figure, he remained useful and had already been placed in two runs earlier in the month. Today's mark of 81 made plenty of appeal to punters who felt the four-year-old had a fitness advantage and was on a winning mark.

I felt inclined to agree as the television commentators talked up the chances of Danny Tudhope's mount. We had to concede weight to this former Group race winner and, had Merry Banter stood her ground, we would be giving weight to an animal recently placed in a listed race. We started to look badly handicapped. At least Theo still had a small apprentice claim which reduced our filly's burden by three pounds.

I'm not sure what I felt as I watched the runners gather behind the stalls from the comfort of the sofa in our back room. Free Love had contested 25 races to date, and I had been present for 23 of them. An emergency closure of the Dartford crossing and a trip abroad accounted for the two absences. In normal circumstances my calendar would have been cleared to make way for a trip to Town Moor. Only an act of God would have prevented me from being there. But these weren't normal circumstances, and I couldn't even invite Pete, who lived a 15-minute walk away, to join me to watch the great occasion on the box. Only outdoor fraternising was allowed.

Free Love looked calm in the paddock and cantered down to the start like the little professional she had become. She's never been difficult to load and once again walked into her starting berth without fuss or hesitation. They were all in and set. Jennie, Joe and I sat in our back-room grandstand waiting for the starter's yellow flag to fall, all eyes on the orange and green jacket in stall 11.

It's one of the great sights in flat racing. When a group of experienced, talented sprinters - and make no mistake, this lot was useful - hits the gate. It doesn't take them long to rattle off sub-eleven-second furlongs as they reach speeds of more than 40 miles per hour. That's twice as fast as Usain Bolt, while carrying a nine stone jockey into the bargain.

It was a level break, but Free Love was out sharper than most along with Abel Handy who was drawn next to her. At halfway, National Anthem led a small group of three towards the far side of the track and, judging by the shadows which stretched across the Doncaster turf, the big horse was a couple of lengths up on Free Love who was doing best of the rest on the near side.

Theo was pushing away, urging his willing partner to close the gap, but as the final furlong loomed it was clear that National Anthem wouldn't be caught. Our filly moved into third but chasing the pace from halfway looked to be taking its toll. However, instead of weakening out of contention, she kept on all the way to the line and held on to third place, two-and-a-quarter lengths behind the impressive winner who made it five wins from nine career starts.

It was a tremendous comeback for our little superstar and the WhatsApp group buzzed in affirmation. Everyone agreed that it was a highly encouraging return, except for Patrick who didn't comment and was presumably still working on his treatise. Although nobody thought we would have beaten the winner with a better draw, we felt Free Love would have been closer.

There was already excited talk about where the filly should next run, and even a suggestion from Trevor that another shot at six furlongs shouldn't be ruled out. It was heady stuff. In an uncertain world, full of dread and loss, we had experienced something uplifting, exhilarating. It only took 58.56 seconds for the future to look that little bit brighter.

8 Blown Off Course

(Doncaster, 5th July 2020)

Monday 29th June 2020

The front page of this morning's Racing Post confirmed that owners were to be allowed back on racecourses starting with a trial on Wednesday. The ROA had been keeping everyone in touch with regular updates, so the news didn't come as a surprise. The stipulations didn't raise too many eyebrows either.

Racing continued to work closely with central government and moves towards anything that resembled normality had to be approved and accompanied with assurances that strict protocols would be in place to keep everyone safe and minimise the risk of increasing infection levels. Only two owners per horse were allowed to attend. Limited access to areas of the racecourse and no hospitality facilities were the draconian givens.

It was all strangely at odds with relaxations which were appearing elsewhere. The initial lockdown rules about taking only one piece of daily exercise close to home had been replaced with unlimited outdoor exercise so long as sensible social distancing was maintained. This had been the case for over a month, but the prolonged hot weather and the draw of some beauty spots had caused some rather predictable problems.

Last week the BBC reported that sun-seekers were urged to stay away from the Dorset coast as thousands flocked to Bournemouth. The tabloids lapped it up with headlines screaming of 'Beach Madness' and revelations that Dorset Police reported gridlocked roads, fights and illegal overnight camping. Apparently, people had travelled from as far away as Birmingham to get a piece of the action.

I suppose our nearest equivalent to Bournemouth beach is

Brighton, and nothing would persuade me to go there on a warm day, pandemic or no pandemic. However, a short trip to the Kent coast has always been a family favourite and within half an hour of Free Love's gallant Doncaster effort last Friday, I was on the road with Jennie heading for Botany Bay, a civilised expanse of sand less than three miles from Broadstairs, the vibrant, bustling seaside town rich in Dickensian history and at ease with its current fusion of tradition and bohemia.

I made sure I registered my unavailability for the afternoon on the NHS volunteer app, although I wasn't expecting a surge of requests. However, I was keen to avoid the embarrassment of a blaring siren which might prompt expectations that I would spring into action and, like a scene from *Baywatch,* sprint heroically across the beach heading in the direction of the nearest pharmacy.

Since my first dramatic call-out in early April, the siren had sounded five further times on my mobile. The first one indicated that somebody just around the corner in Havelock Road needed assistance. I knew where this was going. It was clearly the same lady I helped last time by picking up a prescription, so I contacted her just to make sure that she really needed my assistance. She declined, which was a relief as I didn't fancy another hour or two queuing in Greenhithe.

The only other calls to action came from an elderly lady who was flagged up for help on three consecutive Fridays in May. Somebody must have done some shopping for her at some point, and she was now stuck in a system which automatically generated a plea for help at precisely the same time each week. After my third, fruitless contact she insisted that all was fine and asked me to stop pestering her.

At least I had been of some small use. Pete registered as a volunteer three months ago and was still waiting for the call. It was hardly surprising given the government's initial target of 250,000 had been knocked out of the park. Over 600,000 stepped forward to help. As infection rates fell and the glorious summer continued, work for volunteers dried up.

Our visit to Botany Bay was restricted to some fresh air and a swim. Nothing was open, not even the metal container at the bottom of the stairs leading to the beach which is home to a takeaway café and shop selling a limited range of refreshments and a few buckets and spades.

It was a lovely afternoon. The water was warm and there was plenty of space for families to keep their distance. As only limited year groups were back at school, there were plenty of children running around giving the impression that the nation was on an early summer holiday.

That was three days ago but I reflected on the experience as I thought about the restrictions that faced owners when they were finally allowed on the racecourse to see their horses run. It was time to write another letter to the Racing Post.

Dear Tom,

I was pleased to read in this morning's Racing Post that allowing owners to attend meetings will be trialled later this week, but under stricter conditions than members of the public would encounter if going to shops, garden centres, beaches and, from next weekend, pubs.

This trial may lead to an allocation of one or two badges per horse, but I don't think owners should roll over in gratitude if this is the case. Even if full allocations are allowed (four for single owners, six for syndicates) I calculate that at any one given time a maximum of 300 owners would have to socially distance themselves in grandstand and concourse areas built to accommodate thousands.

The Resumption of Racing Group has worked wonders to get the sport back again, and the safety measures put in place have been positively received by the public and press. Everybody's hard work and achievements should not be underestimated. However, now is the time to move to the next phase of the sport's rehabilitation, keeping in step with relaxations taking place elsewhere.

I was at Broadstairs last Friday afternoon where a well-behaved crowd of around a thousand people enjoyed their legal freedom to have a day out, small family groups sensibly socially distancing from each other. On the same day I was prohibited from going to Doncaster where my filly, Free Love, made her belated seasonal reappearance. The irony wasn't lost on me as I surveyed the busy beach.

Regards, Tony Linnett

It would be easy to rubbish the claims of owners and depict them as affluent whingers who believed they were worthy of special treatment. After all, other elite sports were being acted out behind closed doors and fans were prohibited from attending football, rugby and cricket matches. Next month's Wimbledon Championships had already been cancelled.

But treating owners as just another group of spectators was clearly unfair. They are an integral part of the racing industry. I know the sport is all too often guilty of unhelpful infighting with different stakeholders making competing claims about their particular importance. It's true that without racecourses, punters and bookmakers there is no sport. But there definitely isn't a sport without horses which cost around £25k a year to keep in training and require thousands of stable staff to look after them.

I accepted the fact that I wouldn't be going to the Eclipse meeting at Sandown as a spectator and punter, but if my horse ran at Lingfield or Yarmouth it wasn't unreasonable that I had a chance to be there in person.

Friday 3rd July 2020

Free Love looked set to make a quick reappearance following her promising return at Doncaster a week ago. During one of my regular trawls of the BHA website I spotted a handicap sprint restricted to fillies and mares. The class 4 *British Stallion Studs EBF Fillies' Handicap* carried a bit of extra prize money, presumably a small incentive to reward owners for keeping fillies and mares in training. The first prize was just over £6.5k, which was £2k more than National Anthem netted when completing his hat-trick. In the context of the current prize money structure, it was a decent pot.

The race was on Sunday, again at Doncaster, which meant a gap of only nine days between races. We left it up to our trainer to decide if Free Love was ready to go again so soon after her seasonal reappearance.

It was a very tempting target. When I spotted the race, my first thoughts were about the limited number of older fillies who were sprint specialists and rated 75 plus. There couldn't be legions of them and to prove the point I wasted some time looking at how many of the fairer sex had contested similar handicaps so far this season. It wasn't a huge amount. Geldings tended to dominate these sprints suggesting that Sunday's race might produce only a handful of runners.

Declarations had to be made by 10am, and shortly afterwards the BHA website revealed that Free Love was one of eight intended runners. Two of the eight were due to run at Haydock on Saturday and, if they accepted those engagements, we could be down to just six at Doncaster on Sunday.

Free Love was dropped a pound by the handicapper following her third-placed effort at Doncaster, which seemed quite lenient to me. However, it still meant our compact but relatively small filly would shoulder top weight of 9st 9lbs on Sunday, which was hardly ideal. Another concern was the going. It was currently good to soft with the possibility of further rain over the weekend. We wanted it to dry up as much as it could despite Mick and Theo believing that a bit of cut in the ground would suit Free Love.

I decided to study the opposition in more detail after I had glanced at the main stories in today's Racing Post. An article on owners returning to the racecourse grabbed my attention. My letter to the editor had been printed in Wednesday's RP which was the day of two trial meetings. By all accounts, things went smoothly at Southwell and Kempton which were attended by a meagre number of owners - 50 and 32, respectively.

It wasn't surprising that the figures were so low given the stipulations put in place. The article confirmed that only two owners per horse would be permitted to attend when the new arrangements came into force at all racecourses tomorrow. Owners were asked to arrive no more than 45 minutes before their horse was due to run and to leave immediately afterwards. Separate enclosures or 'zones' would keep owners away from racing staff. There would be no access to the pre-parade ring, paddock or winner's enclosure, and all the bars and restaurants would be shut. That's what awaited everyone once they had registered to attend and undertaken a special online Covid awareness training module. God help them if they tripped up and failed the temperature check at the gate. If they did, it was about turn, jump in the car and drive straight home.

There was no way I was going to drive all the way to Doncaster for that offer. It was possible that Patrick or Mick would consider giving it a go from York. They could get to Town Moor in under an hour. Patrick was back in the WhatsApp group and making noises about going, mainly out of curiosity. He'd let me know in the morning. As the nominated administrator for the group, one of my jobs was to allocate badges via the online booking system and under the new rules this had to be done by 4pm the day before the race. Entry wasn't transferrable, and owners had to turn up with their e-tickets and valid photo ID. It would be easier to book a holiday in North Korea.

Sunday 5th July 2020

The final field was down to seven. Richard Fahey decided to withdraw Spirit Of The Sky from Haydock yesterday where conditions were extremely testing. Aleneva took her chance at the same meeting but finished down the field in a class 4 handicap, so it was no surprise that she was an absentee this afternoon.

It was a tight looking contest. The admirably consistent Rose Hip was favourite with Free Love the public's third choice at around 5/1. The going had improved from good to soft, to good to soft, good in places. There was a strong, drying wind and, with no rain forecast, there was a realistic prospect of good ground when the runners were at the post at 3.25pm.

Patrick decided to take the plunge and make the relatively short trip from York to Town Moor. As usual, he eschewed the convenience of his car and opted for the train. A chance to read the Racing Post and continue work on his treatise over an unhurried cup of coffee meant that his Ford Focus stayed on the drive still waiting for its first run of the season.

As the sole representative of the North South Syndicate to be at the racecourse, Patrick embraced the idea of posting a full report on the WhatsApp group. He even promised to take some pictures.

The team was in buoyant mood aided by our trainer's text message saying the filly was in good order and had a decent chance. The official going description was changed to good and Free Love was now a solid 7/2 second favourite. If she was going to step forward and prove that she had the ability to compete in listed class against her own sex, this was surely the day.

I was glued to Sky Sports Racing from just after 3pm. Until then I had been watching ITV Racing's coverage of the Eclipse card at Sandown where, ten minutes after free Love ran, Enable would bid for her eleventh triumph at Group 1 level.

The omens were good. Theo was interviewed by Simon Mapletoft about Free Love's chances. Our young jockey felt his mount would build on her excellent reappearance and would be suited by the slightly easier ground. It was also noted that the filly had a minor claim to fame as she was the subject of two books. Hence *A Year of Free Love* and *Another Year of Free Love* received a welcome plug.

I know it's difficult to make judgements on television, even harder when your knowledge of horses is restricted to which end kicks and which end should be offered the carrot, but Free Love looked in tremendous condition as she ambled nonchalantly around the paddock, blithely unaware of the importance of the task that lay ahead.

All was calm with the filly on the way down, which was more than could be said for the television pictures which were jumpy and an indication of the fierce wind that would confront the runners head-on as soon as they left the stalls. There had been mention of the strong headwind by jockeys in earlier races which posed a bit of a problem for Theo. Seeking cover at the rear of the field was not a tactic he usually employed on a creature who seemed happiest when bowling along at her own pace.

Free Love made a smart start from stall 5 and was soon at the head of affairs with Rose Hip. Both fillies seemed to be in a good rhythm, although if you wanted to be picky, the pair seemed a little keen and may have been over-racing for the first furlong. At halfway, Andrea Atzeni pushed the favourite into a lead of about a length and Theo set off in pursuit.

This was it. It's absurd to call it a moment of truth, but that's what it felt like. If Free Love could pick off Rose Hip under topweight that would surely be proof that she was back to the glorious form of last summer when, almost a year to the day, she defied a mark of 86 at Windsor and days later was elevated to an official rating of 90. That's the stuff of black type.

For a few fleeting seconds it looked possible, but as they approached the final furlong and Theo's urgings became more desperate, no further inroads were made on Rose Hip's lead. Seen The Lyte, who had been held up last, burst between the two pacesetters and settled the issue in a matter of strides. Free Love plugged on gamely but lost third place close home as her earlier exertions took their toll.

I had that familiar sinking feeling as I watched the final phase of the race unfold. I knew it was all about context and expectation, but that didn't soften the disappointment in any way. On the face of it, our filly had put up a thoroughly respectable performance. Soon after the race the RP had completed its analysis of proceedings. Their race reader described the contest as, *A tightly knit fillies' handicap that looks reliable form. Once more, it seemed like an advantage to race with cover.* Free Love received a mention in dispatches. It was noted that she performed with credit once more, facing up to the headwind more than most.

Our filly had given 5lbs to the winner and was only beaten a total of two lengths. It was another solid effort, but it couldn't be described as a passport to listed race participation.

There were mixed reviews from the others. Trevor was disappointed and felt Theo stopped riding too soon, possibly forfeiting third place. Mick Corringham thought Theo did all he could and observed that maybe it was time to recognise that Free

Love wasn't quite as good as we were willing her to be. Patrick weighed in with his view from the racecourse in one of his more expansive WhatsApp contributions.

Hi.

On my way back. I'll put some photos up later to give a sense of the experience. There was hardly anyone there, which was a bit dismal and only me and one other chap actually watching from the grandstand. Still, it was nice to be back on a racecourse and the staff did what they could to make it a pleasant experience. The track was in great nick.

Obviously, things felt even flatter after FL ran. No particular excuse that I could see other than the entirely plausible one that the race came too soon. There was a really strong and blustery headwind, but all the runners were pretty much in the same boat with little cover to be had. Anyway, I shall be interested to hear what Mick and Theo have to say.

The debate about Theo's ride raged on for a bit. Trevor felt it was a poor tactical effort and our jockey should have taken cover from the headwind. He even had the temerity to suggest a change of pilot, although he accepted that this would probably be viewed as heresy by the group. Patrick pointed out that he had a very small involvement in Spirit Of The Sky through his Racegoers' Club membership and was aware that Tony Hamilton had been given instructions to drop in and find cover because of the headwind. Spirit Of The Sky finished down the field and his jockey reported afterwards that that the filly didn't enjoy the experience and recommended a return to front-running tactics in future. Damned if you do, damned if you don't.

Mick Appleby phoned me after the race to say that he felt Theo made too much use of Free Love and, given the conditions, finding a bit of cover would have been a smarter move. To cap it all, Theo contacted me and said that he thought the race may have come a bit soon after her reappearance. The filly felt a bit flat when he asked her to pick up and struggled to make any meaningful headway on ground that was riding a bit dead.

I know, I know. The real reason Free Love finished fourth was that three horses ran faster than her. Owners tend to avoid such blatant truisms. When the dust settled, we could at least agree that Free Love remained a little superstar. The filly had won four times for us and made the frame on eleven further occasions from 27 starts, which meant she'd reached the first four and a place in the winner's enclosure in more than half of her races. You can't ask for much more than that.

9 The Ecstasy and the Agony

(Windsor, 20th July 2020)

Friday 10th July 2020

The sun was shining, the pubs were open, and infection rates, hospital admissions and fatalities continued to go in the right direction. There was a feeling that we might be over the worst. At the very least there was relief at the respite from the grim news communicated in daily televised briefings that had been a feature of the first two months of lockdown. However, scientists continued to give sober reminders that a second wave was almost certainly on its way and winter would be a challenging time for us all.

There was clearly a tension between those who wanted the economy to reopen, allowing people to get on with their lives, and those who erred on the side of caution, urging that restrictions carry on for much longer.

My optimistic nature put me in the first camp. Could it really be that, after an initial surge in March and April, the virus was running out of steam? Were we looking at the possibility of theatres reopening and crowds returning to outdoor events before summer faded out of sight?

I didn't rush to the pubs on the first day they were back in business after their enforced three-and-a-half-month hiatus. I opted for a pint after a round of golf instead. Dartford's clubhouse reopened last Saturday in line with other licensed premises, and I was able to kill two birds with one stone on Wednesday following yet another indifferent performance on the course.

About three years ago, when there were five vacancies on the golf club board, I uttered the fateful words, 'I don't mind helping out if you're struggling to find people to stand'. I was duly elected, thus fulfilling the axiom that some have greatness thrust upon them.

I knew nothing about running a golf club. I was a late convert to the game and an even later entrant to club membership. A couple of friends had joined the club a few years ago and I threatened to join them once retirement was in sight. Less than two months after I packed in full-time work, my meteoric rise in the world of golf was confirmed when I became a Director of Dartford Golf Club. This meant fellow members could accost me on the fifth fairway to quiz me about a faulty urinal or the deplorable decline in standards of dress. I usually nodded sympathetically while fumbling behind my back to make sure my shirt was tucked in.

I can't say that I was an asset to the Board. When I took up office and was asked where I thought I would be most effectively deployed, I replied that I wasn't joking when I said it should be as far away from golf as possible. If a fellow member moaned to me about the state of the bunkers on the seventh, or the unevenness of the fifteenth tee box, they'd be met with a blank stare or even an expression of guilt. Why didn't I notice these things? I guess I was too busy hacking my way round the course and enjoying myself.

I ended up helping with finance and staffing, which more recently involved preparations for reopening the clubhouse in a Covid-secure way. My pint after playing on Wednesday served two purposes. It was my first taste in months of draft bitter other than the few takeaways I'd carried home in plastic containers from Dartford Working Men's Club, a renowned local hub for real ale. It also gave me a chance to observe the various procedures put in place to ensure that social distancing and hygiene considerations were being followed.

It all looked fine. There was no queuing at the bar, which now had a Perspex screen to protect the staff. Several tables had been removed to ensure generous spacing between groups, which were restricted to a maximum of six. Hand sanitiser was freely available and a one-way system in and out of the clubhouse reduced face-to-face contact in passing. If this was the temporary future of pubs and licensed premises, we could all manage for a few months before things returned to normal.

Thursday 16th July 2020

A visit to the North Norfolk coast contributed to my growing sense of social rehabilitation. I took a flyer about a month ago that campsites would resume business in July in line with government plans for the tiered easing of restrictions. The PM stuck to the timetable, and on Saturday I drove our ancient two-berth Sterling Europa caravan to Woodhill Park camp site, a beautiful expanse of grass overlooking West Runton beach.

When we arrived, we were aware that the shower and toilet blocks wouldn't be open until Monday. Visitors to the site were only allowed if they had their own private facilities. This meant pulling all the junk out of the caravan's tiny shower unit to put it back into use for the first time in years. It also meant that the trip to the disposal point, where the chemical toilet's cassette needed to be emptied, was an even less glamorous job than usual during a brief period when it was impossible to adhere to the strict rule of 'no number twos in the caravan loo.' In a neat division of labour, Joe volunteered to collect the fresh water leaving me to dispose of the filth.

By Monday everything was open, and you had to admire the diligent way that the Woodhill Park staff regularly closed the shower blocks on a rota basis to give them a deep clean. It was the same all over. The Village Inn in West Runton moved all its business into the garden and only opened from noon to 7pm. There was a hand sanitising ritual on arrival, the collection of contact details, a one-way system in and out of the bars, and generous spaces between the outdoor tables.

Some pubs and restaurants chose not to open, or only did so for a takeaway service, but those that did tried hard to reduce the risk of infection and make everyone feel safe. I didn't feel personally threatened by the virus, but if I took the decision to use cafés, restaurants, pubs and anywhere else where people were allowed to congregate, I was happy to follow the guidelines that everyone had worked so hard to put in place.

Our eldest son, Matt, had holiday to use up and nowhere to go so he decided to join us for a few days. He and Joe used the awning as their bedroom and slept solidly, drifting off to sleep to the gentle susurration of the wind and waves. We were that close to the sea. At night, you could walk to the cliff top in two or three minutes and look out due west to watch the shimmering, orange disc of the sun slide into the water, its final moments always quicker than anticipated, almost something of a surprise.

We had a fabulous week in a part of the country that we've only recently discovered. I hadn't really thought of Norfolk as a summer destination. On the few occasions we'd been before it was to places like Blakeney Point, typically in February half-term. I associated the area with bracing walks, driving rain and the wild beauty of remote landscapes that attracted the English middle classes in their droves. It was even money that you'd bump into Jack and Esme.

It was the first time we'd taken a summer holiday in that part of the world, and we were bowled over by the beaches. We all adore swimming and were in the sea at West Runton, Sheringham, Overstrand and Hunstanton. In the evening we either barbecued at the camp site or booked into The Ship at Weybourne, where keenly priced lobster and Cromer crab featured on the menu. After three months of lockdown drudgery, our week on the Norfolk coast was the tonic we all needed.

I kept an eye on developments with Free Love in between playing boules on the West Runton sands. Although a few suggestions for the filly's next run had been put forward on our WhatsApp group, the consensus was to leave it to our trainer. By mid-afternoon, Free Love held three entries: Windsor, Catterick and Sandown.

The fact that Mick had been busy putting her into races suggested that he was happy with the filly's physical condition, and she was ready to run again. It was a matter of which one of the three was the best option.

I didn't fancy Sandown. It's a stiff, uphill five furlongs. The only time Free Love tackled the demands of the Esher track's sprint course was as a two-year-old. It was the fifth run of her career, and it was a complete disaster. She pulled Jack Mitchell's arms out and ran fast for three and a bit furlongs before disappearing quicker than the setting sun at West Runton.

There will always be a place in my heart for Catterick, where Free Love recorded her first ever victory in a class 5 handicap off a mark of 63. But next week's race was a 0-80 class 4 handicap and as the handicapper had eased our filly's rating down a couple of pounds to 80, we would carry 9st 7lbs and be obliged to give weight to all.

The happy hunting ground of Windsor looked favourite. The 0-90 class 3 *Follow At The Races On Twitter Handicap* on Monday would be a warmer affair than Catterick, but it meant a reasonable racing weight. The opposition might be higher calibre, but they would have to give away a few pounds if that was the case.

Saturday 18th July 2020

It was a busy morning packing up camp. Matt had already returned to London leaving me, Jennie and Joe to dismantle the awning and deal with the myriad tasks that needed to be done before the white metal box which had been our home for the last week could be hitched to the car and towed back to Dartford.

I took a break to see how the Windsor race was shaping up. Yesterday evening, Mick had sent me a text to ask if we had any views about our three options. He thought Windsor looked best and I told him we were more than happy to go back to the riverside track where the going looked likely to be on the quick side of good.

It was already 10.30am which meant that the declarations for Monday would be on the BHA website. I sat on one of the picnic chairs that had yet to be packed away and took in the sweeping view of the bay before checking my phone. There were nine declared runners and Daschas was set to carry top weight off his mark of 87. Free Love was allotted 9st 2lbs, but Theo's allowance would knock off a further three pounds. If he used his biggest saddle and went for an extra portion of apple crumble and custard at Sunday lunch, he might only need to stuff three or four pounds of lead into the saddle cloth to bring his weight up to the requisite 8st 13lbs.

Monday 20th July 2020

I couldn't bring myself to go to Windsor. Neither could any of the others. Although racecourses, the press and the BHA all reported how pleased they were with the way things were going, the focus was on the implementation of protocols. It was all very well saying that the temperature checks, segregation arrangements and social distancing enforcement were working a treat, but that wasn't the same as saying that owners were having a spiffing time.

The Racing Post hinted at the surreal nature of the race day experience when it reported on the eerie silence that greeted Serpentine's bizarre Epsom Derby victory at the beginning of the month. Although television coverage continued to be extraordinarily effective at concealing the soulless atmosphere on course, Patrick's personal testimony from Doncaster captured what it was really like. Owners couldn't get anywhere near their horses, jockeys and trainers. His pictures showed a solitary owner sitting in a cavernous lounge, a racecourse steward standing a safe and respectful two metres away. He snapped a similar image of the vast grandstand where an elderly owner sat in resignation (there were no bars or restaurants open) while another racecourse official hovered in the background. It was hardly surprising that very few owners were enthusiastic about attending, given what was on offer. You'd be better off going to the beach.

In theory, Windsor is only 75 minutes from Dartford, but I've taken well over two hours in the past. You have to use the busiest stretch of the southern section of the M25, and the mere mention of the likes of Chertsey, Egham and Staines is enough to induce a feeling of queasiness. It's hard to imagine a more dismal driving experience than that offered by the 20 miles separating junctions 10 and 15.

No, I wouldn't be going all that way for a short, isolated experience that couldn't match what television offered both in terms of spectacle and atmosphere. I never thought there would come a day when I felt like that, but current restrictions made it an easy choice. All the others took the same view, so Free Love would have to do her stuff this evening without the throaty roar of the North South Syndicate to urge her on.

We looked to have a decent chance. The wonderfully named Flippa The Strippa was a non-runner bringing the field down to eight, which was an attractive proposition for each-way punters who would be paid out on the first three places.

I must admit, I have an irrational aversion to each-way betting which I have only partly overcome in the last decade. Prior to that, I wouldn't dream of anything other than money on the nose. My fancy would have to be 33/1 or upwards before I abandoned my tried and trusted win-only policy.

It was Jennie who taught me the value of a more prudent approach. We often go racing together, especially in the summer. We should have been at Newmarket's big July meeting the week before last but that, along with many other plans, fell by the wayside in the wake of the pandemic. Jennie invariably sticks to the Tote and usually has a pound or two each way, or sometimes a place-only bet. It was her regular return to the Tote window to collect her winnings that made me take notice. Her bets may have lacked the boldness of my all or nothing approach, but the compensation was in a purse that always looked a little more well fed than my wallet.

Being a slow learner, I also came late to the notion of having 'a bet for nothing.' It's a bit of a racing cliché. The main thrust of the argument is that there is no point backing a horse each-way unless you really fancy it to win. In other words, don't take an each-way punt on a 25/1 shot in the hope that it might scramble into a place.

It's amazing how some of life's more obvious truisms evade us for so long. Until a few years ago, I wouldn't have dreamt of backing my 5/1 fancy each-way. But if I strongly fancied the beast to win and thought that making the first three was a given, I'd still profit handsomely if the creature was first past the post and break even if a narrow, unexpected defeat were suffered.

There were only two drawbacks to this eminently sensible and rational strategy. If my horse bolted up at 5/1, my £1 each-way bet would yield a return of £8 inclusive of the original £2 stake. However, if the stake was plonked fearlessly on the nose, the total return would be £12, proving conclusively that greed is good. The other flaw in the system relates to the times when my sure-fire selection ran inexplicably badly and didn't even make the first three. This has been known to happen. These situations invoke the feeling of being a mug and make me question the validity of the whole approach, so much so that a period of win-only betting follows as a kind of self-imposed penance. With eight runners and three places, the betting strategy for tonight's Windsor contest would need careful consideration.

I had plenty of time to weigh up the opposition and decided to undertake a detailed analysis of each runner. There are times when my perusal is superficial and mainly focussed on where the pace is likely to be, which in turn throws some light on the significance of the draw. However, on this occasion I made notes on all the runners and priced them up, resisting the temptation to look at what the bookmakers were offering.

I tried to be as objective as I could, but back at Windsor on good to firm ground and dropped to a mark of 80, Free Love looked to have strong claims and I made her the 7/2 favourite in what was undoubtedly a wide-open affair. I had the fast but quirky Glamorous Anna next best at 9/2. Topweight Daschas was a 5/1 shot and Yimou, who arrived on the back of a win over the course and distance, was 11/2 to defy a 4lbs hike in the ratings.

One of the more intriguing runners was Tropics, now aged twelve and rated 82. In his pomp, he contested all the top sprint races and was a winner at Group 3 level. He failed by a nose to win the 2015 running of the Group 1 July Cup at Newmarket and around that time his official rating soared to the dizzy heights of 116. Only last August he was rated 107, but age respects neither man nor beast and it was hard to see him rolling back the years, even off tonight's lowly mark. A well-deserved retirement looked imminent.

I wasn't far off with my predictions. It was a changeable market with Yimou vying for favouritism. Free Love had been briefly available at 6/1, but an online tipping service with a legion of followers had apparently put her up as one of their two bets of the day. The Racing Post's Graeme Rodway was also sweet on our filly. He noted that Free Love had run well from an unfavourable stand-side draw on her seasonal reappearance and backed up that effort with a solid performance into a headwind on ground slower than ideal. Back at Windsor, on a quick surface and racing off a reduced mark, Mr Rodway argued that this was a good opportunity for Mick Appleby's consistent sprinter. This was clearly one of the RP's more astute correspondents.

I was scrambling to get a price following the support for Free Love encouraged, no doubt, by the tipping service and the perceptive Graeme Rodway endorsing her chance. The initial reaction of the layers was to slash the filly's price from an overnight 6/1 to a measly 3/1. However, as the hot and sultry Monday afternoon wore on, more generous offers started to reappear. This was surely an occasion to be prudent, sensible and embrace that 'bet to nothing' strategy. With the bookies paying three places in the field of eight, only a fool would shun the each-way opportunity that was staring me in the face. I had twenty quid to win at 5/1.

Time dragged waiting for early evening to arrive. The *Follow At The Races On Twitter Handicap* was the feature race of the evening, due off at 7pm. What a difference a year makes, I thought to myself as I sat in the garden drinking a non-alcoholic beer about half an hour before the race. Monday and Tuesday are my two dry days and I try to resist backsliding whenever possible. I remember making an exception a year ago on that heady evening at Windsor when Free Love repelled Dark Shadow's challenge by a determined neck. After the backslapping, presentations and photos, we were whisked away to the champagne tent reserved for winning connections. I shunned the mineral water on offer as an alternative to the fizz.

It was just me, Jennie and Joe on the sofa in the backroom as post time approached and Sky Sports Racing turned its attention to the main event. The French windows were flung open allowing the evening sun to flood into the extension. The intoxicating excitement was there, but a wave of regret washed over me as I watched the runners canter to the start. Maybe I should have gone even if the racecourse resembled the *Marie Celeste*, devoid of the bustling, vibrant crowd that its evening meetings invariably attract.

My maudlin musings were rudely interrupted by a loose horse. The cameras homed in on a bay creature who had parted company with his jockey and was cantering in a carefree fashion around the bottom bend which runs close to the Thames. It wasn't Free Love, thank God, and the commentator quickly identified the escapee as Grandfather Tom. The experienced gelding, who really should know better, was almost certain to be withdrawn, reducing the field to seven. This meant the bookmakers would only pay on two places much to the chagrin of those smug each-way punters.

Grandfather Tom's antics caused a slight delay but, at three minutes past seven, the handlers started loading the remaining participants into the starting stalls. I was confident of a big run. Free Love's last piece of fast work, captured on video by Louise, showed her breezing up the Langham gallops with Sampers Seven. Our trainer thought the filly was in great shape and conditions looked ideal. What could go wrong?

Not for the first time, I pondered the importance of the task. We needed to win, or go very close, to keep the dream alive of capturing a decent prize somewhere, a bit of black type being the biggest trophy of the lot. I was beginning to sound like a desperate Charlton Athletic fan pronouncing every encounter as a 'must win game' or a 'six-pointer'. But it was true. Run well, and Free Love moves back towards the mid-80s and class 2 handicaps at Grade 1 tracks. Run poorly, and we drop into the 70s and set the satnav for Catterick.

Fortunately, there was no more time to dwell on these matters.

They were all in. The seven runners stood calmly, appreciative of the small patch of shade at the five-furlong start, before bursting into sunshine, Glamorous Anna and A Sure Welcome setting a furious early pace.

They weren't hanging around. Free Love was further back than usual but she wasn't struggling to keep tabs on the leaders. Theo allowed her to bowl along at a pace with which the filly was comfortable, and at halfway she looked to be travelling well despite sitting in fifth place about three lengths off Glamorous Anna who had now established a clear lead.

As the runners hurtled toward the final two furlongs, Theo made his move. The leader hung right towards the stands rail, A Sure Welcome faded, and Free Love and Yimou charged down the centre of the track taking the race by the scruff of the neck. Glamorous Anna was racing awkwardly with her head on one side, but the rail prevented her from ending up in the grandstand and she was still in contention with 100 yards to go. In the desperate duel between Free Love and Yimou, our filly always looked to have the upper hand, albeit narrowly. The line approached, my screaming reached a crescendo, and when they hit the wire, it was obvious that we had won. It was only by about a head, but she'd done it!

I was in a state of babbling excitement. What a gutsy effort that was. And what an outstanding ride from Theo! The only filly in the race as well. Unbelievable! The hyperboles were rolling effortlessly off my tongue. The cameras followed Free Love and Yimou after the line and focussed on them as they pulled up, but it wasn't even close. Free Love had toughed it out to land a famous victory.

My phone buzzed. It was Ronan texting his congratulations. 'Awesome,' was his single word message, in tune with the hyperbole fest which was still going on in Dartford. I waited until I saw the replay before replying. I really wanted to see this again, to relive every single second of it. Matt Chapman talked the viewers through the closing stages, but he was not so confident about the outcome. He wasn't sure. While all eyes had been drawn to Free Love and Yimou fighting out the finish in the centre of the track, Chapman pointed out that the camera angle favoured the nearside, and it was possible that Glamorous Anna had just held on.

This was obvious nonsense, another example of the flamboyant Sky Sports Racing commentator looking for something mildly controversial to say. A further replay of the finish was shown, this time in super-slow motion. It was frozen as the protagonists crossed the line. The proof was there for all to see. Free Love had clearly bettered Yimou by about a head, but Glamorous Anna, who raced in splendid isolation against the nearside rail, may just have held on.

A nose. After eleven hundred yards run in a blistering 58.86 seconds at an average speed of around 40 miles per hour, a mere two centimetres made the difference between winning and losing. Glamorous Anna netted £6.5k for her owners while Free Love added two grand to her prize money haul. As for how the each-way punters fared, that wasn't high on my list of considerations.

It's impossible to describe how I felt as the reality of Free Love's defeat sank in. I was sure she had won. It was from elation to dismay in seconds as I stared at the freeze frame of the finish and realised that Theo and his willing partner had come up agonisingly short. I went to the kitchen and made two large gin and tonics handing one to Jennie who had the good sense to avoid saying anything about dry Mondays. I sat on the sofa watching the postmortem. The winning jockey, William Cox, explained that Glamorous Anna was a fast filly but has limited vision in her right eye which accounts for her rather wayward running style. It was hard to watch.

But it wasn't long before disappointment was superseded by pride. It was a cracking effort and clear evidence that Free Love retained the considerable ability she had shown as a three-year-old. Within half an hour, the Racing Post had published the full result on its website. The contest was described as *a fair handicap sprint run at a decent gallop*. The race reader's comment for Free Love was complimentary: *In touch with leaders, headway over 1f out, ridden and made strong challenge inside final furlong, kept on well final 110yds, just failed.*

Just failed. The consequences were brutal. A win would have provided funds to cover our training fees for the next three months. As our bank account was nearly empty, and the second-place prize money wouldn't reach it until the middle of August, I informed the others that another £500 contribution would be needed before the end of July. We might be able to have a payment holiday next month.

Another consequence of our narrow defeat would be the impact on our official rating. Although the separating distances were only a nose and a head, the race looked competitive and was run in a decent time. The form had a solid look about it and the winner was bound to go up by four or five pounds which meant Free Love would go up two or even three, making it just that little bit harder to win our next race.

Tuesday 28th July 2020
Free Love showed no ill effects after her hard race at Windsor and we were soon thinking about her next assignment. The weekly adjustments to official ratings were released this morning and they confirmed that she had been raised two pounds to a mark of 82. It could have been worse.

I also noticed during my trawl of the BHA website that a new race had been put on at York on International Stakes day. It was a class 2 five-furlong handicap sprint restricted to fillies and mares rated 0-100. The total prize money pot was £30k which was not to be sneered at in the current climate. It looked far too tempting to miss.

The *Sky Bet Fillies' Sprint Handicap* was like manna from heaven. It was to be run 41 years after Master Willie won the International Stakes (then named the Benson and Hedges Gold Cup) which was my first visit to the Knavesmire. I haven't missed too many Ebor meetings since, and I can't ever recall a sprint handicap for fillies and mares featuring during the August festival. Apparently, the BHA was responding to trainers who were invited to put forward suggestions for races that would cater for horses who had missed out during racing's shut down.

Perhaps the loss of Bath's *Lansdown Stakes* in April, a listed sprint for fillies and mares, had prompted race planners to provide an opportunity for better class female speedsters. I didn't know, and I didn't care. I was sure it was likely to be a one-off and not a race that would become an established part of the four-day Ebor Festival.

We had to go for it. I couldn't resist the thought of having a runner at York on International Stakes day. The race was likely to be our best chance of winning a big pot. I knew there would be some noises from the other boys that we were flying too high and should stick to class 3 and 4 events at Yarmouth and Windsor, but if we only had one crack at something valuable and prestigious during this strange season, this was surely it. If something rated 100 turned up – and that wasn't a done deal - Free Love would get in with 8st 8lbs. Take off Theo's three-pound allowance, and our racing weight would look irresistible.

While I was keen to go straight to York and make it our main summer target, there were some dissenting voices. Pete reminded me that I had as good as sworn a solemn oath never to return to the Knavesmire after our last disappointment there in October.

He was right. We've been out of luck on three occasions at York. Free Love's form figures at the track read 9th, 8th and 11th. The first blow-out was after she had won two on the bounce at Nottingham at the beginning of her three-year-old campaign. Raised to a mark of 88, she was a strongly fancied 13/2 shot to defy topweight in a hot class 3 handicap at the big May meeting. During a period when Mick Appleby's string was badly out of form, our filly threw in a lacklustre performance, gradually fading out of contention in the last two furlongs. Later that season came Free Love's gallant effort from a stinking draw in the big apprentice handicap on Ebor day. Finally, in October we had the double whammy of soft ground and another bad draw.

But distressing memories are short-lived in racing. A poor run on soft going is quickly forgotten when a good opportunity on testing ground presents itself. The inability of a horse to act on a turning track is thrown to the wind when a decent prize at Chester is spotted. And so what if a high draw was a terrible disadvantage last time? It might be different today. It's the ability to allow hope to triumph over experience that keeps us owners going.

York was forgiven. What I said and thought in the heat of the moment last October was forgotten. Maybe the cards would fall right for us this time. Good ground, an attractive racing weight, a decent draw. It wasn't much to ask. Granted the right conditions, why couldn't our little filly make a splash at one of the most prestigious days' racing in the calendar? It was a no-brainer. We had to return to the Knavesmire.

Friday 31st July 2020

It was a scintillatingly hot day. The country was experiencing yet another short burst of temperatures in excess of 30 degrees, encouraging me and Jennie to make an impromptu visit to Frinton-on-Sea. Unfortunately, it was an idea shared with hordes of others and the traffic was atrocious, right back to the pre-lockdown levels that we all know and loathe. It took us three hours to get there, which was hardly surprising as the schools were on holiday; it was a Friday, and the weather was outstanding. We should have known better, but we had a half-baked plan about our eldest son, Matthew, joining us as he had the afternoon off and Frinton looked reasonably easy to get to from his Stoke Newington flat.

People seemed more confident about being out and about and Frinton was busy. Finding a parking space on one of its genteel streets lined with art deco houses was a bit of a challenge, but there was plenty of space on its magnificent sands for couples and small family groups to keep their distance. We only spent a couple of hours there but were in the sea for nearly half of that time. From the water, the scene on the beach looked a picture of good health and vitality. It was hard to believe that we were still struggling to get to grips with a pandemic.

Matt wisely decided to give the seaside a miss, put off by the traffic reports we gave him while stuck on the A12 somewhere near Colchester. Instead, we decided to drop in on him on the way home and arranged to meet up in the garden of the Crooked Billet to have something to eat before completing our circuitous sojourn via the Blackwall Tunnel.

We listened to the news on the radio as we made our way to North London, the car air conditioning on full blast. Apparently, it had been the hottest day of the year with the mercury falling just short of 38 degrees at Heathrow. Elsewhere, temperatures in the mid-thirties were commonplace.

However, the bulk of the reporting was about Covid and there was bad news for racing. Tomorrow's eagerly anticipated trial at Goodwood had been cancelled. It was the final day of the Sussex track's summer festival and arrangements had been made for a limited crowd of annual members and paying customers to attend. The racecourse had spent weeks working out how to safely accommodate up to 5,000 spectators. It was an important pilot event, not just for racing, but for all elite sports, and at the eleventh hour it had been shelved.

The reason for the last-minute cancellation was concern over rising infection rates, but it was difficult to gauge the significance of the numbers. Daily positive tests in England had risen from a seven-day average of around 600 to 800 in the space of a week. You could argue that the increase was a worrying 33%, but in the context of a total population of 56 million it didn't appear that alarming. One thing was certain; while the action played out at Goodwood tomorrow to empty grandstands, the country's beaches would be heaving.

10 Yorkshire Pudding

(York, 19ᵗʰ August 2020)

Wednesday 5th August 2020

It was an ominous start to the month. Contradictory noises were being made about infection rates. The government was worried about an upward trend but there wasn't a sense of accord amongst the scientific community. The surveillance programme run by the Office for National Statistics suggested that infection rates were rising but their findings were based on just 24 positive cases among nearly 30,000 people over the course of two weeks. Some commentators made the obvious point that drawing firm conclusions from such small numbers was difficult.

The other key source of data was the number of cases found by testing. It was true that positive test results were rising. Using a rolling seven-day average, figures were now around 40% higher than they were in the second week of July. However, the number of tests being conducted was increasing and targeting areas where infection rates were highest. The more you test, the more you find, seemed an obvious correlation.

Hot spots included the Northwest where stay at home orders were slapped on millions, including my younger brother Peter, who lives in Altrincham. He was hoping to make his debut at next weekend's annual golf jolly at Tewkesbury but had to withdraw once the government announced the local restrictions put in place to tackle rising infection rates in Greater Manchester.

Another scuppered plan was my intention to meet up with Stephen Cawley, author of three books on the joys of racehorse ownership on a budget. In his self-published *I Really Gotta Horse, Four Hooves And A Prayer* and *Round Ireland With A Horse,* Stephen describes his ownership experiences with racing clubs and syndicates. They provide an entertaining insight into 'penny share' ownership and prove that it's possible for ordinary people on limited budgets to get involved with the sport of kings.

Stephen got in touch to bring his books to my attention, noting how *A Year of Free Love* told a similar tale. We embarked on an enjoyable email correspondence at the beginning of the year and looked forward to meeting each other in person, perhaps over a pint at Haydock. Plans were hatched before the first national lockdown and, although the possibility of sharing racing and writing anecdotes over a drink began to look more promising in the summer, even if a day at the races was unlikely, the new local restrictions for Greater Manchester affected Stephen in Didsbury which put everything back on hold.

At least the news from Langham was more cheering. Last Wednesday, Free Love was filmed doing a nice piece of fast work again upsides Sampers Seven. Her galloping companion had been raised to 86 following an emphatic York victory. This morning our filly was videoed matching strides with Garsman, another ex-Irish sprinter picked up by Mick at the sales when rated in the mid-sixties. In Mick's skilful hands the strapping son of Garswood had won three times and pushed his official mark up to 86. There's no denying Mick's ability to spot potential. If I owned a horse who had shown a bit of ability, but not enough to persevere with, my heart would sink if Mick started bidding for it at the sales.

All seemed fine with Free Love. She was working well and on target for York which was a fortnight away. I thought it would be a good idea to arrange a long overdue get together at the stables and we managed to establish that everyone bar Trevor could make next Wednesday. It would be a chance to see the filly work and have a chat about the future of the syndicate.

There was a tacit agreement that Free Love would either go to the horses in training sale at the end of October or the breeding stock sale a month later. I favoured the latter as I felt that somebody should breed from our filly. She was a genuine, successful racehorse whose career high rating of 90 put her in the top 10% of all fillies and mares in training. She may lack black type, and you had to go back to her granddam to find it, but so what? She was faster than most of the blue-blooded mares that end up in the breeding sheds. She was surely an attractive proposition for a small breeder who knew that Free Love's price at auction would be a fraction of that for a well-related but slow daughter of Dubawi.

I favoured the breeding stock sale for another reason. I couldn't stand the thought of anyone buying Free Love to race her. That would kill me. I knew I was being sentimental and irrational, but the emotional attachment ran deep, too deep perhaps. It's not as if I hadn't had a fair crack of the whip. We had initially agreed a year of fun, and here we were approaching the end of our third season. After York, Free Love might have three more races before we waved goodbye to her. Unless she won, in which case it was game on again.

Even victory at York might not be enough to stave off the inevitable. Free Love would be five next season. That's plenty old enough for a mare to still be in training on the flat. A mare. The name was redolent of the fading blossom of youth. As soon as she turned five on 1st January, she was no longer a filly. On that day, the unnamed creature I first saw ambling around the pre-parade ring at the Tattersalls yearling sales nearly three years ago, had a new moniker. She would be a mare.

No, I couldn't guarantee that we'd keep Free Love in training even if she bolted up at York. The others might think that it was a wonderful conclusion to a project that had exceeded all expectations. The sensible thing would be to sell up, take the profit and maybe go again with another yearling.

Wednesday 12th August 2020

It was short-sleeved shirts for our trip to Langham. The long, hot summer continued to produce temperatures associated more with Andalusia than Rutland, which prompted Mick to ask us to be at the stables at 9.30am. He wanted to bring the last lot forward by about an hour to avoid working the horses in the extreme heat.

I felt that familiar schoolboy excitement as I turned into the drive at the entrance to the yard. Racing enthusiasts go through various rites of passage. In my case, I began as a sixteen-year-old watching the Saturday racing on the telly. A couple of years later, a few small bets added colour and excitement to the experience. In between came my first visit to a racecourse, Lingfield on a cold and damp day in November, where I was almost within touching distance of the novice hurdler, William Pitt, who returned to the winner's enclosure in trails of steaming sweat. Beyond that, appreciation of the sport deepened, and bigger meetings were taken in – Royal Ascot, Glorious Goodwood and York's Ebor meeting. Kris, Le Moss, Triptych. I even ventured abroad, going to the Arc via an arduous coach and ferry trip when I was in my twenties.

While all of this was happening, one ambition trumped all others. Wouldn't it be just glorious if one day, somehow, I could own a thoroughbred racehorse, and instead of being a face jostling for space and peering in from outside the parade ring, I could be in there, talking to my trainer and jockey in the nerve-jangling moments before my horse ran? Wouldn't it be fabulous if somehow it could be magically arranged?

I always thought it would need a bit of magic. That's why I often threw a few pennies at the ITV 7 or Tote Jackpot. That seemed my best chance of being able to afford a racehorse. When I started off in the world of work, the cost of keeping a horse in training was more than I earned in a year. There was a hefty initial purchase price as well. Racehorses have never been cheap - apart from the ones who have demonstrated beyond all doubt that they couldn't catch a cold.

I never thought I'd be an owner. Then along came racing clubs, syndicates and the notion of shared ownership. A door had opened for ordinary racing enthusiasts, and I walked through it without looking back.

I suppose I'm slightly envious of the opportunities now afforded to younger racing enthusiasts. It's so much easier these days to take a small share in a horse or be part of a racing club. Some schemes offer involvement for a flat fifty quid a year. You may be one of a thousand owners but you're a bona fide shareholder and your name will go into the draw for badges whenever your horse runs and, as Stephen Cawley illustrates in his books, one day your turn will come. You'll be standing in the paddock with a dozen equally excited penny-share owners, listening intently to your trainer's thoughts on your horse's chance before a jockey, maybe even a famous one, walks over to the eager group and tips his cap in a time-honoured gesture of deference.

Yes, it's so much easier now to get involved, but I wasn't complaining. I was just grateful to have arrived. I turned these thoughts over in my head as we approached the entrance to the yard where horses from a previous lot were being washed down.

As soon as I stepped out of the car, I was hit by a dense wall of heat. It shouldn't have been a surprise, but it was only 9.30am and the air conditioning had been on for the entire journey. Had I bothered to check the temperature before I switched the engine off, the display would have told me that it was already 28 degrees. No wonder Mick wanted to complete the morning exercise early and get the horses washed and back in the cool of their stables as soon as possible.

We were gathered at the top of the all-weather gallop by 9.45am. Mick was in his usual position, chatting to a small group of new owners who had moved Narjes to him. Briefly rated in the mid-70s some three years ago, the six-year-old mare's official mark had slumped to 54 and her owners were hoping that the Langham Magician could conjure up a revival.

I talked briefly to the Narjes gang before picking Mick's brains about York. He thought we'd get into the race. After all, how many female sprint specialists can there be who are rated in the 80-100 bracket? We both thought that a maximum field of 22 runners was unlikely. Mick mentioned that the owners of Sampers Seven were also keen on the race. Seconds later, Free Love and Sampers Seven were charging up the gallop, working upsides at a decent clip.

You can't read anything into these pieces of fast work. The horses are travelling at about 90%, and in a race it's the final 10% that makes the difference. Nevertheless, it was pleasing to see Free Love moving so smoothly, about half a length ahead of her York rival. It was an encouraging work-out. At least I could say that while keeping more absurdly optimistic thoughts to myself.

It was another great visit to Langham. Back at the yard we made a real fuss of our filly, her proud owners posing for photographs as they patted their pride and joy. The warmth of the sun was unrelenting and, as I stood next to Free Love, gently stroking her neck and playing with her ears, it was hard to believe that anything could be wrong with the world. Brilliant sunshine, a racehorse in flying form, an imminent entry for York on International Stakes day; what more could I want? Maybe world peace and the end to the global pandemic.

We didn't keep Free Love in the sun for too long. She was soon hosed down and back in the stable block where she could shelter from the intense heat of another day when noon temperatures would exceed 30 degrees. After one last round of pictures of Free Love in her box, we said our goodbyes and made our way to Oakham for a light lunch in the Wheatsheaf and a chinwag about the future.

The conversation over sandwiches and a pint of Everard's Tiger was about the future of the syndicate. We all agreed that this was probably our last season and the filly would be sold as a potential broodmare in the autumn - unless she hosed up at York and deposited twenty grand into the pot which would allow us to have one more year; one last chance for black type, perhaps.

Even if York proved to be a glorious success it didn't guarantee another season. Voices around the table suggested that a victory on the Knavesmire would increase the filly's value, making selling an even more attractive proposition. But then we wouldn't have a horse. Was I the only one who could see this?

I offered to do some research on what it would cost to breed from Free Love ourselves. Wouldn't that be a fantastic adventure? I swear I could hear the tumbleweed as Pete, Patrick and Mick lowered their heads to avoid eye contact and took slow and silent sips from their pints.

We departed in good spirits but with nothing long-term decided. It was very much a case of 'wait and see'. We had about two grand in our racing account and prize money to come from Windsor of roughly the same amount. We had enough to pay the end of August bills and, who knows, if Free Love hit the jackpot at York, we wouldn't need to put our hands in our pockets until the beginning of the new flat season next April.

Wednesday 19th August 2020

We knew the day after the stable visit that Free Love would get into the race at York. There were only 19 entries and on Monday the final declarations revealed a field of 13. Keep Busy and Lady In France headed the weights. They both had a listed race win to their names and were rated 101 and 100 respectively. The contest wasn't lacking in quality. Free Love would be getting plenty of weight from both, though. She would carry an attractive looking 8st 5lbs after Theo's apprentice allowance was deducted.

The draw didn't look great. We were berthed in 11 which was our third high draw on the bounce at York. I tried to convince myself that it might not be such a disadvantage in a field of 13, but I was irritated that we could find ourselves on the wrong side of the track once again. You need all the cards to fall right in these sprints, and stall 11 was a knave, not an ace.

There was no way that I was going to be absent for this one. In any event, the race day experience for owners had markedly improved in recent weeks. We were no longer required to turn up half an hour before our race and leave straight after its running. Racecourses were beginning to provide food and refreshments for owners, following the same government guidelines adopted by pubs, restaurants and hotels. These establishments had reopened their doors in the first week of July and I was able to book a budget hotel for me, Jennie and Joe which ruled out the need to drive to York and back in a day.

It felt as if we were edging back to a more normal way of doing things as we sped up the A1. A day at the Ebor meeting followed by a few drinks in the city centre is a ritual I've observed for decades. The racecourse gave owners an allocation of six badges and offered a three-course lunch to those who attended. Our table would be completed by Patrick and Sally, and Mick Corringham. Trevor was a non-runner as he was self-isolating ahead of a cruciate ligament operation on Friday, and poor Pete was unable to be there as he was a victim of Covid, in a rather roundabout way.

Following a blood test, he was called into hospital by the Urgent Care team. His hastily arranged appointment was for 11.30am today. Pete agonised about going. He desperately wanted to be at York but resigned himself to missing out as he had been called in quickly by a team that had 'urgent' in its name. In the circumstances, he felt he had to go to the hospital and was obviously worried about what he might hear. Apparently, he received a phone call from the hospital about an hour before he was due there to confirm that the consultation would be conducted by telephone.

Pete was livid. He had received a letter which confirmed a face-to-face appointment. It even gave him helpful information about parking at the hospital. It was clearly a cock-up. Due to Covid, lots of consultations were now taking place by telephone or Zoom. However, in Pete's case, a standard letter was incorrectly generated telling him to be there in person. I can only assume that, when the first patient turned up at reception with their appointment letter, the penny dropped, triggering a mad scramble to get in touch with all subsequent visitors.

My old Reading University pal spent most of his career working in NHS training and administration, and he was aware of the pressures currently on our services. That didn't stop him from being irritated and disappointed, but he knew there was nothing to be gained from bawling down the phone at the unfortunate bearer of bad news, telling them that this unforgivable error had prevented him from watching his racehorse in action. 'Toff Slates Our Heroes in Racing Outburst,' was a Daily Express headline lurking in the wings.

Pete conveyed all of this to me in a phone conversation shortly after we arrived at the racecourse. I was sipping a complementary glass of champagne in the lounge on the top floor of the Ebor Grandstand when he called. This vast, carpeted area had been converted into the owners' dining room for the day. It had space for around 50 socially-distanced tables and, although the racecourse had dropped its insistence on jackets and ties for gentlemen and smart attire for ladies, nearly everyone in attendance opted to dress up.

I felt Pete's pain as he told me about his exasperating experience. When he asked me how York was looking after the owners, I instinctively held the champagne glass behind my back as if to hide it from his gaze. I avoided the subject of the splendid looking three-course luncheon menu and mumbled something about some food being put on. It wasn't the time to enthuse about how well we were being treated.

I steered the conversation towards the race. Pete was negative about the draw. He wasn't sure about the ground either. York hadn't seen anywhere near the amount of rain that was originally forecast and the official going was 'good'. We both doubted the accuracy of that description. The final going stick reading of 6.7 suggested that Free Love would encounter a surface on the slower side of good. Even worse, it might ride a little dead or loose. It wasn't what we had hoped for, but it wasn't the quagmire that we feared a few days ago.

We all agreed that Free Love should take her chance and, soon after my chat with Pete, Mick Appleby called to wish us luck. He thought our filly would be suited by a little juice in the ground but mentioned that the Sampers Seven gang were having second thoughts about running. They intended to wait until their jockey, Silvestre De Sousa, reported back after his ride in the first race.

Half an hour later, Silvestre finished 20th of 21 in the opener. He must have told Mick that the going was unsuitable for Sampers

Seven, and before I moved onto my main course, a tannoy announcement confirmed that Free Love's galloping companion was a non-runner. She joined Electric Ladyland and Princess Power who were also withdrawn because of 'unsuitable going'. With Maygold already scratched on veterinary grounds, the field was down to nine.

It was difficult to work out exactly how the track was riding. The first race was a typically competitive handicap sprint run over the straight five-and-a-half-furlong course. Twenty-one runners fanned across the track, but the far side always seemed to have the upper hand and it was Acclaim The Nation from stall nine who landed the spoils, chased home by Soldier's Minute who was berthed in two. Now that Free Love's race was down to nine runners, I hoped that her comparatively high draw wouldn't have too much impact on the outcome.

It wasn't long before the official result for the first race was posted on the Racing Post app. I'm not a stopwatch expert, but I have a rudimentary understanding of what the figures mean. Acclaim The Nation's winning time was only 0.6 seconds outside the standard time for the race. That suggested good ground with just the slightest hint of give, but it was at odds with how some of the jockeys and trainers felt the course was riding.

Over the years, I've come to regard the Knavesmire surface with some suspicion. The course is responsible for its fair share of shocks, especially when rain arrives. I remember being part of a stunned crowd gawping in collective disbelief at Golden Horn's inability to reel in a 50/1 outsider, Arabian Queen, in the 2015 International Stakes. The colt had won the Derby and Eclipse before his stuttering effort at York and would subsequently win the Irish Champion Stakes and Arc de Triomphe. The Pegasus of his generation didn't have hooves of clay that day in August; they were made of lead.

Maybe there's something about this particular patch of Yorkshire turf that some horses don't like. I've seen plenty of good one's flop inexplicably at the Ebor meeting. It was more of the same as I watched Cloudbridge, even money favourite for the second race on the card, the Group 2 Acomb Stakes, run deplorably. The Godolphin-owned colt, who had been an impressive winner of his sole start to date, finished last of the eight runners beaten nearly 20 lengths. Maybe some horses just don't get on with the Knavesmire. Perhaps Free Love was one of them I pondered rather gloomily.

It was a strange afternoon. The meal was top class, and I couldn't fault the racecourse for the way in which we were looked after. The safety measures were rigorous and well-honed during a three-month period of behind closed doors racing. But the absence of a crowd killed the occasion stone dead.

I went to the parade ring before the big race to get a close look at the five runners in the International Stakes. My route took me past a section of the racecourse that is usually buzzing. The champagne bars and gardens opposite the paddock, normally the home of laughter and excited chatter, were eerily empty and silent. It was the same for the parade ring. The stepped viewing area, invariably packed and requiring sharp elbows to secure a space, had a smattering of curious watchers, none of whom looked to be associated with the five runners who made up this year's contest.

I made my way back to the top floor of the Ebor stand and decided to watch the race from the outside viewing area. In 2012, when the mighty Frankel attracted a crowd approaching 30,000, I couldn't get near the grandstand when I returned from the parade ring, where I caught a few glimpses of the great horse only by virtue of elevating my six-foot three-inch frame on tiptoes. The place was jammed, and I had to watch Frankel put his International Stakes rivals to the sword from the running rail about 50 yards before the winning line. It's not where I usually choose to watch races. I prefer the panoramic view afforded by a decent spot in the stands where I can see the whole contest unfold. But wherever you were on that scintillating day in 2012, the atmosphere was electric.

Eight years later, I found myself with three other people watching Ghaiyyath make all the running to gallop his four rivals into submission in the 2020 renewal of the big race. The imposing son of Dubawi powered home by three lengths from the multiple Group 1 winner, Magical, and in doing so probably became the highest rated racehorse in Europe, if not the world. I clapped along with my three companions on the grandstand as Ghaiyyath scooted clear. This isn't racing, I thought to myself as I made my way along a deserted concourse to the winner's enclosure. The horse deserved better than the feeble reception he received from the handful there to witness his triumph.

The hour was upon us. The *Sky Bet Fillies' Sprint Handicap* was the penultimate race on the card so there had been plenty of time for a leisurely lunch and to analyse our chances. Free Love had been a 20/1 shot in the morning but, following the withdrawals and a little bit of late support, she was now half those odds. We all thought our Windsor nemesis, Glamorous Anna, was likely to blaze a trail and hoped Theo could edge over and follow her through. The two 100-rated fillies looked obvious dangers despite their big weights, but I wasn't too worried about the warm favourite, the hideously named Dancin Inthestreet, who had looked unlucky in a big Royal Ascot handicap and similarly unfortunate at Newmarket a month later. She was turning into one of those serial hard-luck stories that punters like to back, and bookmakers love to lay.

Owners weren't allowed into the paddock, but Free Love looked well enough from our vantage points on the viewing steps. It was a drab, overcast day with dampness in the air, and none of the fillies could be described as gleaming in their coats. I was just grateful that the heavy rain forecast for late afternoon hadn't materialised.

Free Love cantered calmly down to the start and, as I watched her circle behind the stalls, I was hopeful of a decent run. Yes, I knew there was our York hoodoo to overcome, the ground might be a little more dead than ideal, and the opposition was as warm as could be expected for a class 2 handicap at the Ebor meeting. But our form figures for the season read 342 and the filly was returning to the fray following a nice 30-day break since being touched off by a nose at Windsor. We were entitled to be thereabouts.

They were all loaded and ready to go. Free Love had been nibbled at and 9/1 was now the offer. It was nice to know that the public didn't think our filly was out of place in this exalted company. Nor did she look it from the start. Dandy's Beano was out like a rocket accompanied by Glamorous Anna with Lady In France close up. Theo had Free Love handy in midfield, tracking Glamorous Anna and at halfway he looked poised to strike.

With two furlongs left to run, Dandy's Beano began to fade, and Theo asked Free Love to make her effort. For the briefest of moments, I thought our filly was about to overhaul the weakening pacesetters and go in pursuit of Lady In France and Keep Busy who were duelling for the lead. But 100 yards later it was obvious that Free Love could do no more than plug on without making any impression on the leaders. She crossed the line in seventh place beaten just under five lengths by Lady In France who repelled Keep Busy's persistent challenge by half a length.

It was a deflating experience watching those last 300 yards. Getting plenty of weight from the race's black type performers, Free Love just couldn't pick up when it mattered. She travelled sweetly for half the race before being unable to find the type of finishing speed she had shown at Windsor. I knew it was a better class of race, but she was weighted to be involved.

I walked back to the parade ring to see if there was any chance of getting a word with Theo. I knew I wouldn't be able to see Free Love. Being able to pat your vanquished equine heroine and feel the raised veins on her sweating neck after she's valiantly given her all, was an experience denied to owners in these strange times. I thought how much I missed it as I walked briskly to the paddock to see if Theo was about.

The others must have dawdled as I was on my own when our jockey came over to speak to me, him on the inside of the parade ring, me socially distanced on the other side. Theo felt that Free Love just couldn't go the pace from halfway because of the quality of the opposition. A return to class 3 handicaps was his recommendation.

I couldn't really argue with his feedback, but I wasn't so sure about our filly being outclassed. Glamorous Anna had been raised again following another victory, this time at Goodwood and had to concede 9lbs more to Free Love than she did at Windsor. We were a nose behind her there but more than two lengths adrift today. Our Little Pony, a close fourth this afternoon, was half a length in front of Free Love at Doncaster but had extended her advantage to more than three lengths in today's contest. We were one pound better off with the atrociously named filly as well.

I had to conclude that Free Love ran about 7lbs below expectations. I knew that some of the other boys would say that the filly wasn't up to this level and maybe we shouldn't have run at all, especially given our record at York, but show any race reader the result and they would reasonably conclude that Free Love should have finished a couple of lengths closer, which would have put her in the frame and in line for a decent bit of prize money. In the end she finished seventh in a race where the money went down to sixth. I wouldn't be buying an 'I Love York' tee-shirt in town tonight.

A strange day at the races was followed by an odd evening in town. Some pubs had 'no room at the inn' signs as customers had pre-booked tables for the evening. Others employed bouncers on the door making sure that large groups weren't admitted. At seven (Mick's partner Alison had joined us for the evening), our group fell into that category. We had to split up and approach pubs at agreed intervals to try to gain entry in twos and threes. It was like being sixteen again. To cap it all, some establishments threw in the towel, locking up early at 10pm. My naïve notion that we were edging back to a form of normality had been thoroughly dispelled by the end of the evening. The only thing that was normal about the day was another disappointing run at the Knavesmire for Free Love.

11 Fade to Grey

(Windsor, 7th September 2020)

Friday 28th August 2020

What do you do with a four-year-old filly who is reaching the end of her racing career? Sell her at the December breeding stock sale? Wrong! The correct answer is that you persuade your fellow owners that a breeding project would be a life-affirming experience and they would be fools to spurn the opportunity.

I had only mentioned the possibility of breeding from Free Love once or twice in passing. I can't recall Pete jumping to his feet screaming 'I'm in!' as he simultaneously plonked a five-grand wad of notes on the table to signify his enthusiastic commitment. In fact, I can't remember anyone saying anything about my whimsical proposal. Swiftly moving the conversation on to something else was the usual response.

But wouldn't it be great to breed from Free Love? Wouldn't it be fantastic to undertake such a project with all the research and learning that would be needed to make a go of it? I knew nothing about breeding thoroughbred racehorses. That's why I was making a visit this morning to the man who had bred Free Love.

I'd only met Brendan Boyle once before. That was when we shook hands on a price of 10,000 guineas for lot 1383 who had been led out unsold at the Tattersalls Book 3 sales in October 2017. After Free Love started racing, we'd been in touch with each other a few times via Facebook Messenger and today I was taking up Brendan's offer to visit him to pick his brains about what would be involved if we decided to breed from our filly.

Home Farm Stud lies about 10 miles north of Newmarket. I love driving through the headquarters of British racing. The whole area is steeped in the story of the thoroughbred racehorse. From the village of Six Mile Bottom - named after its distance from the start of the historic racecourse - the London Road runs straight and true, a handful of studs dotted either side of this ancient thoroughfare, which only pauses for a vast roundabout one mile south of the town. In the middle stands an enormous bronze statue of the dramatically rearing Newmarket Stallion, sculpted by Lady Astor and installed in September 2020, its £200,000 cost met by the racing industry and its supporters. It screams, 'This is Newmarket, home of horseracing'.

By 11am I was driving through the entrance of the stud, its impressive new sign confirming that it was the base of Brendan Boyle Bloodstock. I parked behind a stable block and as soon as I got to my feet, Brendan was over to bump elbows and welcome me to his operation.

I didn't know what to expect. It was the first time I'd visited a stud and although I discovered from Brendan's website that he offered a wide range of services including boarding mares, rearing foals, and preparing yearlings for sales, I hadn't a clue how it all worked.

Brendan whisked me through the barn showing me some of the broodmares he was looking after. Most were owned by clients who paid a monthly fee for upkeep which, I soon learned, increased but didn't double when a foal arrived. He also owned his own broodmares, but I can't remember how many. Brendan is an energetic individual who talks and moves with urgent purpose, and I was struggling to keep tabs on the barrage of information being thrown at me.

I knew for sure that at least one broodmare in his ownership was Peace And Love, and once we had completed our whistle-stop tour of the stable block, we emerged on the other side of the building to face a large grass paddock where a couple of mares and foals were idly nibbling the turf.

'Do you want to see Peace And Love?' Brendan asked while opening the gate to the enclosure. He looked down at my inappropriate footwear, assuring me that I'd be fine, before marching off towards the horses with me following in his wake. And there I was, in the middle of a field somewhere between Newmarket and Bury St Edmunds, standing next to Free Love's mum while stroking a beautiful three-month-old foal by Gregorian who was Peace And Love's latest offspring.

The young filly was a beauty. I'd never been anywhere near a thoroughbred foal and it's fair to say that I was enchanted by Free Love's half-sister.

'You can have her if you want,' said Brendan, almost casually. 'You can lease her from me with nothing to pay until next October. I don't think I'll send her to the sales. She'll need a bit of time. But I'll lease her to you and take her back after her first season.'

I didn't know how to respond. I'd come to Home Farm Stud to learn about breeding, and now had visions of Brendan helping me to shove a light bay Gregorian foal into the back of my Zafira, sealing the deal with a firm pat on the back, while telling me that I wouldn't regret my decision.

The Master of Home Farm was loquacious and persuasive but, having assured him that one horse at a time was enough for me, we turned our attention to the costs involved if I decided to breed from Free Love. He could help with a discounted stallion nomination. I think he mentioned something about getting Gregorian for a couple of grand. We also talked about boarding rates.

Over coffee, Brendan continued to outline the options while I turned the figures over in my head. There would be a daily rate for boarding Free Love who would need to be covered sometime between April and May next year. A foal would arrive the following spring and, 18 months later, The North South Syndicate would be the proud owner of a broodmare in foal (assuming Free Love was covered again) and a yearling who could be offered at one of the big autumn sales. We'd get all of this for around £30k.

Brendan knew his stuff. He'd been in the game for over 30 years, taking on various roles including Head Lad to the successful Newmarket trainer, David Loder. But most of his experience has been in breeding bloodstock and preparing young horses for sales. He spent ten years managing Ashbrittle Stud in Somerset before deciding to go it alone. Peace And Love was part of his leaving package when he parted company with the west country breeding operation to set up his own business.

One of the longest, hottest summers in recent memory was now behind us, and I drove back to Dartford through light rain and early autumnal gloom. A quick check in my mirror confirmed that the Gregorian foal wasn't in the back of the car. 'Look what I've got!' I imagined myself saying to Jennie when I arrived home.

Returning to less fanciful matters, I chewed over the breeding options as I joined the A11 south of Newmarket. Without a farm or land of our own, the syndicate would have to pay at every stage to breed from Free Love. We didn't have the means to put our filly out to grass for a few months in our own field. We'd have to pay a daily rate for her keep – and the keep of her offspring – for as long as we owned her.

It seemed to me that we had little chance of making any money out of the project. I suppose like most owner-breeders we'd have to view it as a rewarding hobby, breeding horses to race rather than sell. Now, if we had a scrap of black type, that would be completely different. It was something I had discussed briefly with Brendan during my visit. He thought Mick Appleby had missed a trick by not aiming at a soft listed race abroad when Free Love was on top of her game following her win at Windsor last year. I confessed that the decision to aim elsewhere and go to York for the big apprentice handicap was ours. Maybe we should have been more single-minded about grabbing a bit of black type in Germany, Italy or some other backwater of European racing.

From a commercial perspective, it made sense. Once we knew we had a mid-80s rated sprinter on our hands, perhaps we should have gone flat out to find suitable listed race opportunities abroad. After all, we only needed to hit the first three on one occasion to enhance the value of Free Love and that of her future offspring. It would make anything Brendan bred from Peace And Love more marketable as well which accounted, in part, for his enthusiasm for the approach.

I hadn't given up on black type. The handicapper sided with me and took the view that Free Love was a little below par at York. Her rating was left unchanged on 82 despite the fact that three of the horses who finished in front of us were dropped a pound. Work that one out. Neither had I had thrown in the towel on the possibility of breeding from Free Love. I needed to do a bit more research. Perhaps a trip to Langham was in order. Mick does a bit of breeding and maybe he could give a second opinion. As I approached the familiar sight of the industrial sprawl either side of the Thames, which told me that I was nearly home, I made a mental note to arrange a visit.

Saturday 5th September 2020

There were around 1,800 positive Covid tests today. It was hard to tell whether it was the start of a worrying trend or just a small uptick in numbers which had been low throughout most of June, July and August. The schools were back, pubs and restaurants remained open, and the rule of six still applied. Gatherings for significant family events, such as weddings, were restricted to a maximum of 30 people, and last Sunday Jennie and I celebrated our pearl wedding anniversary with 25 family members and friends. The occasion doubled up as a toast for Joe's eighteenth birthday which was in March but couldn't be marked in any meaningful way because of the lockdown.

The weather just about held for our gathering. The sun made valiant but unsuccessful attempts to break through, but dry and 18 degrees meant we could be in the garden with Joe in charge of the new charcoal-burning barbecue. Much to Jennie's irritation, Joe and I prefer the Neanderthal experience of flames, choking black smoke and incinerated sausages to the joyless, suburban alternative of a gas contraption. In any event, since buying the new grill at Easter, Joe had become a real pro. He insisted on the very best charcoal and total control of all cooking. God help me if Joe caught me trying to turn the lamb skewers while he popped into the kitchen for a beer.

It was inevitable at any social occasion these days for the conversation to settle on the current state of the pandemic. We all tried hard to avoid it, but the daily news was saturated with Covid updates and everyone had a view on the return of schools, the furlough scheme, wearing masks in shops, the state of the economy, the possibility of crowds returning to sporting events, and the latest figures. You couldn't avoid the figures. The evening news invariably kicked off with the latest number of positive test results and fatalities. Familiarity with these morbid statistics had become part of our lives.

At least I had been able to talk horses for a bit last Sunday. Pete was there and we discussed possible races for Free Love as well as the alarming story in a recent edition of the Racing Post about racing's 'funding crisis'. The Racecourse Association's (RCA) chief executive, David Armstrong, reported that racecourses were on target for a £300 million loss this year. He was genuinely concerned for the future of some tracks and warned that prize money levels could not be improved until crowds returned. Racecourses were still receiving funds from media rights – what slice of this cake ended up on racing's plate was a cause of contention – but the RCA's assertion that things couldn't improve without the return of spectators was bleakly realistic.

We knew that Free Love was likely to be declared for Windsor today, and just after 10am it was confirmed that she would face eight rivals in the class 4 *Sky Sports Racing Sky 415 Handicap*, a 0-85 dash for three-year-olds and upwards. Last weekend Pete told me that he was seriously thinking of breaking a family holiday in Pembrokeshire to drive to Windsor and back in a day if Free Love ended up running there.

I thought he was mad. It would be at least four hours from Nolton Haven to Windsor, and for what? York pulled out the stops for the Ebor meeting, but I wasn't sure that the Thameside track would be pushing the boat out on a Monday evening when the fare was mundane and the owners unlikely to feature Michael Tabor or Sheik Mohammed.

Monday 7th September 2020

Although Pete and Trevor had first call on the tickets as they were unable to come to York, neither took up the offer. Pete decided that the journey from the west coast of Wales was too much to do in one day, and Trevor was at an early stage of recuperation following his knee operation. Since Patrick was the only other owner able to make it, I offered one of the spare tickets to my eldest son, Matthew.

I didn't know what to expect at Windsor, but I soon found out that it wasn't York. Once we were through the ID verification and temperature checks, we were directed to drive beyond the usual carpark until we arrived at the back of the course where a marquee was home to a handful of owners. There was no complimentary glass of champagne followed by a three-course lunch. It was a sandwich box and a packet of crisps.

We had access to the owners' lounge, but the furniture had been stripped out and stored in the private boxes making it clear that, although owners were permitted to watch races from this facility, they shouldn't hang around and make themselves comfortable. We couldn't get to any other part of the course. The main grandstand was out of bounds which was irritating as the owners' viewing area is set at an angle around 50 yards beyond the winning post. It provides a head-on view of the straight which is an odd and unsatisfactory way to watch a race.

It was a far cry from 8th July 2019 when the course was packed, and we abandoned the quirky perspective of the owners' enclosure and positioned ourselves instead in the compact main grandstand to witness Free Love overcome Dark Shadow in a hotly contested class 3 handicap. That was my last visit to Windsor. It was all sun, fun, crowds and champagne and I felt gloriously alive.

About half of the parade ring for tonight's meeting was accessible from the owners' zone so we were able to get a decent view of Free Love before she went to post. Our filly looked to have a good chance; a view shared by the public who made her 9/2 second favourite with only
hat-trick-seeking Spoof favoured in the betting.

I was less convinced. I couldn't get away from Free Love's flat run at York. I knew she was beaten less than five lengths in a class 2 contest which featured some smart fillies, but she lacked her usual zip. She hadn't run badly, but she hadn't run well, and I wasn't sure what to expect tonight. The weight also bothered me. Yes, we were down in class but that meant the filly was only three pounds below the top-rated horse and was accordingly allotted 9st 7lbs. I didn't think she had the physical size to give weight away to inferior opponents, which is why I favoured 0-90 or 0-95 class 3 races where Free Love was likely to get a weight that didn't require Theo to fill his saddlecloth with slabs of lead.

The going was another potential negative. It had dried out to 'good', but I eavesdropped on a conversation between a jockey and trainer after the first and heard the rider report the ground as 'dead'. Like York, this opinion was contradicted by the race time which suggested a decent enough surface.

It was all irrelevant now. The horses were being loaded for the feature race of the evening – it wasn't a star-studded card – and Free Love moved forward in characteristically calm fashion to take her place in stall 5, smack bang in the middle of the pack. There could be no excuses on that score.

I had to rely entirely on the small screen sited on the far side of the track to see what was going on as nothing could be gleaned from watching the horses charge head-on towards the only vantage point provided for owners.

Free Love made a decent start. I could see *that* much as I craned my neck in an attempt to get a reasonable view of how the race was unfolding. She was in midfield, tracking Spoof who was disputing the lead in the centre of the track flanked on either side by Doc Sportelllo and Grandfather Tom. At halfway I was happy. The filly was travelling well and, although she had a wall of four horses in front of her, she was following Spoof who made his decisive effort with two furlongs to run. Theo went after him, but there was nothing there. All Free Love could do was plug on at the same pace making no impression on the leaders.

One hundred yards from the finish, our jockey dropped his hands and accepted the situation making sure that the filly didn't have an unnecessarily hard race. It was a blanket finish and Free Love was beaten only a shade over three lengths in seventh place, but I found no comfort in that statistic. It was a bitterly disappointing performance.

The handicapper would no longer regard York as an aberration, an anomaly. That was two flat runs on the bounce and Free Love was heading towards an official rating of 80. The slim chances of black type were fading to grey.

It was a glum walk to the paddock where I hoped we'd be able to have a socially distanced word with our jockey. I videoed the conversation for the benefit of the other owners who couldn't be there. Theo had only ridden two winners since racing resumed in June and the rides seemed to be drying up. He was all the rage when he had his seven-pound apprentice claim but, now it had been cut to three, the clamour to use him had subsided. As he talked through the race he sounded as if he were trying to justify his riding tactics to himself rather than to me.

'I know I was following the right horse. I must have been. He's gone on to win it,' he explained. I didn't disagree with him. On her A-game, Free Love would surely have been able to hang on to Spoof's tail and mount a challenge inside the final furlong. I asked Theo about the ground which he described as a bit dead, but it's the way of racing that winning riders think the ground is perfect while losing ones find fault in it.

Our young jockey departed just before Mick Appleby phoned. Mick thought that the filly didn't see too much daylight and never got into the race. He felt Theo should have positioned Free Love more handily. Maybe so, but he rode her almost the same way last July when coming from a midfield position to lead close home.

I finished the conversation with Mick by letting him know that I intended to make a quick visit to Langham on Wednesday. I wanted to discuss the autumn sales and ask him about breeding. One thing was for sure. We wouldn't be talking about listed races.

12 When the Going Gets Soft

(Nottingham, 14th October 2020)

Wednesday 9th September 2020

I didn't mention my stable visit to the others. It was better for me to go solo as I intended to drop in on Anne and Robin Bickers, who had happily retired to Oakham more than 15 years ago. There was nothing to see anyway. Free Love wouldn't be working so soon after her disappointing effort at Windsor. She wouldn't be doing much for a while, in fact. Mick sent me a text yesterday reporting that the filly was sore in her back and shoulders and his 'back man' had given her a thorough 'going over'. It sounded like something from a D H Lawrence novel.

I arrived towards the end of the break between the early and late lots. Mick had already returned to his usual position at the top of the all-weather gallop, and after gulping down a quick mug of tea, I went to join him. Under a dark and sullen sky, I was a desultory observer of the morning's final gallops and canters. I only exchanged a few words with Mick as a couple of owners were there to see their horses in action and they wanted to quiz their trainer about running plans.

I decided to wait until morning exercise was finished before interrogating Mick about breeding plans. After the other owners had departed, we went into the small office where the yard's racing secretary, Jane Hales, was beavering away behind a computer surrounded by piles of paper. Jane made the entry there and then for the Tattersalls breeding stock sale at the end of November. With a click of her mouse, a cool £850 left our syndicate's account.

I discussed with Mick our intention to race Free Love right up to

146

the time of the sale, which could mean two or three more runs depending on how long it took her to recover from the soreness she picked up at Windsor. At least we had an explanation for her flat effort on Monday evening.

After the sale entry had been sorted, the conversation turned to the possibility of breeding from Free Love. I knew this wasn't an adventure for the faint hearted, but Mick gave me a bit of hope. He was sure that the rates charged by the small, local stud he used to look after his mares and foals would be a fair bit cheaper than Newmarket, and the £12 a day figure he mentioned sounded within our compass. By 'our' I meant The North South Syndicate, although at this stage I was the only member keen on pursuing this exciting new dream.

We talked about stallion fees, veterinary checks and the timescales involved. Mick raised the possibility of Free Love being covered in the spring and continuing to race after she was pregnant, which was a common enough practice. Fillies sometimes showed improved form in the months that they were allowed to race after conception.

It was a fascinating chat that confirmed my ignorance of the bloodstock industry, but I felt I was learning all the time. I left with contact details for a local stud and some figures which I mentally examined as I drove away heading for Oakham. I was two minutes from Anne's house when a terrible thought interrupted my financial calculations. I hadn't been to see Free Love!

I couldn't believe it. I had become so absorbed in the conversation about breeding that time ran away from me. I was a little behind schedule when I said my goodbyes at Langham and rushed to the car before speeding off to Oakham. I was wracked with guilt, picturing a mournful Free Love waiting in her box for a special visitor who failed to materialise. I felt like a parent who had forgotten about their young child's class assembly.

There was nothing I could do about it now. I would have to return before the sale for a final visit to Langham. That was the only way to ensure a last chance to get up close to Free Love, to stroke her neck and play with her ears and snap one final round of photos before somebody else took charge of the story.

I didn't stay long in Anne and Robin's garden. We talked briefly about our old times at Edenbridge Primary School, where Anne was the Special Educational Needs Coordinator when I was promoted to headship in January 2000. Twenty years. My youngest, Joseph, off to university in a fortnight's time, hadn't even been born.

I was home by late afternoon and was soon settled on the sofa with a mug of tea watching a recording of the first day of Doncaster's St Leger meeting. It was a big deal for sport, not just horseracing. It was over a month since the eagerly awaited trial of crowds returning to racecourses was scuppered at the eleventh hour, leaving Goodwood with a mountain of unsold food and a thumping bill for their troubles. Today, Doncaster was set to try again, and 2,500 spectators had bought tickets for the first day of the four-day meeting at Town Moor which would climax with the running of the final Classic of the season on Saturday.

No stone had been left unturned. The ITV presenters, led by Ed Chamberlin, were at pains to show the precautions taken by Doncaster to minimise the risk of Covid transmission. Apart from the usual temperature and health checks on arrival, masked racegoers were directed to one of 30 mini zones where they would be required to stay for the duration of the meeting. The usual social distancing and hygiene protocols, including the rule of six, were expected in these segregated enclosures.

Although I admired the thoroughness and understood that this was an important trial for all sports not just racing, I didn't fancy it. Being unable to move around would frustrate me. Visiting the

148

paddock, applauding the victors on their return to the winner's enclosure and meeting up in the bar to chat about what we fancied in the next, are intrinsic parts of the experience. It was a start, I suppose. We had to be thankful for that.

It turned out to be a false start. Not long after Tarboosh won the listed Scarborough Stakes (in which Wise Words, only three-quarters of a length in front of Free Love at Leicester last September, finished an excellent fourth) Ed Chamberlin addressed his TV audience with the solemnity of a presenter on duty at a royal funeral. The trial was dead in the water. After today, the plans to accommodate small crowds on the other three days of the St Leger meeting had been scrapped.

You could write a book about the sorry saga. The local MP backed the trials but the Mayor and her joyless Public Health Director, Doctor Rupert Suckling, were opposed. There seemed to be a bit too much petty politics going on, with local councillors and health gurus feeling they had been side-lined in what was a government backed test case for all elite sports.

It was true that confirmed cases were beginning to creep up nationally, but it was hard to take Dr Suckling's assertion seriously that there had been a worrying acceleration in local rates to 10.6 per 100,000. I made that about 1 in 10,000 which meant the odds of having an infected individual in the crowd at today's meeting was 3/1 against. It was probably less, given the temperature checks in place.

The local public health supremo also made some strange claims about the dangers of crowds descending on the town after their day at the races. He talked about, 'Public disorder risks across the borough.' The inference was that racegoers would be raucous and unruly and therefore a danger to the local community. He stopped short at advising parents to lock up their daughters.

I was irritated by the provincial nature of the decision making. Rupert Suckling stressed that this was his call alone and not a directive from central government. I would have preferred Oliver Dowden, the Minister for The Department of Digital, Culture, Media and Sport, to have pulled the plug and explain what the implications were for the trials planned for other sports. A national response was needed for a national strategy.

Whatever the rights and wrongs of the decision, everyone in racing could at least agree that it was disappointing and a huge setback. A trial was planned for Warwick on 21st September, but it was hard to know how that would fare as reports began to circulate about the government considering what steps it would need to take to keep infection rates under control.

Wednesday 16th September 2020

Tom Marquand landed the St Leger on Saturday, picking up the spare ride on Galileo Chrome. The horse's regular pilot, Shane Crosse, tested positive for Covid the day before the final classic was run, so up stepped young Tom to ride yet another winner at the highest level, adding a little more radiance to his already stellar year.

Free Love had been hiding her light under a bushel since Windsor, but this morning we had evidence that she was on the mend. It was only a five-second video clip of the filly doing a gentle solo canter under Erika, but it was a good sign and made me feel optimistic that she was over her setback and it wouldn't be long before we saw her on a racecourse again.

I decided it was time to give the boys a report on my stable visit including what I found out about breeding.

Morning gents,
Sorry for the delay in giving you a report about my visit to Mick's yard last week. The main purpose of the visit was to confirm Free Love's entry in the

Tattersalls December fillies and mares' sale and to pick Mick's brains about what would be involved if we decided to breed from Free Love ourselves.

I'm pretty sure that I won't get a majority for the latter, but I promised myself that I would do some research and make everyone aware of what's involved. I'm nearly there. I had a useful conversation with the local stud that looks after Mick's own mares and foals. One of his home-breds, Mops Gem, makes her debut today. I know Mick likes her but he's not renowned for readying two-year-olds for a winning debut.

As for Free Love, you know that Mick reported her as sore in the back and shoulders the day after Windsor. His physio had to spend about an hour with her, but Mick didn't think it was anything serious, and we discussed Free Love running two or three more times until the end of November when the sale takes place. It was good to see the video of her cantering this morning.

The sale entry fee was a whopping £850. We've had our VAT return and once that comes out of the account, we'll have about £1,500 left so I'm afraid another £500 each will be needed on or before the 30 September.

I see Free Love was dropped two pounds to 80 yesterday. Every little bit helps. You'd like to think that was a winning mark, but her last Windsor effort was so much below the previous one against Glamorous Anna and Yimou that it's hard to know what to expect next time she runs. Mick will look at entries towards the end of the month. We probably want a race between now and a return to Nottingham in October. The Goodwood apprentice race is on the agenda (Theo not eligible), but it all depends on how the filly recovers. There's a race at Leicester as well. I told Mick that we wouldn't mind a spin on the all-weather in November. That seems a better option than just leaving her in her box until the sale.

That's all for now. I'll send the madcap breeding project figures to you later this week. I'm sure the majority vote will be for taking the money and running. It's hard to know what Free Love would fetch at auction in the current climate. Similar fillies went for around £8k - 20k last year but we are living in different *times.*

Regards, Tony

Although I had the figures for the breeding venture, I wanted to have one last look at them before I knocked them into shape and sent them to the others. In any event, my email conveyed news about the need for a further £500 contribution to keep the current show on the road. I suppose I could have said, 'While I'm on the subject of money, the breeding project will cost about five thousand each over the next three years so why not transfer five-and-a-half grand and be done with it?'

I left Mick's last week with contact details for Judith Jones at Sinneyfields Farm who could not have been more helpful when I called her on Monday to talk through how she and her husband could help. There were scans and other veterinary fees to build into the costs, but the core expenditure would be the keep for Free Love from January onwards, and for the foal who would arrive around 15 months later.

The stallion fee was the main variable. Judith suggested a local option and clearly had faith in the ability of Music Master to make it as a commercial sire. However, if we were breeding to sell, choosing a more fashionable stallion might be shrewder. The only problem was that sexy sires came with sexy price tags. They also come in and out of fashion with alarming speed. We could choose an expensive, fashionable young stallion who had made a great start at stud only to find out three years later, after a couple of disappointing crops, that our foal was shunned by buyers.

That all presupposed that the object of the exercise was to breed to sell, but I knew that wouldn't happen. I'd want to keep the youngster for ourselves and would be working flat out to persuade the others that we needed to put the son or daughter of Free Love into training to complete the owner-breeder dream. We could always sell the next one…

Thursday 24th September 2020

It was blowing a gale in Norfolk. Jennie and I had spent a sleepless night listening to the howling wind tear through the silver birches that surrounded our caravan. At 7am, Jennie pulled back the blind on the rooflight to check that the tree swaying directly over our van wasn't about to crash in on us.

We were due to go home tomorrow after an impromptu five-day break. We dropped off Joe at Leeds University on Saturday and decided to mark the departure of our third and final child with a short holiday. After nearly three decades of family vacations, we were on our own. This was rather irritating as, had Joe been with us, I could have sent him outside to face the teeth of the storm and assuage his mother's anxiety about the state of the trees, which she felt were on the verge of toppling onto the roof of the van.

It was an incredible turnaround. On Tuesday, we had been swimming at Wells-next-the-Sea. It was the last hot day of the year and the Zafira's temperature gauge read 25 degrees when we eventually found a parking space in town. Our dilatory approach was in stark contrast to the ruthless organisation of other day-trippers, who ensured that the beach car park was full hours before we arrived. This meant a 25-minute walk from the harbour to the beach carrying all the mandatory paraphernalia needed for a day at the seaside.

The long haul along Beach Road, which is as straight and unrelenting as Newmarket's Rowley Mile, was worth it, though. At the end of our slog, we were greeted by a wonderful expanse of golden sand ahead of us, and colourful beach huts crouching in front of towering pine trees to our left.

153

The beach at Wells' is fabulous for both swimming and lounging, whatever the time of day. When the tide is out, a narrow channel of fast-moving water, locally known as 'the run', is full of shrieking bathers. It's only about 30m wide and easy to swim across to the far side where the deserted sand resembles a lunar landscape. It was one of those magical late summer experiences that would linger in the memory for years to come.

This morning's tempestuous conditions could not have been more of a contrast and the stormy weather was set to continue, prompting a decision to leave a day early if we could find a short break in the wind and rain that would make it possible to take down the awning and pack it away. There were other important decisions to be made, not least what to do about Free Love who was due to run at Pontefract this afternoon.

While Jennie was pondering her mortality, Mick Appleby had been texting about the going at Pontefract. Our trainer must have been happy with the way the filly was moving following her small setback, and towards the end of last week he made a couple of speculative entries. One at Chelmsford drew an unenthusiastic response from the other owners. The other was for Pontefract. I've never been to the West Yorkshire track but knew that the sprint course was a little quirky. After an undulating first three furlongs, a gentle left-hand bend guided the horses into a short finishing straight. I looked at some video replays of past five-furlong races there and was undecided about Free Love's ability to handle its demands.

We all agreed to resist interfering and let Mick decide where to go. He plumped for Pontefract and the class 4 0-85 *Follow @WilliamHillracing Handicap*. However, since being declared on Tuesday there had been further rain. Although the overnight going description was 'good to soft, good in places', the forecast was for continuous rain in the Pontefract area from about 9am onwards. The other boys didn't want Free Love to run on testing ground so by 8am, following a brief conversation with our trainer, the decision was made to withdraw our filly.

The other evasive action taken that day was our tactical retreat from Kelling Heath. By midday, the wild weather had temporarily calmed and within two hours we were packed up and heading home for Dartford. The next band of torrential rain and high winds wasn't due until the early evening, and we made sure we wouldn't be there to greet it.

Saturday 26th September 2020

The Covid numbers were looking increasingly worrying. My optimism, based on the fine weather and low rates of infection throughout June, July and August, now seemed misplaced. The talk was all about preparing for a difficult winter. Earlier in the month, Northumberland joined Manchester and Liverpool as an area requiring targeted interventions. We were due to join my two brothers for a week in Bamburgh but, like the reunion we planned for six couples in Barcelona at the beginning of the month, it became just another holiday to fall by the wayside.

A few days ago, the return of crowds to racing was shelved despite the success of the Warwick trial. The Racing Post's front page gloomily predicted that it would be at least six months before spectators were allowed back. At least owners were still able to see their horses run, but their appetite for the soulless experience of sport behind closed doors could hardly be described as insatiable.

During the afternoon I provided an update for other owners attaching a breakdown of the costs involved of breeding from Free Love.

Morning gents,

I hope you are all well and ready for another six months of lockdown. First things first. Your next £500 payment is due on or before 30th September (Wednesday). We have just over £2k in the pot so we're not in bad shape

As far as our next run is concerned, although the straight five at Redcar next Saturday would suit, the weather forecast looks grim. At this rate we might have to seriously consider going to Chelmsford to avoid soft ground.

By the way, did anyone notice that the five-year-old, Dandy's Beano, who finished one place behind us at York was third in last Friday's fillies and mares' listed race at Ayr? She was rated 85 and has only been put up two to 87. A small price to pay for doubling her value.

Finally, attached is the financial suicide package, otherwise known as the breeding project. As you know, I visited Brendan Boyle, Free Love's breeder, to talk things through with him. He confirmed that Newmarket is expensive for anything to do with racing. I also talked to the small stud that looks after Mick Appleby's mares and foals. I sent the attached estimations to them just to double check the figures which they confirmed as accurate.

In brief, we'd all need to pay around £125 a month for three years to get to the stage where we had a yearling. At that point we would be about £22-23k out of pocket and our assets would be a broodmare and a yearling.

There you have it. Any thoughts?

Regards, Tony

Sunday 4th October 2020

I didn't set a deadline for thoughts to be shared. Indeed, it wasn't compulsory to make any comment at all. But it was now more than a week since I laid out the plans for the North South Syndicate's breeding empire and deafening silence was the only response.

I took the hint. Free Love was going to Tattersalls on 2nd December where she had been allotted a lousy slot towards the end of the catalogue on the final day of the sale. Hopefully, she would be bought by a small breeder looking for a keenly priced new broodmare. If that happened, I'd know she was in good hands, and I could follow the progress of her offspring for years to come. The story would have finished, but my vicarious involvement could last until I was ready to meet my maker.

I thought there might have been a bit of interest in Dandy's Beano's black type heroics. Here was an experienced and thoroughly exposed sprint handicapper who had tried her luck in a listed race and snuck into third place as an unfancied 40/1 shot. That could have been us. You just need to be in the right place, at the right time, with all the cards falling in your favour – physical wellbeing, draw, going, pace etc. Until her exploits at Ayr, Dandy's Beano had won five of her 27 races, none of which had been above class 4. Her highest official rating was 85. Given Free Love's most recent flops it seemed ridiculous to cling to ambitions of black type, but I knew if she turned up for a soft listed race restricted to her own sex and she produced the type of performance that saw her touched off by a nose at Windsor in July, she could do it. More accurately, she could have done it. HMS Black Type had surely sailed. We'd missed the boat.

There was no run for Free Love at Redcar yesterday. Rain swept across the whole country and although the meeting survived (Ascot was cancelled) our trainer was the first one to say that Free Love should stay in her box as the going would be atrocious wherever we went.

Wednesday 14th October 2020
In contrast to the weather, our patience was running dry. Since cutting out of Redcar, various options were considered. We even had an entry for Musselburgh at one point as our trainer searched

high and low for a reasonable opportunity on decent ground. In the end, we opted for Nottingham today, accepting that the filly needed to run even if conditions weren't ideal. The other option was Southwell in two days' time, but we told Mick that we would prefer to return to a track where Free Love had won two from four, including a victory on good to soft.

The going at Nottingham was soft when Free Love was declared on Monday, but a relatively encouraging forecast gave hope that our filly might be racing on something a bit better. Unfortunately, the Met Office prediction was wide of the mark and unwelcome rain arrived this morning, ensuring that Free Love would encounter genuinely soft ground in the class 3 *MansionBet Proud to Support British Racing Handicap;* yet another race supported by a bookmaking firm during a period when local businesses must have viewed race sponsorship as a low priority.

The turf season was nearing its conclusion, yet it was the first time that Pete would have the chance to see Free Love in action this year. We arrived at about midday and while we went through the usual checks, I asked one of the racecourse staff how many owners they were expecting. I was told that if everyone on the list turned up, it would be 43. There were over 90 horses declared for this afternoon's nine races meaning at least 360 owners were entitled to attend. The figures spoke for themselves.

Wearing a mask was now compulsory in all indoor areas of racecourses and could only be removed when seated to eat and drink. I didn't object to wearing a face covering but the mixed messages issued by government ministers and scientists about their effectiveness were irritating. However, if it helped suppress the spread of Covid, I was happy to wear one and put up with the minor inconvenience of my steaming spectacles.

As soon as I was seated, off came the face-covering and my vision returned. The owners' lounge looked empty. It stayed that way for much of the meeting. Patrick strolled into the room looking relaxed and unhurried. As usual, he had let the train take the strain; something I frequently promise myself that I will do next time, usually as soon as I hit the first traffic jam on the M11.

All three of us were a bit glum about the going, Pete edging more towards despondent. As usual, I tried to talk up our chances, reminding my two friends that Free Love had run well on heavy ground at Haydock as a two-year-old. All was not yet lost. They were less convinced, and the betting public was on their side. Our filly was easy to back at around 16/1.

The first race was a maiden for two-year-olds run over a mile and it looked hard work out there. Set Point was a convincing winner for Hugo Palmer, but my heart sank when the time was announced. It was almost ten seconds above standard. They were only youngsters, but ten seconds suggested a surface akin to Passchendaele.

The sprint races would be a better guide and, rather unusually, there were three five-furlong contests on the bounce from race five onwards. We had a leisurely lunch while waiting for the first of these which was a nursery handicap in which Mick had a runner. Fantasy Master was an 80/1 shot when he won a Nottingham maiden last month under Tom Marquand. He showed that there was no fluke about the performance when gamely following up this afternoon off a mark of 76 with the same pilot in the saddle.

You always take heart when your trainer has a winner ahead of your own horse running. I'm not sure why. Some see it as a good omen, others as an indication of the stable's wellbeing. We took it as a bit of both. The time was encouraging as well. It was 2.5 seconds outside the 58-second standard which suggested the ground was soft but far from heavy. The following race confirmed that view. It was a treat to have a listed contest on the card and the admirably consistent Dakota Gold was favourite to win the *Rous Stakes* for the second year running. The soft ground specialist made no mistake, galloping his opponents into submission and breaking 60 seconds while he was at it. His official rating was 109 - a fair indication of what's needed to win a mixed-gender listed sprint.

The going is bad but not terrible, I thought to myself as we headed for the paddock where Free Love was being led round by Erika. It was a class 3 event in which the top-rated horses both had a mark of 87. Free Love was dropped two pounds to 80 following her Windsor flop and was set to carry nine stone. Theo's claim took the actual weight carried down to a handy looking 8st 11lbs.

The progressive three-year-old, Shepherds Way, was on a hat-trick and looked a formidable opponent as did Wrenthorpe and Fantasy Believer, a couple of horses guaranteed to enjoy the underfoot conditions. The last named was in the same ownership as Fantasy Maker and a stable companion of Free Love.

Our filly looked relaxed and in good shape as she walked around the parade ring. It was the usual deal. Metal barriers divided the large, oval paddock in two. The side nearest to the main racecourse entrance was reserved for owners, the other half was for trainers, jockeys and stable staff. I was getting used to it by now. Unlike Windsor, we had access to the main grandstand which provided a decent view of the track as well as a large screen located directly opposite. It wasn't difficult to find a good spot. There were only three other onlookers on the spacious terrace.

As Free Love cantered down to the start, I reflected on how much I liked Nottingham and how it had been a lucky track for me. My first ever visit was during half-term in October 2009. I had taken a 5% share in South Cape through Heart of the South, which I split with Trevor and a racing enthusiast no longer with us, Derek

160

Maidment. My close friend and fellow headteacher, Colin Turtle, kept me company and was rewarded with a win. I can still feel the thrill of being in the winner's enclosure with the horse in which I had a 1.67% share. Nearly a decade later, Free Love revealed her first glimpse of ability at Colwick Park when showing speed for three furlongs in a novice event, and the following April she returned to Nottingham to record two impressive handicap wins inside 20 days. Yes, the place had been kind to me.

Free Love had touched 20/1, but 14/1 was the best offer as she walked nonchalantly into stall 10. It didn't look a good draw to me despite some views that on soft ground high numbers were favoured. I always thought the middle to far side was the best place to be. It wouldn't take long to find out.

Talk about a six-pointer. Run well and we maintain our rating of 80, or maybe improve on it. Run poorly and we drop into the 70s which would extinguish any hope of extending the season for a few months, perhaps taking in a winter all weather campaign to make up for lost time. It was mid-October, and it was only the sixth run of the season for Free Love. By this time last year, she had won three times and already tucked ten runs under her belt.

The ready and waiting excuse was the ground. As the last of the runners was led forward, I was already preparing my speech for the others. 'We had to run somewhere but she didn't act on the ground so I think we can put a line through that performance. The draw didn't help either.' I was rehearsed and all set to put the case for the defence as I watched the ten runners burst into action with Wrenthorpe making a flying start from stall one.

Free Love was easily best away of those on the near side and, at halfway, she was a handy fourth, two or three lengths off Wrenthorpe who was still dictating the pace. The well backed Shepherds Way was floundering in the mud and already beaten. Our filly appeared to be travelling sweetly which didn't surprise me. Her natural pace allowed her to keep tabs on the leader. It was her ability to pick up in the ground that was questionable.

It was crunch time. With a furlong-and-a-half to run, Theo asked his charge for her effort and, with no immediate response evident, I thought we were booked for a plugging on fifth or sixth. Wrenthorpe wasn't for catching, but under a right-hand drive Free Love edged left towards Case Key and Royal Context who were vainly chasing the leader. Getting closer to other horses seemed to spur her on and in the last 100 yards our filly set her head low and galloped all the way to the line passing Wrenthorpe's pursuers to grab a hard-fought and incredibly game runner-up spot.

I was ecstatic. It was a huge effort and much more like the filly we knew and loved. The three of us scampered down the steps at the back of the grandstand and squeezed as close as we could to the winner's enclosure where only the first and second were allowed to return. We exchanged a few socially distanced words with Mick and Theo who were both really pleased with the filly's return to form. Our trainer observed that it proved Free Love could act on the ground which opened a few more options for what was left of the season.

There was no crowd, nor could we enter the enclosure to pat our little heroine on the neck where her veins stood proud, providing evidence of her gallantry. It may have been different, disappointingly quiet and lacking in atmosphere, but the sense of elation was still there. It was a 0-90 handicap and our little 10,000 guinea bargain had run her heart out. I watched with a deep sense of pride as Free Love was led around by Erika before she disappeared to the racecourse stables beyond the pre-parade ring.

Back in the owners' lounge, a member of staff was on hand to offer a glass of champagne to the winning connections while they watched a replay of Wrenthorpe's triumph. This little ritual is usually conducted in a small hospitality room under the main grandstand, but Covid protocols dictated that owners should stay in their allocated zone. The presentation of a trophy to the winning owner took place just beyond the food servery and in front of a large television which was showing a recording of the race.

I recognised the winning owner. He was one of the Nottingham six who crammed into the grandstand to watch the race a few minutes earlier. We got chatting, and he told me that it was the gelding's fourth course and distance victory from five attempts (he was only beaten a head in the one race that evaded him) and all the wins were achieved on soft ground, including success in last year's running of today's race. He was a real course specialist who adored the mud. 'And he had a better draw than us,' I thought of saying but decided against such a sour observation. Instead, I maintained my congratulatory tone with as much sincerity as I could muster.

On the one hand, I felt aggrieved about bumping into Wrenthorpe, King of Nottingham, but on the other hand, it made Free Love's effort even more meritorious. More than anything, I was relieved that she had left behind those flat runs at York and Windsor, bouncing back to form on ground that was far from ideal. It was going to be a chatty and upbeat journey back to Dartford.

13 End Game

(Southwell, 9th November and 11th December 2020)

Thursday 15th October 2020

My mobile buzzed. It was 08:42 and there was a short text from Mick to say that Free Love was fine after her great run yesterday. The second part of the brief message informed me that a 'foreigner' had offered £15k for the filly.

There were no further details about the mysterious buyer, and I had no idea what Mick meant by a foreigner. As he is Barnsley through and through, with an accent to match, I wondered whether he was referring to somebody from Oldham or a similar location on the wrong side of the Pennines.

In racing, the idea of a tight-lipped, foreign buyer conjures up images of only one person - Sheik Mohammed. If it wasn't the Godolphin supremo who was interested in Free Love, it was probably somebody with Middle East connections. I was reminded that our filly's full-brother, Lawless Louis, was sold to race in Qatar at the end of his three-year-old career.

I was intrigued and immediately called Mick for more information. He had no idea who had made the enquiry, which was fielded by his racing secretary, Jane Hales. Jane was unable to throw much light on the situation. She told me that it was quite common for the office to be contacted in this way and, more often than not, it amounts to nothing.

I felt duty-bound to put the others in the picture despite my reluctance to sell. The Tattersalls sale was only six weeks away and there might be a majority vote for taking the cash now. It wasn't an unreasonable offer. It would be three grand back each, which was halfway to having another crack at ownership. But I was keen to complete the journey and put up a strong case for turning down the offer and getting two more races out of Free Love – and a win.

I argued that we'd probably get £15k for the filly at public auction, or very close to that figure. We might get more, especially if Free Love signed off the season with a win. I produced an analysis of last year's broodmare sale that suggested a value of between 10,000 and 20,000 guineas for our filly. Now that Free Love was back in good form, why not race on and take our chances at the sale?

That afternoon, I made a visit to Crayford dogs where I told Richard Hennessy all about the elation in the camp following Free Love's effort at Nottingham, and this morning's mysterious foreign buyer. I've only known Richard since I joined Dartford Golf Club which was less than five years ago. In his younger days he refereed football matches at a decent level, was a top-class cricketer, and now he plays off a golf handicap of eight. I can't compete with that. Today I was his guest at an afternoon meeting which featured two greyhounds in which Richard had significant shares.

Although I hadn't been to the dogs for nearly a decade, I was familiar with the nuances of the sport. The tight Crayford circuit, barely 300 metres in circumference, was built as a replacement for the big, galloping track that was demolished as part of the development to create a Sainsbury's superstore. I was a frequent visitor to the old Crayford. When we were sixth-formers, Patrick's dad, Joe, would often lock up shop early on a quiet midweek evening, getting away from his off licence in Sidcup just after 9pm. We'd arrive at the track in time to see the last three or four races by which time the gates were open and we could waltz in for free. I have fond memories of sipping a small glass of keg beer, cigarette in hand, as I tried to crack the forecast for the upcoming A5 contest.

Joe didn't pay too much attention to the form but dabbled in systems instead. Traps 1, 2 and 6 in a forecast combination was one of his favourites. On other occasions, he might spend all evening backing the field to beat trap 2. He usually seemed to do ok. Patrick and I, on the other hand, studied sectional times, bend positions, variations in racing weights and the subtleties of trap positions which made it all the more irritating when Joe landed a juicy forecast through his more random and quirky approach.

I must have been a lucky charm for Richard. His two dogs, Twins Jetto and Allowdale Mia, bolted up. Both grabbed an early lead and, once they had clear sight of the lure, neither looked likely to be caught. Richard fielded a few congratulatory calls and texts from friends and co-owners who couldn't be there. His experience wasn't dissimilar to mine at Nottingham yesterday. There were about a dozen owners present, only allowed to be unmasked when seated at spaciously separated tables. The bar was shut, and a solitary waitress was employed to provide a table service of tea and instant coffee.

We did our best to roar Jetto and Mia home, but the atmosphere was subdued and unnatural. We were in a strange, twilight world that had no end in sight. Alternative strategies to dealing with the pandemic had received short shrift from the World Health Organisation, including suggestions from reputable scientists. The Great Barrington Declaration, published about a week ago, advocated a different approach involving 'focused protection' of those most at risk which would avoid or significantly reduce the harm that lockdowns and restrictions caused to wider society.

The declaration called for individuals at significantly lower risk of dying from Covid to be allowed to resume their normal lives; going to work, socialising in bars and restaurants, and gathering at sporting and cultural events. I could see the sense in it even if the WHO and a posse of experts rushed to condemn the proposal as irresponsible and unworkable. As far as Western Europe was concerned, the timing for a Great Barrington approach now looked wrong. Infection rates were creeping up and winter was approaching. It was time to fasten your seatbelts. We were in for a bumpy ride.

Wednesday 4th November 2020
It was a beautiful, crisp morning and bright sunshine was already melting the frost as Pete and I set off for Langham. We should have been heading for Nottingham, but due to a misunderstanding, Mick hadn't entered Free Love for today's class 4 handicap. It may have been a blessing in disguise as the ground at Colwick Park was likely to be even more testing than when Free Love chased home Wrenthorpe exactly three weeks ago.

I was initially disappointed when I found out that Mick and I were at cross purposes. He thought we had decided to draw stumps and head straight for the sale on the back of a good run. I thought today's race at Nottingham represented our last opportunity for a final fling on turf and we were now faced with the prospect of a valedictory visit to Southwell, which is not where I envisaged Free Love's racing career finishing.

Despite the brilliance of the weather, the mood in the car was sombre. There were over 25,000 positive Covid tests in the UK yesterday. An alarming move in the wrong direction began at the beginning of October and was showing no signs of easing up. Boris Johnson shunned calls for a two-week mini-lockdown or 'circuit breaker' as it was referred to by scientists, politicians and the press, preferring to stick with regional interventions for those areas with the highest concentrations of infection. The new tier system introduced last month kept millions of people in a state of local lockdown which wasn't good news for my brothers in Altrincham and Durham.

We arrived at Mick's at the usual time and were soon at the top of the gallops watching Free Love work infinitely better than her companion, the moderately rated Jorvik Prince. It was further evidence of the filly's wellbeing. On Saturday, Louise had sent a video clip of an equally smooth-looking piece of work in the company of the useful Fantasy Believer. Free Love looked ready to run and after her gallop we had a quick chat with Theo about the filly's next race, which was likely to be at Southwell next Monday.

The Southwell assignment was a class 4 handicap for horses rated 0-80, which meant it was the weakest race Free Love had contested this season. Unfortunately, that also meant she had plenty of weight to carry. She was set to shoulder joint top-weight of 9st 7lbs. Theo was unperturbed. He felt we were better class than most of the field and would have no problem conceding a few pounds to most of our opponents. He made course specialist, Queen Of Kalahari, the one to beat.

Before we left, I popped into the office to pick up the racing plates Free Love had worn at Windsor. During my last visit to Langham, I met up with Kate and Eamonn O'Brien, who run a small syndicate like ours. They've had a lot of fun and great success with their young stayer, Call My Bluff, who started his winning run in a handicap at Goodwood in August. To commemorate the great event, Kate had the four racing plates worn by the gelding engraved and presented to the other owners.

They looked great and I only wished the idea had been brought to my attention before Free Love had won her four races. The set Jane had put aside for me were worn by the filly when she finished seventh at Windsor. It wasn't an ideal memento for the other owners. A winning shoe was preferred, but it would be nice for everyone to have a souvenir of the adventure to go with the pictures and memories we had accumulated over the last three years.

I left the office clutching four horseshoes in a paper bag and noticed a van parked in the yard which obviously belonged to the farrier. Its back doors were open revealing trays of different sized plates, nails, hammers, rasps and other tools of the trade. I found its owner and introduced myself to our farrier, Ed Dodd, who had a list of horses to replate that morning, including our own Free Love.

Until today, my only contact with Ed had been via email to pay his monthly bill. Now, after a quick elbow bump, he cheerfully offered to shoe our filly straight away which gave me and Pete a chance to watch him at work. Free Love stood calmly, totally unfazed as Ed plonked her near foreleg on a metal hoof stool while two of her co-owners asked inane questions about the farrier's trade. Twenty minutes later, our filly had a gleaming new set of aluminium shoes, and I possessed the four plates she had worn when runner-up at Nottingham.

Monday 9th November 2020

The day after last week's stable visit, Boris Johnson announced that tiers were no longer in vogue and the whole country would start a four-week lockdown instead. It was no surprise given the way infection rates continued their inexorable rise. It was back to staying at home unless it was for education, food shopping, outdoor exercise, medical care or work that could not be done at home. Pubs, restaurants, non-essential shops and entertainment venues all had to close. We were back to where we started in March.

Fortunately, elite sport could carry on behind closed doors and, at least for now, owners would be allowed to see their horses in action. But it was the same deal as in early June when racing finally resumed. Only two owners per horse would be permitted to attend, arriving no more than 45 minutes before their horse was due to run. There would be no refreshments and owners were expected to clear off almost as soon as their horse crossed the winning line.

It wasn't the most attractive proposition I've ever been offered, and I wasn't surprised when the others declined to pitch in for a badge for tonight's meeting at Southwell, agreeing to let me drive Trevor who was still unable to get behind the wheel following his knee operation.

There were a dozen runners for the *Class 4 Betway Handicap* which was due to be run under lights just after 6pm. Free Love had been left on 80 following her excellent effort at Nottingham, which struck me as lenient. The punters favoured Queen Of Kalahari who had a ridiculously impressive course record. She had won five of her eight starts at Southwell, improving her rating by 26lbs in the process. Despite her prolific success, the five-year-old mare's official mark was still only 74, meaning Free Love would be conceding 6lbs to the Queen of Southwell.

I like Southwell. I know it's associated with low grade racing and fibresand specialists, but it caters for small owners who can only afford cheap horses and, let's face it, a win is a win. It doesn't matter if the equine apple of your eye is rated 48 (Queen Of Kalahari's starting point) and has a 1 in 27 strike rate. If she turns up in a class 6 handicap worth two grand to the winner, and somehow manages to make it 2 in 28, you are in paradise.

We arrived a little early and dutifully waited in the car park until it was 5.15pm before donning our masks and making our way to reception. It wasn't the usual point of entry for owners and, once through the ID and temperature checks, we emerged at the back of the grandstand with the well-maintained lawns and paddock to our right. Like Nottingham, the facilities had been cut in two. A line of low-level, metal Heras fencing kept owners on their side of the parade ring and prevented them from accessing the winner's enclosure, where only the first past the post would be allowed to return.

If Nottingham was quiet, Southwell was deserted. The lounge on the top floor of the main grandstand was set aside for owners. I counted three other souls present when we sat down at a numbered table with a cup of instant coffee we had made for ourselves at the unmanned refreshments table. It was a long way to come for one race and a sachet of Nescafé.

Despite the subdued atmosphere, Trevor and I were in an upbeat mood, feeling positive about our chances. So were the others judging by the messages on the WhatsApp group. Free Love was generally a 9/2 shot with 5/1 fleetingly available from time to time. I thought our filly was entitled to be favourite, but the betting public sided with Queen Of Kalahari who was solid at around 5/2. Trevor decided to have his maximum bet each-way as he couldn't see the filly being out of the first three. I agonised about embracing such a sensible strategy but decided that £25 on the nose was the way to go. As ever, the betting was inconsequential to what was really at stake, which was more than the winner's purse of five grand.

It was only three weeks to the sale. In twenty minutes, Free Love would race one last time for the North South Syndicate before starting a new life as a broodmare. It didn't seem the right place to finish – on the sands of Southwell, under lights, witnessed by a handful of owners and stable staff - but if this was to be where the story concluded, let's go out with a bang, I thought to myself, as I gulped down my coffee, put on my mask and made my way to the paddock.

Free Love looked alert and on good terms with herself as Erika led her around. It was a cold evening, and the filly was wearing a rug which made it hard to see the condition of her skin, not that I'm in any way qualified to pass judgement on such a thing. She looked happy enough, though, and that was good enough for me.

Down at the start, the cameras homed in on Free Love before

she entered the stalls. The commentator was talking about her awkward draw as the filly ambled into stall one. I thought it was ok. The middle to far side was the place to be at Southwell and I'd rather we were widest of all instead of being drawn high nearest to the stands' rails. Admittedly, three or four would have been better, but that was being fussy.

Our filly negated any problems presented by her wide draw by making a smart start. After two furlongs she edged over to the centre of the track and was disputing the lead with Queen Of Kalahari and Poyle Vinnie. Free Love was travelling well and, as the pacesetters approached the final furlong, it was obvious that we were going to go close. With 200 yards to run, our filly was a neck ahead of Queen Of Kalahari with Dark Shot trying in vain to make up late ground. It was a two-horse shoot-out.

We were roaring on Theo and Free Love, two lone voices on the near empty grandstand steps. With a hundred yards left there was nothing in it, but Queen Of Kalahari kept on dourly to grind out victory by half a length, our filly falling on her sword in her attempt to concede six pounds to the incredibly tough winner.

So close. I really thought we had it. In that pulsating final furlong both jockeys put their sticks down and pushed away on two fillies who were giving their all. We were just outstayed by a mare who was making it six wins from nine runs at the track, a remarkable achievement at any level.

If that was it for the North South Syndicate, we were going out on a high. Of course, it would have been better to win, but you can't ask any more than for your horse to give their all, going down with all guns blazing. If you're not going to win, that's the way to lose.

We walked towards the Heras fencing barricade to see if we could get a word with Theo. In normal circumstances we'd be in the winner's enclosure talking the race through while patting our filly, heaping praise on her. But we were living in different times and a socially distanced conversation which we would video for the others was the best we could hope for.

Theo appeared on the other side of the fencing after he had weighed in, his saddle hanging across one arm, helmet and cap in the other hand. It was obvious that he was delighted with Free Love's effort and uttered phrases like 'ran her heart out,' and 'gave her all'. He was in no doubt that we had come across a mare in exceptional form and our filly had run above her mark of 80 in defeat.

We chatted briefly about the future. There was a possibility of one more run before the sale, maybe at Newcastle, but our jockey was sceptical, feeling that Free Love would need a little time to get over her exertions. It's the price you pay when you have a horse who gives everything whenever they run. Theo felt that coming back to Southwell would be ideal. There were plenty of sprint races coming up at the track, but they were all after the sale.

We broke all the rules and stayed for one more race before starting the journey home. There were no pubs or restaurants open where we could discuss our options over a pint and something to eat, but service stations fell into the essential shop category, and we stopped at the one on the A14 near Cambridge.

We were both ready to eat and grateful for small mercies when we discovered that McDonald's was open. Every other outlet was shut. York had been complimentary champagne and a three-course meal. Today's lockdown treat for owners was a small burger and regular fries washed down with a tea.

On the way home, we chatted about whether Trump would win the election, what was happening with Brexit, and the breaking news about the Pfizer/BioNTech vaccine which had been 90% successful in large-scale trials. Even the most doom-laden scientists agreed that it was a huge breakthrough.

Thoughts of saving the world gave way to the idea of salvaging the syndicate and we returned to the subject of horses for the final stage of our journey. Trevor and I were singing from the same hymn sheet. We both felt it would be a shame to call it a day while the filly was in such cracking form. There were plenty of all-weather opportunities during the winter and another breeding stock sale at the beginning of February. Why not race on until the end of January? I felt another meeting of the syndicate via Zoom was imminent.

Tuesday 17th November 2020

The surgeon could see that I needed help visualising the procedure he would be performing on my heel within the next few hours. He clicked his screen and up popped an animation of a neat incision into the flesh to expose the achilles tendon, which was then detached before some superfluous bone at the back of the heel was neatly chamfered to prepare a surface on which the tendon was reattached. It was easy, bloodless and tidy. A mellifluous, transatlantic female voice accompanied the short film and talked through the operation in a matter-of-fact way. She could have been describing how to replace a dishwasher filter.

I had waited about a year for an operation to address an ongoing problem which surfaced towards the end of my undistinguished amateur football playing career. It had got to the point where it was painful just walking and, after trying all sorts of physio, I threw in the towel a couple of years ago and went to see my GP about making a referral to discuss the possibility of surgery.

I reminded myself that I was lucky to be called in for the operation at a time when lots of elective surgery was being shelved. But when I took in the scale of the procedure, I can't pretend that I

174

didn't have last minute reservations about going through with it. The surgeon's confidence helped me to keep my resolve.

'It's classic Haglund's. I've seen it hundreds of times. We just get rid of this lump, reattach the tendon, and 6-8 months later you'll be fine.'

This was clearly his speciality, his signature operation.

I awoke from deep, dreamless sleep at about 5pm feeling queasy and grateful that I had obeyed instructions not to eat anything after yesterday's evening meal. Apparently, the surgeon had dropped in on me to tell me that the procedure had gone well but I had no recollection of his visit. Not long afterwards, Jennie collected me. I was in bed by 10pm and soon asleep, still feeling the effects of the general anaesthetic.

Friday 20th November 2020

The Zoom meeting went well. It was decided to withdraw Free Love from the sale and keep her in training until at least the end of January. If she won a race, we might be encouraged to have one last turf season, but for the moment the deal was a two-month extension which would conclude at the Tattersalls sale in February. We all thought it would be a shame to call it a day just when the filly had hit a decent vein of form.

There were grumbles about how much money we would lose by pulling Free Love out of her appointment with the auctioneer next month. Tattersalls boasted that it was Europe's premier breeding stock sale and gave it a price tag to match. There would be a £650 penalty for withdrawal to add to the £850 entry fee we had already shelled out, making the total cost of our non-sale a whopping £1,500. However, even after settling that bill, the extra cash we needed to continue wasn't above what we had agreed in May. I pointed out to the boys that the money saved by the 'payment holidays' we took at the end of August and October would pay for the small extension to Free Love's racing career.

I felt positive about our decision. I wasn't ready to call time on the adventure, especially as 2020 had yielded just seven runs and four measly visits to the racecourse. The season had been a non-event. There were loads of opportunities on Southwell's fibresand during December and January, and a little bit of research revealed that last year's class 3 sprints at the Nottinghamshire track drew small fields. There was no need to look any further afield. It wasn't inconceivable that Free Love could win a couple, banking enough prize money to encourage the North South Syndicate to have one last, pandemic-free season.

Saturday 5th December 2020

If a week is a long time in politics, a fortnight is an eternity. Towards the end of last month, the Prime Minister outlined plans for Christmas which seemed confusing and contradictory. The country was still a week away from coming out of a second national lockdown and the nation's appetite for turkey with all the trimmings seemed dulled. Nevertheless, Boris Johnson was keen to promote the idea of small family gatherings which would give everyone their annual chance to fall-out with each other, reviving simmering enmities, which are an established Yuletide tradition.

I just wanted the whole thing to be over as quickly as possible and was happy to scrap Christmas for one year if it meant our lives could return to normal in the spring. More accurately, by the start of the flat season.

Infection rates were bumping along at around 12,000 a day, but falling as the lockdown ended and gave way to the new tier system last week. The government was determined to signal urgency and went for medium, high and very high. Maybe it was a compromise, satisfying the backbenchers who wanted low, medium and high, as opposed to the scientists who wanted catastrophic, really catastrophic and Armageddon.

It looked like lockdown but with a different name and, to make matters worse, Kent was shunted into tier 3 following a surge in cases in its more built-up and populous areas. For months, I had regarded Manchester and Liverpool with detached pity. Now it was us. I was so sure that Dartford would evade the most punitive tier that I wasn't aware what it involved until I read the small print. I knew the basic stuff about pubs, shops and the ban on household mixing, but now I had to get to grips with the nuances of the travel rules, especially as Free Love had an entry for Southwell next Friday.

But the idea of travelling anywhere in my current condition was a bit fanciful. Jennie described it as insane. I was still in a cast and not allowed to put any weight on my right foot for another five weeks. If our filly ran at Southwell, I was resigned to staying put and watching the race on television.

Free Love was one of 16 entries for Friday's 0-85 class 4 handicap at Southwell, another race sponsored by Betway. Queen Of Kalahari was an absentee, but there were a few useful types in there including Mulzim, Doc Sportello and, course specialist, Crosse Fire. I was surprised and disappointed by the size of the initial entry and hoped it would thin out to a single figure field. Anything above that and the stall position became something that could make or break our chance. At least our new mark looked fair. The handicapper had given Queen of Kalahari a four-pound hike following her sixth course win, and Free Love was nudged up a couple back to 82.

I was unsure where owners stood for Friday. Last Wednesday, Nottinghamshire moved seamlessly from lockdown into tier 3. Small crowds had started to return to racecourses in tier 2 but those located in tier 3 areas were prohibited from accommodating the public, though owners were still allowed to attend. Then there was the issue about travelling between tiers. Apparently, citizens should not travel out of tier 3, but after closer reading of the guidance it was clear that it was just that, guidance. The exhortation to stay in your plague-pen was advisory, not mandatory.

I was tired of the restrictions but not inclined to ignore them. If we all did our bit, it would help the country to get out of this mess sooner rather than later. However, if Southwell offered tickets to owners and some of the boys wanted to go, that was their call. Along with everyone else involved in ownership, as individuals or through partnerships and clubs, we were helping to keep the show on the road for little reward. I would keep my plastered foot on the sofa and watch from home.

Friday 11th December 2020

It was sunset as we crossed the Trent beyond Newark and cut across the fields flanking the A617 near Kelham. The last rays of the sun were diffused by the low mist which hung on the landscape, transforming the setting into something almost mystical in character. I made this wistful observation from the back of Pete's car, my plastered leg stretched across the length of the rear seats.

All my good intentions went out the window yesterday when Southwell confirmed an allocation of four owners' badges and Pete volunteered to drive. I felt compelled to go despite the potential discomfort of six hours in a car and negotiating the racecourse on a pair of crutches. Jennie thought I was mad and, to coin a racing term, she's not a bad judge. But what if Free Love won and I wasn't there to see it? It was a possibility that induced mild panic attacks whenever I thought of it.

We arrived at the track about an hour before our race to find it shrouded in dense fog. I managed the tricky business of using the lift to the top floor of the grandstand where some welcome hot food was provided. The first race had already been run but, as the runners made their way down to the start for the next, the visibility seemed to be deteriorating. It was impossible to pick up the action until the horses were about 150 yards from the line. The big screen on the other side of the track was not much help, the cameras doing only a marginal better job than the naked eye.

We were next up, and we made our way to the parade ring to get a glimpse of Free Love. The fog had become thicker just in the last ten minutes and, when we arrived at the paddock, Mick Appleby informed us that a decision would be made about carrying on once the runners were down at the start and the officials and jockeys were able to judge if it was safe to continue.

Only two of the original 16 entries failed to declare, which was sod's law. Fields of 14 are a rarity at Southwell but we had managed to cop one tonight. At least the draw had been kind for a change. Our filly was berthed in seven, ideally placed to follow the pace wherever that might be. It was a wide-open contest and, although Birkenhead was a solidly supported 3/1 favourite, Free Love was one of a gaggle of rivals all around 10/1 or shorter in the betting.

The cameras picked up the runners clearly once they arrived at the start and were milling behind the stalls, but they circled aimlessly for several minutes as the official off time came and went. This looked a good chance for Free Love who had continued to work well since her last run behind Queen Of Kalahari. In a luckless year, it would be a final stroke of misfortune if the meeting was now abandoned, robbing our filly of her last chance to win a race as a four-year-old. The horses continued to circle while officials talked earnestly with each other on walkie talkies. It was nearly ten minutes past post time when, much to my relief, the first horse was loaded into the stalls indicating that the race would go ahead.

My confidence was tempered by the size of the field, but I felt we must be thereabouts if reproducing the quality of our last run. Sure, we could have done with a bit more rain. Without it, the Southwell surface can become dry and deep, but our filly had the class to cope. She just needed to break well and keep out of trouble in the first half of the race. If she could do that, she would surely feature.

All eyes were glued to the big screen. It looked like an even break, but the camera deployed at the start remained the one in use for the first furlong of the race. Free Love appeared to get out well, but it was hard to tell based on the sight of 14 equine backsides disappearing into the mist. The camera angle switched and picked up the runners after they had completed a couple of furlongs. Our filly was in the firing line, sitting in fourth or fifth place no more than a length off the leader.

We were again treated to a rear view as the field raced towards the final two furlongs where another camera picked up the climax of the race. Although viewing was difficult, with cameras alternating between different perspectives as they tried to overcome the fog, I saw enough to know that Free Love had gradually lost her pitch and, as they approached the final furlong, she had more in front of her than behind and was fighting a losing battle.

It was a bitter disappointment. Our filly trailed in ninth, beaten six lengths behind the veteran, Duke Of Firenze. Our old friend Dark Shot was third, confirming the impression that Free Love had run well below expectations. I headed for the lift as Pete, Trevor and Patrick went on ahead for what would be a stony-faced debrief with Theo. The lift doors opened, and I hobbled onto the damp lino floor where one of my crutches skidded and sent me sprawling to the ground. This is my racing nadir, I thought to myself as I hauled myself up, masked, glasses steaming, unbloodied but unquestionably bowed. My love affair with Southwell was waning by the second.

I reached the others who were stood by the dividing fence waiting for Theo to arrive. We let him go first. He could sense our disappointment as he explained that the filly broke well but the pace was strong which took her out of her comfort zone.

'But she's never had trouble laying up with the pace, including in better class races. I can't accept that those class 4 handicappers took her off her feet,' I interrupted in exasperation.

Theo took my point and changed tack saying that maybe something would come to light over the next day or two to explain the poor performance. Mick Appleby was also there, listening stoically, allowing our jockey to say his piece. When Theo departed it became clear why Mick had held his counsel. He thought it might be time to try another jockey.

It wasn't the first time that the subject had been raised. There were some grumbles after the fillies' handicap at Doncaster, where Theo had Free Love racing into a fierce headwind throughout. The eventual winner sought cover in the small field of six and shot clear when manoeuvred around her toiling windbreaks in the final 150 yards. Hindsight is a wonderful thing, though. Should our jockey have been more aggressive tonight once he had made a good start? Could the loss of position during the middle part of the race been avoided? Or was it simply a flat run, just one of those things? Maybe it would transpire that something was amiss, as was the case after the filly's run at Windsor. I knew one thing for sure, if anyone came out with the old chestnut that 'they're not machines, you know,' I'd beat them about the head with my crutches.

Monday 14th December 2020

During the weekend, members of the North South Syndicate freely aired their views about the jockey situation. It's fair to say that the camp was split. I was aware that retaining the same jockey for such a lengthy period was unusual. It's true that there have been some famously successful partnerships such as Enable and Dettori, but it's not something you associate with class 4 handicappers who have lost their last 16 races.

It was a sobering statistic. Since beating Dark Shadow at Windsor last July, our filly had put together a long losing run. The fact she had found the winner's enclosure by making the frame (first four) in half of those races explains why her handicap mark remained static and respectable. You could argue that she'd been too consistent for her own good.

In my heart I knew we should have tried a different pilot an age ago. Theo had been on board for 14 of those 16 straight defeats and, although I didn't feel he was at fault for any of them, most owners and trainers would have experimented with different jockeys just to mix things up, to see if a change brought about a little bit of improvement. Somebody new could also provide a different perspective about Free Love's attributes and the best way to ride her.

I knew I was being soft and sentimental by wanting Theo to retain the ride. He was part of the story. But maybe, like me, he was too close to it. I agreed with Mick that I would talk in person to Theo about the situation. After all, he had ridden Free Love to all four of her victories and was clearly attached to the filly. She meant a lot to him at a time when his riding career was faltering. He deserved to hear it from the horse's mouth.

I managed to secure a majority vote to tell Theo that the owners were thinking about a new jockey, but he would keep the ride on Free Love for her next race. It wasn't a case of giving him one last chance. It was more about giving him notice of a change which was inevitable in a game where owners chop and change trainers and jockeys in search of that elusive win.

I sent Theo a text and arranged to call him in the afternoon after he had finished his work at the yard. It wasn't the easiest of conversations, but it wasn't the hardest either. He accepted that most owners or trainers would have tried two, three or more different jockeys during Free Love's losing sequence. Whether the new riders would have brought about a change in fortune is something that he doubted. I couldn't disagree.

It turned out to be a lengthy but positive chat. Theo took it well. I asked him to be open-minded about any feedback he received from Mick and from his jockey coach, John Bramhill. I observed that while it's important to be confident, being pig-headed isn't a good look in any walk of life. I also assured him that if we made a change, he shouldn't see it as a direct criticism of the way he had ridden the filly. We'd just be trying something different in our attempt to get back on the winning trail.

Friday 18th December 2020

I watched with a mixture of irritation and frustration as Mick Appleby's Zapper Cass, a seven-year-old journeyman sprinter, landed this afternoon's five-runner 0-90 class 3 handicap at Southwell off a mark of 82. He was the top-rated horse in what was a weak field for the class and money. Our old pal Dark Shot was third. It was exactly the type of race that I thought Free Love could mop up during a short winter campaign at Southwell. Instead, our filly remained in her box having looked sore and not fully sound the day after my conversation with Theo.

Who knows if Free Love's untimely bout of lameness was the reason for the below par effort on the Southwell sand last Friday? At least we may have found a legitimate reason for her lacklustre performance. I imagine Theo was feeling vindicated as well. On one level, being lame was better than running inexplicably poorly. On every other level it was a disaster. We're told that there's no use crying over spilt milk, but on the way home from Southwell last week we found out that the rest of the meeting had been abandoned due to the enveloping fog. Had our race not gone ahead, we would have run and started favourite in this afternoon's contest instead.

Mick's first reaction was to suggest that it was a good time to give Free Love a break, but there was no commitment from us to keep the filly in training next year. As there wasn't a plan for us to breed from her either, she was heading to Tattersalls in the first week of February. We either threw in the towel now, or asked Mick to see if the filly came right in time to squeeze in one more run before the sale.

It all looked a bit tight, and I resigned myself to the fact that it was probably game over. What I found most depressing was that the foggy, mask-wearing, hobbling experience at a deserted Southwell was likely to be the last time I saw Free Love in the flesh. The way the data was going - there were over 35,000 new cases yesterday - suggested that next month's sale would be behind closed doors. Like most people, I couldn't wait to see the back of 2020, but the depressing reality was that 2021 promised to deliver more of the same.

14 Promised Land

Wednesday 6th January 2021

It had been a quiet Christmas. A week before the big day the whole of southeast England was thrown into tier 4. I didn't know anything existed beyond the three tiers that were already in place. It was like an eleven plus question. What comes next in the following sequence? Medium, High, Very High, _ _ _ .

I thought the answer might be 'Oliver Cromwell' as the new tier was clearly designed to ban Christmas. Out went the idea of cosy three-household bubbles who could meet up for a few days. Instead, we were instructed to stay in our own households. I was relieved that the Met Police supremo, Ken Marsh, was reported as saying that police would not 'be knocking on people's doors on Christmas Day' to check whether the rules were being observed. Our two eldest children, Matthew and Celia, faced spending Christmas Day alone in their respective London flats after their partners fled the south to stay with their families in the sunny uplands of tier 3 areas. Matt and Celia came round to us. It was unthinkable that we should leave them in solitary confinement for the day, whatever the rules said.

By the end of December nearly the whole of England was living under tier 4 restrictions which made a nonsense of the idea of a targeted local approach. Nobody was surprised when a weary Boris Johnson announced a third national lockdown in a televised address on Monday evening. The decision followed a steep rise in infections and hospital admissions across the country. The alarming increase in cases was attributed to a new Covid variant which scientists believed was up to 70% more transmissible.

I thought back to June and July when I naively believed we were out of the woods. The weather was fabulous, and everybody was

185

outdoors enjoying the sunshine while the numbers plummeted. By contrast, today's figures made sombre reading. There were over 62,000 new cases and more than 1,000 deaths. The number of patients being treated for Covid in hospital was rapidly approaching 30,000 and there were warnings that the NHS was three weeks away from being overwhelmed.

Thank God the cavalry was coming in the form of vaccinations. About four weeks ago, Margaret Keenan, a 90-year-old grandmother, became the first person in the world to be given the Pfizer jab. The historic event took place at University Hospital, Coventry. And only on Monday, 82-year-old Brian Pinker achieved his five minutes of fame by being the first person to receive the Oxford AstraZeneca version. The UK's ambitious vaccination programme had started.

Monday 18th January 2021
During the first two weeks of lockdown I busied myself with the final arrangements for the North South Syndicate. I managed to get a free entry for the February sale. Tattersalls took pity on me when I asked them if they would consider a discount as we had just spent £1,500 on an auction that didn't take place. Every little bit would help as I prepared to wind down the account.

I chased up the other boys for their final £500 contributions which would pay for the January training bill as well as the veterinary checks and transport costs associated with the sale, which was now less than a fortnight away. The February breeding stock auction is a much smaller affair than the one from which Free Love was withdrawn in early December, and we were allocated a good-looking slot in the catalogue. Free Love was lot number 175 which was towards the middle of the 256 horses for sale, most of which were fillies and mares. Mick's small consignment from Langham Stables consisted of Free Love, Fenix and Gold Brocade. They would enter the sales ring just before a large draft of beautifully bred Godolphin fillies went under the hammer. We couldn't have asked for a better pitch.

I was idly flicking through the online catalogue when I received an email from Paul Davis. I'd got to know Paul during the last few months after he bought one of my books. We commenced an email correspondence and soon discovered we thought along the same lines about racing, only Paul was way ahead of me in so many respects. Although we both started off as enthusiasts who desired greater involvement with the sport, the height of my ambition was the type of ownership project that was now coming to an end with Free Love. Paul had gone way beyond that.

He lives in Stow-on-the-Wold but all the great plans to pop down and see him fell at the first fence when local restrictions morphed into tiers, and then national lockdowns. As was the vogue in these strange times, we had managed a couple of virtual conversations via WhatsApp video, which wasn't the same as talking horses over a pint in an idyllic Gloucestershire pub, but it was better than nothing.

Paul has shares in a few horses and is the lead member in the partnership that owns Acey Milan, a chaser who finished fourth in the 2018 Champion Bumper at the Cheltenham Festival. Paul still bursts with pride and boyish enthusiasm when speaking about that day. During our virtual chats and email correspondence, I learned that Paul could ride. He also helps at Martin Keighley's yard in Condicote where he looks after the trainer's racing club horses. To cap it all, he holds a staff licence which means he can go to the races and assist with saddling and leading up Martin's runners.

It's an impressive CV and it was no surprise to find out that he was on the ball with the latest developments in the bloodstock world. His email this afternoon informed me that Tattersalls had decided to make the February sale completely virtual. Even the horses would be absent.

'How was that going to work?' I thought to myself as I digested the news. More to the point, what impact would it have on the market? With nobody allowed to attend and buyers bidding online based on the pedigrees printed in the catalogue and video clips of variable quality uploaded by vendors, it was easy to envisage Free Love being picked up for buttons. I made the others aware and said we needed a Zoom meeting to discuss our strategy. It was all well and good saying that we weren't prepared to let our mare go for a derisory three or four thousand guineas, but what happened next if we took that stance? We had less than a fortnight to work out what to do.

Wednesday 20th January 2021

Free Love lost her race against time. Although Mick reported that she was over the soreness suffered after her last run, she had only been back in light work for about a week and our trainer felt it would be too much of a rush to get her ready for one last roll of the dice.

The news came as no surprise. There would be no last chance saloon for the syndicate where an eleventh-hour win at Chelmsford or Newcastle induced a dramatic change of heart. Free Love was going to the sales. The story had run its course.

Faced with such an unsatisfactory conclusion, I chewed over the alternatives. I convinced myself that keeping Free Love in training wasn't such a stupid idea. In one of the many idle moments provided by the lockdown, I looked at the BHA's database for the official ratings of all horses in training. I wanted a feel for Free Love's value both as a racehorse and as a potential broodmare. She may lack a pedigree rich in black type, but her race record was harder to dismiss. Those who were disdainful of her bloodlines would do well to note that her current rating of 81 placed her in the top 15% of all fillies and mares in training. When Free Love was rated 90, she was in the top 8%.

The figures shouted that it would be a sin to allow such a talented mare to slip through our fingers for a pittance. If I couldn't muster any enthusiasm for breeding, perhaps I could secure support for keeping her in training for one last season. It might mean buying out some of the existing owners, but it was worth giving it a go.

I phoned each co-owner individually to make sure I understood their position. Mick Corringham wanted out. He had lived the dream of racehorse ownership and was grateful for the wonderful memories the experience had given him, but he had sold his flat, sorted out his finances and moved in with his new wife, Alison, and wasn't prepared to commit another four grand to the project. He was content to finish after three seasons, which had given him much more than he had anticipated.

Pete may have lacked Mick's decisiveness when we chatted, but he was pretty sure that he wanted to sell. When I asked him about the idea of setting a reserve on Free Love to prevent somebody picking her up for an absurdly low price, his certainty began to crumble. Nevertheless, at the end of an angst-ridden conversation I was left with the impression that Pete wanted out – I think.

Patrick was sitting comfortably on the fence. All things being equal, he thought it was time to sell. But, on the other hand, he didn't want to see Free Love snaffled up for an insultingly low price. Then again, he was quite happy to consider another ownership project in the future and his involvement wasn't reliant on how much cash he got back from Free Love's sale. I concluded our discussion wishing that the sofa in our back room was as comfortable as Patrick's fence.

I had an ally in Trevor. He knew we had a smart little sprinter on our hands. A long time ago, his dad had shares in horses trained in Kent by Tom Long. He had one good one, but the rest didn't amount to much, which is the story for most. Trevor knew that Free Love retained her ability and was capable of being competitive in class 3 and 4 handicaps. She was unlucky not to get her head in front last season and he felt that to walk away from such a genuine and proven performer would be folly, especially if she were sold cheaply. He knew that we could buy half a dozen similarly priced yearlings over the next twenty years and the odds were stacked against any of them turning out to be as useful as what we already had. Trevor was in. He wasn't prepared to look a gift horse in the mouth.

We agreed a strategy. I would try to find two or three racing pals who were interested in buying out those owners who wanted to call it a day – providing the price was right. There were two obvious candidates to approach. It had to be Tim Cogan and Kieran Scott. I've known the pair for more than forty years and a shared interest in horseracing was the start of both friendships. Tim is a knowledgeable and keen racegoer who has hinted at getting involved with ownership at some point. Kieran, being the more impulsive of the two, has a history of shared ownership, typically being the junior partner holding between 10% and 20% of horses that his good friend Chris Hughes sources and places with the Newmarket trainer, Chris Wall. They have always bought fillies and tried to secure the best bloodlines they can afford, reasoning that a well-bred filly who doesn't make a huge splash on the racecourse has a higher residual value than a similarly talented colt or gelding. They're also cheaper to buy in the first place as everyone wants a Derby winner who will go on to become a famous stallion.

The time was right for Tim. He was in. I couldn't give him a precise figure, but he was happy to pay around two grand for his 20% share. It might be less if Trevor and I bought the filly back at the sale or bought out the others privately for an agreed price. I was unhelpfully inexact, but Tim understood why.

I thought Kieran would be a tougher nut to crack. He surprised me in November when he announced that he had pushed the boat out and gone halves with Chris Hughes for a Murhaarar yearling filly. They secured the youngster for 14,000 guineas and Kieran was committed to at least a year of sharing upkeep costs for a horse based at Newmarket. He told his wife, Caroline, that this was to be his last big ownership adventure. Like Pete, he probably gave a solemn oath that the guttering would be the next thing on the list followed by a shower replacement or maybe a new garden patio. Kieran didn't completely dismiss the idea of getting involved with Free Love. He just needed a few days of skilful negotiation before a decision could be made. It made the Brexit talks look easy.

Monday 25th January 2021

It was all looking good for Wednesday's Zoom meeting with the boys. Kieran got the green light to enhance his burgeoning bloodstock portfolio, meaning the partnership was saved. All we had to do was agree a price with the others.

At 9.30am this morning a large spanner was thrown in the works. Jane Hales contacted me to say that an offer of £13k had been received for Free Love. Somebody perusing next week's catalogue was obviously trying to do a bit of private business. Mick's secretary asked me how I wanted to proceed, and I asked her to forward the email and I would deal directly with the potential buyer.

In one fell swoop, the value of a 20% share had soared to £2,600. For a split second I considered ignoring the approach. After all, it was Jane who told me that she deals with lots of queries that rarely come to anything. But the email suggested that this was something different, something more credible. The sum of £13k was in black and white. So was the name and contact details of the man making the bid.

I did a little research before emailing Shafir Edry. He appeared to be a bloodstock agent based in the ancient Biblical city of Beersheba in South Israel. Nearly all the pictures on his Facebook account were equine related. He posted with pride about importing a consignment of European racehorses which he had bought for various clients. Free Love could end up in worse places, I thought to myself as I flicked through photos of stables, paddocks and horse transporters. I sent an email to put the prospective owner fully in the picture.

Morning Shafir,
I hope you are healthy and in good spirits.

I am the lead member of the small syndicate which has owned the filly, Free Love, since she was a yearling. I know you have been in touch with our trainer, Mick Appleby, about buying her for a client

At the moment, we are unsure whether the filly will be sold or if we will race on for one more turf season. There are five owners and if the majority want to sell and I am unable to find new partners to buy them out, then we will be interested in your offer.

I am very keen to make sure that the filly ends up in good hands if we decide to sell. Are you able to tell me where your client is based and whether they intend to race Free Love or breed from her?

….If I have the right Shafir, your Facebook account shows you are based in Israel and Brendan Boyle, Free Love's breeder, is one of your friends. It's a small world!

Regards, Tony

Sami, as he preferred to be called, responded with his mobile details and within ten minutes we were chatting about his proposition. He told me he wanted a sprinter as Beersheba racing is all about speed.

192

The plan was to race for a year then breed, preferably using Sami's own Galileo colt as the stallion.

There were worse fates. One of them, as far as I was concerned, was Free Love being bought to continue racing in the UK in somebody else's ownership. After my brief conversation with Sami, I became resigned to an unusual but attractive end to the story. Free Love might become a local sprinting superstar before starting a new career as a successful broodmare. In the city of Abraham, her descendants might be as numerous as the stars in the cloudless Israeli sky.

I've always wanted to visit the Holy Land and I wistfully imagined me and Jennie making a pilgrimage which took in a trip to Beersheba, where I could reacquaint myself with Free Love, stroke her nose and admire one of her offspring happily mooching around in a sun-drenched paddock. It was a romantic notion, I know, but the whole adventure had been an affair of the heart, so why not finish somewhere miraculous? The promised land.

Wednesday 27th January 2021

Before this afternoon's Zoom meeting I had to go back to Kieran and Tim to tell them that the share price had risen to £2,500. I thought it would be a deal breaker and during the last 48 hours I had become accepting, even positive, about Free Love heading for a new home in Israel.

Soon after speaking to Sami, I set out the complete financial package in an email for those who wanted to stay involved. It explained that eight monthly payments of £400, starting on 1st February, would get us to the autumn breeding stock sale. As usual, calculations were based on an unsuccessful season in which no prize money was won. On the face of it, this wasn't the deal of the century. The total outlay was £5,700 each for our two new partners with no guarantee of a return. However, in Free Love's eight unsuccessful efforts in 2020, she still amassed over £7,000 in place prize money. A similar record in 2021 would ensure that she maintained a value of around £10k, meaning that Kieran and Tim might be only two grand out of pocket after their summer of fun. We must all pay for our pleasures, after all.

I was surprised how quickly the pair responded. They were both in, although Kieran was at pains to point out that the agreement had to be finite, finishing in the autumn. His inference was that my original one-season adventure had already exceeded its sell-by date by over two years, and he wasn't prepared to sleepwalk into an ownership deal that meandered into the future with no indication of when it might end. I gave him a solemn oath that it would finish with Free Love becoming a broodmare at the end of her five-year-old campaign. What I didn't disclose was my aching desire to become and owner-breeder myself. I thought it was best to keep that card close to my chest.

In the afternoon, the five members of the North South Syndicate met via Zoom to discuss the dispersal of their equine asset. Mick, Patrick and Pete were unaware that I had been actively trying to find new owners to buy out their shares. They knew I might have a go at saving the partnership but, until I had concrete offers, I had no intention of saying anything along the lines of, 'Kieran said he might be interested,' or 'Tim's not sure but he's thinking about it, and I might have a chat tomorrow with Jennie's brother-in-law, Gareth'. No, I needed to bring signed and sealed offers to the table, which is now what I had.

We started the meeting with a recap of everybody's position. Mick and Pete wanted out. Patrick was more in the 'I suppose so' camp as he felt it was time to wind down the operation. At this point I disclosed that I had some buyers and asked everyone if they were happy to agree a value of £12,500 for Free Love. It was a little less than the Beersheba bid, but Sami wouldn't be able to pick up the mare for about a fortnight and the cost of her keep until collected would have to be met. There was also the chance of the deal falling through. Mick, Patrick and Pete said they would be happy to take £2,500 each which avoided the risk of gambling and getting less if Free Love was sold cheaply at next week's strange virtual sale. Nobody knew how that peculiar lockdown innovation would work.

Nearly there. I revealed with a flourish that I had two definite new owners, Kieran Scott and Tim Cogan. If necessary, Trevor and I would split the fifth share and take on 30% each but I was fairly confident I could find another partner if needed. It wasn't as if I had exhausted all possibilities. When Patrick heard the identity of the two mysterious buyers, he hopped off the fence with elan. These were two of his oldest racing pals and there was no way he'd bail out if Kieran and Tim were joining the party. Peter soon followed suit, and Tim and Kieran agreed to split Mick Corringham's share. We were back in business.

Did it! I had another season of Free Love in the bag. I wouldn't be finishing on a low, sprawled on the lino at Southwell. Nor would I be waving goodbye to Free Love as she stepped onto an aeroplane heading for the Holy Land. There was a chance of a final fling in the sunshine. It might be Nottingham in June or Windsor in July. It could even be for a tilt at a listed race at Bath or Ayr. Wherever we ended up racing, there was the prospect of friends being there and crowds back on our racecourses. Living the dream of racehorse ownership on a budget would have one last hurrah. All we had to do was roll out the vaccine and pray for deliverance.

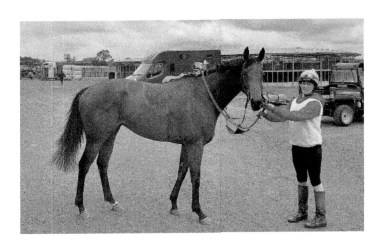

'Don't I know you?' Free Love gives a knowing look to the author during a socially distanced visit to Mick Appleby's yard. June 2020

Tony Linnett with his youngest son, Joseph, at a near deserted York racecourse on International Stakes day, August 2021.

Free Love's dam, Peace And Love, with her latest foal in Brendan Boyle's paddocks near Newmarket. August 2021.

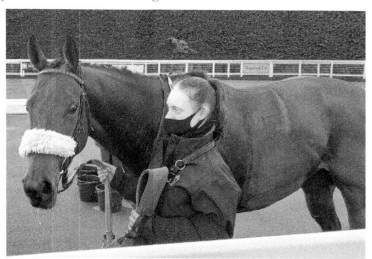

A masked Erica Parkinson with Free Love at Nottingham. The filly was a gallant runner-up to Wrenthorpe, October 2020.

PART II

1 Here We Go Again

Monday 1st March 2021
Free Love was back in full training following an eleven-week stint on the easy list. Apart from a couple of canters in mid-January, which merely confirmed that Mick would not be able to get her ready in time for a final run before the sale, our mare had spent the bulk of the period resting in her box or ambling around the spacious paddocks at Langham.

While Free Love relaxed during her near three-month absence, it was easy to believe that the world was coming to an end. The UK was on the verge of a no-deal Brexit which seemed a crazy position to be in considering that the pandemic was already making life difficult enough for businesses and their employees. Days before Christmas, with a deal yet to be reached, France imposed a ban on UK freight because of concerns over the newly identified Kent coronavirus strain. The variant was suspected to be responsible for rocketing infection rates, particularly in southeast England. About one-quarter of food, medicines and other goods passing through British ports had been blocked by President Macron's decision, resulting in a crisis at Dover. The daily news relayed pictures of thousands of stranded lorries whose drivers faced the prospect of spending Christmas in their cabs.

The poor drivers were eventually allowed to cross the channel to Calais and return to their various European homes, but only in time for New Year's Eve, not Christmas. No doubt their celebrations would have been as muted as mine. Like everyone else – apart from supermarkets, Amazon and PPE suppliers – I waved goodbye to 2020 pleased to see the back of it. Surely 2021 had to be better.

It wasn't a great start. On the sixth day of the new year, I watched the television with incredulity as a mob broke into the Capitol Building in Washington, USA, sending members of Congress fleeing as Electoral College votes were being counted to confirm the presidential victory of Joe Biden. Five people died in the violence, including a police officer. Many of the rioters came directly from a rally at which the outgoing president, Donald Trump, spoke for more than an hour, insisting that the election had been 'stolen'.

If I hoped to find sanity and solace in the world of racing, I was sadly mistaken. The front page of this morning's Racing Post was all about the photograph of top Irish trainer, Gordon Elliott, sitting on a dead horse who had suffered a heart attack on the gallops. The picture was circulating on social media over the weekend and any thoughts that it might be a fake were dispelled when the trainer admitted that the image was genuine.

I viewed it once, and once only. That was enough. Elliott was grinning and making a Churchillian-style victory salute as he sat astride the stricken animal, Morgan, a seven-year-old gelding who had scored four times in 21 visits to the racecourse and surely deserved a more dignified ending than the one bestowed by his handler.

As the story wore on and reached the attention of the national press and the wider public, anger became the dominant emotion. Elliott's tawdry actions could not be justified in any way. It didn't matter if the motives for somebody posting the picture were vengeful and destructive. It didn't matter if this was just an isolated 'moment of madness'. And I'm afraid it didn't matter that the horses in Gordon Elliott's charge receive the highest levels of care and attention from the large band of dedicated staff employed to feed, clean and exercise the 200 or so thoroughbreds housed in one of the most successful and prestigious jumping yards on the planet.

What Elliott's stupidity evoked – and 'stupidity' was the most charitable word I could use – was much more than universal condemnation of his disrespectful and repugnant actions. He also gave licence to the anti-racing lobby to seize on the incident as evidence of the moral bankruptcy of the sport.

The newspapers were full of it. Journalists with little knowledge of racing were happy to put the boot in, conflating the appalling image of an Irish trainer on a dead horse with cruelty and poor equine welfare in general. One writer in a popular broadsheet wrote about how he had enjoyed racing for the best part of 35 years, always looking forward to the Cheltenham Festival which was rapidly approaching. He was now disgusted by the sport and vowed never to watch it again.

It wasn't the most rational or fair response to the scandal, but it was a view echoed by plenty of others. A letter to another reputable daily, from Kenneth Jarret, was irritatingly ignorant yet depressingly predictable in tone. He wrote:

The anger stirred up by the media over a trainer sitting on a dead horse pales into insignificance when one counts the number of horses euthanised on the racetrack because they've probably been too frequently raced. Racehorses and their jockeys risk their lives every day of the week for the benefit of the gambling industry and the rich and famous.

Mr Jarret sounded as if he'd made up his mind long before Gordon Elliott gave him the ammunition to take aim at the sport of kings. As far as he was concerned, racing was the ugly pursuit of monied toffs and unscrupulous bookies, who couldn't care less about the welfare of its participants so long as the poor creatures made money for them.

Try telling that to Shelley Bennett. I met Shelley through Heart of the South Racing. We both had shares in Lightning Spirit, a half-sister to The Shuffler. A little later we were in the Good Luck Charm partnership, which only came to an end in December when the old warrior competed in his 93rd and final race, a class 6 handicap at Lingfield. Shelley was there. Sky Sports Racing picked out a small group of masked, socially-distanced owners standing on the steps of the parade ring. It was a far cry from the full ownership experience, but I knew Shelley would be there even though she wouldn't be allowed to get close enough to make a fuss of GLC, as he was affectionately known, for one last time.

It's fair to say that Shelley is besotted with her horses. They are her great passion. Despite being unable to drive because of a visual impairment, no train journey is too difficult for her if it means a chance to see her horses racing or working on the gallops. Her first thought is for their safety and well-being. That was brought home to me at Brighton in April 2016 when Good Luck Charm was a creditable third behind Fingal's Cave in a class 4 handicap. Shelley burst into tears as GLC returned to the winner's enclosure, overwhelmed by his gallant effort and relieved by his safe return.

'My God, Shelley. What are you going to do when he wins?' I asked while watching her dab her cheeks with one hand and pat her equine hero on the neck with the other.

It's not a scene that would fit in with Mr Jarret's unshakable world view. And that was the real scandal of the Gordon Elliott affair. It painted racing in a dismal light and tarred everybody with the same brush. It didn't matter that owners, trainers and staff loved the horses with which they were associated. The accusation was that the sport itself was barbaric. The shrewd Irish pundit, Kevin Blake, perceptively summed up the sport's dilemma. 'Horseracing faces an ongoing battle to retain its social licence in a world that is slowly but surely moving against animal-based pursuits. Sadly, this incident and its fallout represent a significant defeat in that fight,' was his disturbing observation. Only time would tell the extent of the reputational damage inflicted on racing by the actions of one man.

Tuesday 9th March 2021

It was a glorious morning as I walked through the allotments on my way to the Tesco Express on Dartford Road. The sun shone with unseasonal warmth as I made my way past neat plots being prepared for planting. I was in an upbeat mood. Nearly four months after my achilles tendon operation, I was now walking with the aid of just one crutch. As I negotiated my way through the narrow, grassy pathways edged by fragrant rosemary shrubs and dormant blackberry bushes, I overhead unhurried conversations between gardeners idly leaning on rakes and spades. Thankfully, their opprobrium was aimed at Harry and Meghan's televised interview with Oprah Winfrey rather than Gordon Elliott.

Holding a loaf of bread in my one free hand, I returned home by the same shortcut feeling optimistic about life. The Government's roadmap for working our way out of lockdown looked feasible. Pupils returned to school yesterday and the next relaxation was planned for 29th March when the 'rule of six' would apply for outdoor settings. At cautious intervals, shops, leisure centres and hospitality services would return, including outdoor events with limited crowds. From 17th May onwards, it would be possible to see Free Love in action at a racecourse with bars and restaurants in operation and some spectators present.

Like nearly everyone else, I just wanted an end to lockdowns and restrictions. I had coped with the last four months pretty well given my circumstances. For most of that time my ankle was either in plaster or a surgical boot and needed to be kept elevated as much as possible. I developed a routine of writing in the morning and watching the racing in the afternoon. It was the writing that kept me sane. There was also my voluntary work for the prison. Although my current physical state prevented me from visiting, there was still plenty to do, and I made sure I kept in touch with how the pandemic was affecting the inmates of HMP Isis. Education and training, family visits, physical exercise and most forms of social contact all fell by the wayside as prisoners were kept behind their cell doors for up to 23 hours a day. But there were no protests or riots. The prisoners were aware that life outside was hardly a bowl of cherries either.

But there were surely better times ahead. The number of new cases, hospitalisations and fatalities were in steady decline, while vaccination rates were soaring. We needed good news following 12 months in which the country had been in a state of near paralysis.

I often thought about how times and perceptions have changed. It's a good thing that diets and health care have improved markedly in many parts of the world during the last century. But do these advances now walk hand in hand with an unrealistic expectation of what science can do for us, particularly for those fortunate enough to live in relatively affluent countries?

It's true that the Covid pandemic caused last year's excess deaths to rise to their highest level in the UK since World War Two. There were nearly 697,000 deaths in 2020, which is about 85,000 more than would be expected based on the average for the previous five years. It's not a good figure, but it's not one that justified the wilder claims that Covid was the biggest health crisis since the Black Death. For the record, that fourteenth century disease is thought to have wiped out between one-third and a half of the earth's population.

Centuries later, Spanish Flu swiftly followed the First World War during which approximately 20 million military and civilian lives were lost. It is thought that the ensuing influenza pandemic may have accounted for up to three times as many victims as the war itself.

I wasn't belittling the crisis, nor was I inured to the personal tragedies behind the figures. Although I hadn't experienced a catastrophic, premature loss of a close family member through Covid, it wasn't hard to empathise with those who had. I remember visiting Falconwood Crematorium on a searingly hot day last May when nothing was open, and Jennie and I had time to go for yet another walk. Part of the itinerary included a visit to the Memorial Chapel, but it was shut due to Covid restrictions and there was no opportunity for Jennie to read the copperplate script entry in the Book of Remembrance showing that her mum, Cecilia Wormald, had died on 15th May 1973. She was thirty-seven when struck down by encephalitis, leaving behind three young daughters whose lives were changed forever.

I was acutely aware that the pandemic had produced tragedies like the one Jennie and her two sisters experienced nearly 50 years ago. I wasn't insensitive to that fact, but it felt like it was time to move on. We needed to roll out the vaccines, cautiously reopen society in stages, and learn to live with Covid. The idea of 'winning the war' by eradicating the virus was absurd. Christopher Witty, the Chief Medical Officer for England, tried to steer the public away from the notion of a final victory against Covid by saying that we'd end up accepting a tolerable level of annual hospitalisations and fatalities. That, as much as anything else, would allow us to open the economy and get people interacting again. And what better place to interact than on a racecourse?

Saturday 20th March 2021

I received a couple of video clips from Louise. One was from last Wednesday, the other from this morning. They were both solo canters undertaken beneath overcast skies and accompanied by the familiar soundtrack of the early morning traffic speeding along the nearby road to Melton Mowbray. In the first canter, Free Love looked quite keen, and Erika was sitting tight against her making sure that the mare wasn't too exuberant. The second piece of work was much sharper and Free Love looked to be moving well.

It was clearly time to organise a stable visit, and by the end of the day, I had a tentative agreement via our WhatsApp group that Saturday 17th April suited all six owners. In an ideal world, I would have liked to have gone earlier. Free Love had returned to full training later than last year, but her break had been shorter. I was still hoping that she might be ready to race by mid-April which would make it possible to chance an entry for the listed *Whitsbury Manor Stud Lansdown Stakes* staged at Bath the day before our planned visit to Langham.

I was like a dog with a bone. On the face of it, it was barking mad to give a second thought about entering an 81-rated five-year-old mare in a race of this calibre. But unless we wanted to shell out thousands to go abroad in search of a morsel of black type, the Bath listed race and the *Land O'Burns Stakes* at Ayr in late June, were the only two targets worth considering. They were niche contests, both over the minimum trip and both confined to fillies and mares. In the last ten years, five horses rated 80-85 had gate-crashed the party by making the first three at either Bath or Ayr. That means that 8% of the placed horses were of roughly the same ability as Free Love. Not great odds, but good enough for an incurable optimist.

Wednesday 31st March 2021

Pete and I decided to seize the day and we were on the road to Langham just before 7am. The Government's lockdown exit strategy was proceeding according to plan. As there was no early evidence that the reopening of schools had caused a spike in infections, the small easing of restrictions due to start on Monday went ahead. I thought it was kind of Boris Johnson to mark my 63rd birthday with a return of the rule of six for outdoor settings and Jennie invited two couples to join us in the garden to mark both occasions. Over a drink I suggested to Pete that we should shoot up to the stables on Wednesday, mainly on the grounds that we could.

Apart from being a pleasant day out for two gentlemen of leisure, today's visit was a chance to gauge how close Free Love was to making her reappearance. It was a near miss for Mick Appleby. He was at Newmarket trying to buy a horse for a new racing club. He would therefore avoid the painful experience of me and Pete quizzing him about the Bath listed race. I'm sure trainers are used to owners thinking their geese are swans, but it must be hard to remain diplomatic and measured during a conversation with two syndicate members who are wide-eyed and almost foaming at the mouth when discussing plans for their five-furlong goose.

Pete was driving as, like all good racehorses, I had suffered a minor setback. The wound at the back of my heel refused to close, became infected and required me to visit Darent Valley Hospital on a weekly basis. When penicillin didn't work, my surgeon opted for a Crimean War approach, cleaning out the gaping flesh with a combination of carbolic soap and brute force. The pain was excruciating but at least I wasn't offered a leather tawse to bite on while he rummaged around in his kit bag looking for a saw. A week or so later, I was still hobbling around with the aid of a crutch and only driving locally. There was no return to golf, no long lockdown walks and no absence of pain either.

The traffic was light, and the two-and-a-quarter hour journey flew by as we chatted about anything and everything that came to mind. We probably shouldn't have been sharing a car, but we were both glad of the company and a chance to converse with another human being by means other than Zoom. Pete is well-read and follows current affairs closely so there's never a shortage of conversation topics. We talked horses for a bit, agreeing that the incredible achievements of Rachael Blackmore and Henry de Bromhead at the Cheltenham Festival had provided the good news story that racing needed following the furore over Gordon Elliott's dismal behaviour. Vaccination passports, the Met's handling of the Clapham Common vigil for Sarah Everard, and the impact of Brexit on the Scottish fishing industry were other subjects put under the microscope. Before we had time to touch on the breaking controversy of the publication of the report from the Commission on Race and Ethnic Disparities, we were turning left off the A606 and driving through the entrance to the Mick Appleby Racing and Breeding complex.

It was a beautiful morning. We were sipping mugs of tea outside the owners' portacabin when a string of about a dozen horses, walking in single file, returned from the gallops and were led into the main yard to be washed down. Ten minutes later, we were parked at the top of the all-weather gallop waiting for the last lot to exercise. Free Love was due for another piece of solo work. I wasn't sure how exacting it was going to be, but I messaged Mick before we left Dartford to ask him for a rough idea of when our mare would be ready to race again, and he replied that the end of April would be about right.

It looked like farewell to Bath, as well as a nice class 3 handicap at Epsom on 20th April, but I convinced myself that if Free Love worked well I could always get back to Mick to ask him if an earlier reappearance was possible.

There was only me, Pete and Louise watching the horses at work. Louise was busy taking videos of each canter and gallop which she would send to the respective owners. Most of the horses in this final session were going solo. A hooded Sampers Seven tore up the all-weather strip looking as if a return to the racecourse was imminent. The veteran sprinter, Caspian Prince, was taken gently for the first three furlongs before being asked to stretch out up the final incline. It was quite a sight watching the globe-trotting 12-year-old chestnut have his final prep before heading to Musselburgh for a valuable sprint handicap on Saturday. Even to the naked eye, it was obvious that this was a seriously fast horse. He showed scorching pace. Still rated 100, and winner of over £800,000 in prize money, Caspian had a lofty mark of 118 in his pomp and had twice captured the Investec Dash on Epsom Derby day. He's all about raw speed and boy, did he still have it. I wasn't looking for similar fireworks from Free Love but having seen two of Mick's better sprinters put through their paces, expectations had now risen.

At last, it was time for the star of the show. Free Love was the final one on the worksheet and I trained my binoculars towards the bottom of the gallop where Erika was making sure that her partner went very steadily to begin with. I anticipated a change in gear as the pair met the rising ground, but Erika sat tight, only allowing her mount to proceed at a snail's pace. It reminded me of the slow bicycle races we had as kids where the idea was to try and keep riding as slowly as possible without putting your foot on the ground and coming to a halt. It was as if Erika was trying to canter as slowly as she could without allowing the horse to break into a trot or walk. If Caspian Prince was an exhilarating blur, Free Love was a perplexing super slow-mo.

'What was that all about?' I quizzed Louise hoping that she could provide a plausible explanation. After all, I know nothing about training racehorses and the slow bicycle race technique might be a new, pioneering method that Mick was now employing.

'I don't know,' was Louise's less than reassuring reply.

I looked at Pete. He made no comment, but his pained facial expression said it all. It was how he looked when he realised it was his turn at the bar.

The horses started filing back, Free Love cutting a rather sullen figure walking about 20 yards behind the main group.

'Everything ok?' I ventured when Erika and Free Love finally drew level.

'She just didn't feel herself. She felt a bit stiff and wasn't moving fluently so I decided to hang on to her,' Erika replied.

It was a long way to come for one of the slowest canters in the history of racing. Looking on the bright side, I suppose we got value for money. It took Free Love about ten seconds to crawl past us while Caspian Prince was gone in the blink of an eye. We gave the horses a good head start before clambering into Louise's car and slowly making our way back to the yard. By the time we reached the main driveway, we had caught up with the string. Free Love was at the back of it, still detached from the last in the line. I put it down to our mare not being in a sociable mood rather than lacking the pace to keep up with the others.

Back in the yard, we weaved our way through the bustling group of horses being washed down by their work riders. Some of the animals stood compliantly, calmly accepting splashes of cold water and the attention of their grooms. Others were more skittish, wheeling away from their handlers, prompting me and Pete to give them a wide berth as we walked towards Erika and Free Love.

The mare looked fine. She may have been a little big. The fact

209

that I couldn't see the definition of her ribs suggested she had a few pounds to shed. And while her summer coat was nearly there, a bit of winter wooliness remained. As I talked to Erika, and she explained why she wasn't happy with the feel Free Love gave her, I realised that I knew nothing at all. I may understand how racing works, but my ignorance of the creature at the heart of our sport is almost absolute.

After the horses were dispersed to the barns and walkers, Theo joined us and we chatted about plans for the season. I confirmed that he would be aboard for Free Love's reappearance. This was something that had been agreed in December and I wasn't prepared to renege on the promise even if the ownership of the group had changed. Beyond that first run, it was down to the six people who now made up the North South Syndicate. I explained that we still might shoot for a bit of black type, but it depended on what the others thought. Now that Bath had been ruled out, the only other realistic chance would be at Ayr in June. We'd have to see how Free Love fared when she returned to action. We'd soon know our fate.

Before we left, we were told that the vet would be making his rounds in the afternoon, and he'd have a look at the mare. Last year she was given an injection in both front fetlock joints and moved considerably better after the treatment. If injected, she wouldn't be allowed to race for 2-3 weeks which put her reappearance somewhere towards the end of April, which is what Mick had already told me. Perhaps we'd get more precise information when all six of us visited on 17th April. As to what sort of report we would send to the others following this morning's underwhelming workout, Pete and I could talk about that on the journey home.

Saturday 10th April 2021

Racing's redemption was complete. As the race unfolded, there looked to be an inevitability about Rachael Blackmore's historic Grand National victory. Minella Times was always handy on the inside, travelling well and jumping like an old hand. When the favourite, Cloth Cap, weakened dramatically shortly after the Canal Turn, all eyes were transfixed on the yellow and green hoops of the J P McManus eight-year-old who breezed into the lead at the second last fence and kept on strongly on the long, stamina-sapping run-in to score by an emphatic six-and-a-half lengths.

It didn't matter that there wasn't a paying crowd and only a small number of owners were allowed to be there. The world's most famous horse race attracted around nine million viewers in the UK and its global audience was estimated to be more than 100 million. The national news would now carry extensive coverage of the first female jockey to win the great race, the feel-good story completely overwhelming the bad press received through the Gordon Elliott affair.

The remarkable achievements didn't stop with Rachael. Henry de Bromhead saddled both the winner and runner-up. It completed a four-timer for the self-effacing Irish handler following his stunning Cheltenham Festival hat-trick of the Champion Hurdle, Champion Chase and Gold Cup. And to cap it all, ten of the first eleven horses to cross the finishing line in Aintree's big race were trained in Ireland. Perhaps we should send Free Love to Henry and Rachael and ask them to prepare her for next year's Supreme Novices' Hurdle?

There is no doubt that Rachael Blackmore is a fine rider, one of the best of her generation – male or female. Henry de Bromhead is also a masterful trainer and his extraordinary feat of winning those four iconic races in the same season is unlikely to be repeated in my lifetime. But, more than that, you couldn't wish for a pair of more modest, grounded and thoroughly likeable ambassadors for the sport. It made me feel proud to be part of racing, even if only through the shared ownership of a cheaply bought sprinter.

Friday 16th April 2021

Tomorrow's planned stable visit was off. Since my trip to Langham at the end of March, Free Love had received treatment for her troubling fetlock joint and had cantered once. Mick wasn't happy with how the mare was moving and had arranged for the vet to have another look at her today. The absence of video clips told me that things weren't going well.

Racehorses are fragile creatures, and most owners know that setbacks come with the territory. I had a share in a Heart of the South horse who was troubled with lameness at the start of his four-year-old career. Bone chips were diagnosed as the problem, and they were removed by keyhole surgery. The rather inauspiciously named The Shuffler was given time to recuperate, but when he was put back into training the lameness recurred whenever he built up to faster work. By the end of September, it was agreed that he wouldn't race again, and a nice home was found for the gelding on a farm in Kent. I had spent a whole season waiting anxiously for news of progress, hoping that we might get back on a racecourse before the turf season slid out of view. It wasn't to be, and the experience served as a reminder of how lucky I had been so far with Free Love. In between a couple of minor problems, our sprinter had run 33 times in three seasons.

We'd had a fair run for our money. However, our new shareholders, Kieran and Tim, might not be so phlegmatic. At least they had bought into a mare with a residual breeding value, and it wouldn't be a case of just giving her away if persistent health problems forced the curtain down on her racing career.

Later that afternoon I received some encouraging news. Mick

informed me that the vet and farrier had taken a good look at Free Love's feet and decided that she would benefit from having pads fitted. After the mare was plated with her new shock absorbers she appeared to move better, and Mick said that he'd crack on with her and monitor the situation.

I let everyone know the news and by early evening settled down to watch the feature race from Bath, the *Whitsbury Manor Stud Lansdown Stakes*. The only two fillies in the original entries rated over 100 were Liberty Beach and Keep Busy. They both had marks of 109 and I knew we couldn't beat either, but beyond that pair the field looked rather ordinary. It was both surprising and frustrating that neither was declared, and although 14 runners lined up for the listed sprint, only three of them were rated over 90. Top of the lot on a mark of 96 was Wise Words, who Free Love had run to three-quarters of a length off level weights at Leicester in her three-year-old season.

One of only two realistic chances for black type had slipped away. The other one was in late June at Ayr and the way things were going, you couldn't guarantee Free Love being ready to run in that one either. I watched in sombre resignation as the lightly raced and improving Declaring Love just resisted the strong late challenge of Wise Words. The first three home were rated 88, 96 and 93. It was unlikely that Free Love would have troubled the judge, but it was further evidence that these listed sprints restricted to fillies and mares are often weakly contested. As if to underline the point, the fully exposed Wings Of A Dove was beaten less than three lengths in fifth place off a mark of 78.

But running with great credit to finish fifth doesn't win any prizes. The sales catalogue won't read 5th in the Lansdown Stud Stakes, Bath **L**, the upper-case L in glorious black type. In my heart I knew that a creditable mid-division placing beaten only four lengths would be the most likely outcome if we ever had a tilt at a listed race. But you never knew. Maybe we just needed all the cards to fall right.

Saturday 24th April 2021
It was just a gentle solo canter under a pale blue early morning sky at Langham, but it was a great relief to receive the eight-second video clip which confirmed that Free Love was back on the gallops.

I passed it on to the others and revived the conversation about a stable visit. I reckoned we were about a month behind schedule. It wasn't just the listed race at Bath that had slipped away. There was also a class 3 handicap at Epsom's spring meeting last Tuesday which had been a possible early season target. Theo had talked before about how the track and the race might suit our filly. He nearly won it on our old adversary, Dark Shot in 2019, failing by a neck to land the £12,500 prize.

I was there two years ago, enjoying the early days of my retirement from primary headship, marvelling at the fact that a meeting which had been barred to me for 30 years because it always fell in term time, was back on the agenda. Free Love had already bolted up on her seasonal debut less than a fortnight earlier and I remember leaning up against the rail by the finishing line where the also-rans congregated (only the first past the post are accommodated in the winner's enclosure at Epsom) to offer a few words of commiseration to young Theo.

Two years later, the 2021 renewal of the race took place behind closed doors with only a smattering of masked owners permitted to attend. The first-place prize money had plummeted to a few quid short of six grand. It was another illustration of the debilitating impact of the pandemic on the sport. It was left to Dark Shot to provide an illusion of constancy. Off a lowly mark of 71, in a weak-looking six-runner contest, he once again chased home the winner, this time the 84-rated Recon Mission. That could have been us, I thought to myself, as I watched the televised coverage from Epsom.

There was no use crying over spilt milk. If we were lucky, Free Love would be ready to race towards the end of May. It wasn't a disaster. In any event, things were going well elsewhere. Pub gardens had opened on 12th April and, by the time our mare made it to the racecourse, crowds could be back for the first time in what seemed like an eternity. Going racing might be fun again.

Saturday 8th May 2021

This morning's video bulletin from Langham sparked a frenzied conversation about a stable visit. In contrast to the recent sedate, solo canters, today's footage showed Free Love working upsides. It was the first time since she returned to full training at the beginning of March that our mare had attempted anything so strenuous.

Her galloping companion was Arceus, a lightly raced three-year-old son of Camacho with a modest official rating of 58. In visibly heavy rain, the two sprinters sloshed their way up the stiffly rising finish of the all-weather gallop at a decent clip. Neither rider was doing any more than letting their mount stride out in a comfortable rhythm, so you couldn't read anything into the fact that Arceus was nearly a length clear of Free Love as the pair passed Louise's mobile phone. I hoped not anyway.

It looked like we were back on track, which was the main thing. A visit to Mick's yard to witness Free Love in action was on the agenda again. It would be a chance to see her on the gallops and quiz our trainer about the management of the foot problems that had mucked up the schedule. We still looked about three weeks away from seeing Free Love back on a racecourse, and that relied on things going well from now onwards.

It might be a blessing in disguise, I thought to myself. May 17th was the date set for the next relaxation of restrictions. Meeting indoors with family and friends, and the return of modest crowds to sporting events, were two significant freedoms that were due to be restored.

We settled on Wednesday 19th for our visit. As usual, trying to find a date that everyone could make proved to be an insurmountable challenge. I thought we had achieved the impossible until Patrick announced that he was having his second jab on the selected day and didn't think the Health Secretary, Matt Hancock, would be too impressed if he delayed matters to watch a horse run around a field in Rutland.

He was right, of course. The impressive speed of the vaccination roll-out was enabling the UK to drop its sick man of Europe tag. There were pockets of resistance in the population, but the take-up remained reassuringly high and early signs suggested that getting the jabs provided encouraging protection from the variants that were doing the rounds.

Following hot on the heels of the Kent, South African and Brazilian mutations came the Indian variant which was thought to spread more easily than other versions of the virus. B.1.617 was the snappy name given by scientists to the Indian mutation, but I couldn't see the public embracing numbers instead of easily remembered place names. The danger was attaching blame to certain countries for the emergence of a new threat. My mind cast back to Donald Trump's rasping intonation of 'Chinese Flu' in the early days of the pandemic.

Maybe the meteorologists' alphabetical approach to naming storms should be employed. Alice variant, Brian variant, Charlotte variant and so on. And if that approach ran into gender difficulties, what about using famous racehorses? The Nijinsky variant sounds quite classy. Throwing in the occasional gelding would also satisfy the non-binary lobby. Imagine the kudos of having a Covid-19 mutation named after your horse. I saw myself holding court while leaning against the bar. 'Unfortunately, our filly just missed out on black type, but she did have a strain of a deadly virus named after her.'

The scientists and the politicians didn't seem unduly worried about variants. Of course, it was easy for the press to sell a few more papers by squeezing a quote from one of the more cautious epidemiologists, which led to headlines about threats to freedom and eternal lockdowns. If journalists wanted something more jolly, they just needed to talk to a junior minister who insisted that we were still on track. The tone of the newspapers' front pages seemed to alternate daily.

Yesterday's Racing Post carried a headline confirming that the country was generally on track. From Monday 17th May, crowds would be allowed back on racecourses. The larger sports stadia would be permitted to accommodate 4,000 spectators or half their capacity, whichever was smaller. I'd already taken a punt on tickets for Sandown's Brigadier Gerard evening meeting at the end of May which now looked certain to take place in the presence of a healthy number of paying customers. It felt like we were coming out of hibernation.

Wednesday 19th May 2021
The miserably wet April had given way to an arid but cool May, devoid of sun and warmth. It was a real stroke of luck that we picked one of the month's few decent days for our stable visit. It was still a morning for quilted jackets and sweatshirts but, by the time we were at the top of Mick's all-weather gallop, the porcelain blue sky dotted with delicately sculpted alabaster clouds resembled the ethereal quality of a Titian painting. It was the perfect setting to watch

thoroughbred racehorses surge up the hill, nostrils flared, hooves pounding, and a reminder of why ownership is so absurdly exciting.

Maybe 'surge' wasn't the most appropriate word to describe Free Love's piece of work which was no more than a gentle solo canter. Since her last gallop, our mare had been re-shod and was apparently a bit sore afterwards. She missed her next scheduled exercise and last Saturday only managed a three-furlong spin at the bottom of the gallops which wasn't captured on video by Louise. Clearly her feet problems were still ongoing.

Erika seemed happy enough when we chatted with her back at the yard where she washed down Free Love and posed for the latest round of pictures. She felt that the mare was moving well and was over any soreness she had recently experienced. During our chat with Mick, he advised stepping up the work and looking for a race within the next 2-3 weeks.

It all felt positive enough, although a chance conversation with Ed Dodds, the farrier, tempered our optimism. Ed turned up just as we were getting ready to leave and soon found himself surrounded by four members of the North South Syndicate who quizzed him about the state of Free Love's feet.

The affable farrier explained that there had been little growth at the back of the mare's heels and special pads had been fitted between the aluminium plates and her feet to stop her feeling any minor discomfort when she moved. He said that without the pads, it was a bit like a human donning a pair of shoes with paper-thin soles, making the wearer sensitive to every stone or uneven piece of ground walked on.

Ed knew that Free Love hadn't had a decent break during the winter. She had raced until mid-December and stayed at Mick's until resuming training not much more than two months later. The previous season she was turned out at Castle View Stud for a few

218

months. If time wasn't an obstacle, Ed's advice was to put her in a field for six months to allow natural growth at the back of her heels. That would take us to the end of the flat turf season which we all knew wasn't an option.

It was a case of managing the problem in the best way possible. As Ed showed us the bewildering array of pads and paraphernalia he employed in his work, Mick remarked that one of his stable stars, Danzeno, had terrible feet and for years had been treated with all the tricks of the farrier's trade. As Danzeno was still rated 105 at the ripe old age of ten and was more than capable of strutting his stuff in heritage sprint handicaps, it made me feel that maybe Free Love's problems could be overcome with a bit of tender loving care.

We left Langham in an optimistic mood and headed for the Wheatsheaf in Oakham where we had a table booked for lunch. Two days ago, restaurants and bars were allowed to restart indoor service, and we were looking forward to a more familiar pub experience. Of course, in many ways, it was still far from normal. Punters were expected to sign-in on arrival, sanitise their hands, wear masks when not seated, and follow the rule of six.

There were five of us in total. The whole of the southern section of the syndicate was present plus one of our new owners, Tim, and his eldest son Oliver. Other abnormal practices included Perspex screens around the bar, staff in visors and menus that could only be accessed via QR codes. We were all used to these rituals by now, but you had to question the logic of some of the things we were being asked to do.

An article in the BBC News app reminded everyone that at the start of the pandemic a lot of focus was on surfaces. People washed groceries and avoided touching buttons at pedestrian crossings. Councils shut playgrounds and cordoned off park benches. But Dr Eilir Hughes, a GP and campaigner for more protective PPE for

NHS staff, contended that it's been all but impossible to find an outbreak that could be linked to an infected surface.

The Welsh medic went on to explain that it would take an unlikely chain of events for infected droplets on an object to be transferred into someone's respiratory system just by touching it. It seems they would have to lick their fingers or put them up their nose, and I had no intention of doing that with one of the Wheatsheaf's pepper pots. Even then, the likelihood of enough virus surviving this chain of events to make someone ill was slim. That all made complete sense to me and, although Dr Hughes recognised that keeping your hands clean was important for all sorts of reasons, he cautioned people to avoid 'hygiene theatre' where we focussed excessively on washing hands and surfaces or avoiding touching objects. There was a danger of concentrating on performative strategies rather than effective ones.

I didn't mind a little theatre if it kept everyone happy and, more importantly, kept the hospitality industry open. Apparently, it employs around 3 million people in the UK which is around 10% of the total workforce. I don't know the average age of someone working in the industry, but I bet it's on the young side. What a miserable last 14 months those youngsters must have had.

We washed down our sausage baguettes and chicken paninis with a pint or two of Everard's Tiger while talking excitedly about options for the coming season. As usual, I had interrogated the BHA website and printed a list of suitable race options from the end of May onwards. Given Free Love's current official rating of 81, I included everything from class 4 and above but only over the minimum distance and on turf.

There were plenty of opportunities on the horizon, including a couple of new initiatives. The Racing League and Sky Bet Sunday Series seemed to be throwing a lot of money at handicaps for horses in the 70-90 bracket which was right up our alley. Details appeared a bit vague at this stage, but July and August looked to be two months full of lucrative opportunities for Free Love – providing she stayed sound.

Wednesday 2nd June 2021

Free Love was entered for a class 3 handicap at Windsor next Monday. Since our stable visit, she had completed a sharper looking solo canter and two faster pieces of work upsides a pair of Mick's run-of-the-mill handicap sprinters. This morning's video clip showed her working with the smart Nigel Nott. It looked like, barring an act of God, we would begin our new campaign at the riverside track next week.

Everything seemed to be moving in the right direction. As Free Love's health improved, so did the nation's. By the end of May, nearly half of the UK adult population had been double jabbed. Jennie and I joined the club three days ago with a trip to Gravesend where the cheerless 1970s Woodville Halls Theatre complex had been turned into a huge vaccination centre.

The first tentative steps back towards a more convivial and natural way of life were being taken by those who felt healthy and confident enough to venture out. Crowds were back at racing with a maximum of 4,000 paying spectators allowed to attend. This new freedom prompted me and Trevor to take in a very low-key Lingfield meeting the day after our visit to Langham. It wasn't a joyous return. It was 13 degrees, windy, and drizzling for most of the afternoon. Punters were required to wear masks indoors unless seated to eat and drink. Although there were plenty of tables outside, hardly anyone wanted to brave the foul weather so finding a spot to sit down in the warmth was as difficult as unearthing winners on the unseasonably heavy ground.

As we stood on the terraces before the claiming stakes, one of many class 6 contests on a distinctly moderate card, I noted two fellow punters in front of us sipping coffee from takeaway cups. I didn't think anything of it until a steward homed in on the pair and informed them that they must sit down when consuming food or drink. They dutifully sat down on the steps and the steward moved on happy with his work.

'I feel so much safer now,' I quipped to the coffee drinkers.

'Don't,' replied the compliant punter with a roll of the eyes. 'But it's not worth having a row about it.'

He was right, of course. Yes, it was all a bit absurd, and I struggled to see how 'following the science' was evident in this tiny example of 'Racecourse Covid Protocols', but here we were. After a prolonged period of the public being barred from racecourses, we were back on a track and prepared to jump through any number of hoops to be there.

Sandown Park was infinitely better a week later. The Brigadier Gerard Stakes evening is one of my favourite meetings of the year and Sandown might be, on balance, my favourite racecourse. We had to go through the same booking rigmarole as we did for Lingfield. This included confirming that all online Covid guidelines had been read and understood. Although photo ID was supposedly required on entry, we breezed in without being asked to show anything. Temperature checks had also been dumped.

As you would expect from a Grade 1 track, Sandown had cracked the table service arrangements with all drinks ordered via the Jockey Club catering app. It helped that the weather was decent enough to enjoy a drink outside and it felt close to normal as I sat on the terrace at the back of the grandstand overlooking the parade ring, sipping a beer, and discussing the likely winners of the evening's feature races with my eldest son, Matt.

Our in-depth analysis yielded no fruit. The admirable veteran, Euchen Glen, returned to form with a decisive victory in the four-runner Brigadier Gerard Stakes. He was the 20/1 outsider of the field. Half an hour earlier, Henry de Bromhead scored with a rare runner on the flat when Lismore sprang a 14/1 surprise in the Group 3 Henry II Stakes. It seemed almost unfair that the Irish handler who had dominated Cheltenham and landed a one-two in the Grand National should now start plundering graded races on the flat.

Sandown made me feel buoyant about the ownership experience we were likely to get at Windsor next Monday. The last-minute decision to keep Free Love in training as a five-year-old was fuelled by the desire to have one final season, free from the wearying restrictions we had all endured for longer than we cared to remember. We would still be required to wear masks indoors and crowd limits were set to stay for another month or two, but it would surely feel as close to normal for the first time in the twenty months that had elapsed since Free Love concluded her three-year-old campaign.

Monday 7th June 2021

There were just eight declared for Free Love's reappearance race at Windsor this evening. The hardy Yimou, rated 85, was set to carry top-weight with our mare just four pounds below that mark. Considering it was a contest open to horses rated up to 90, the *Fitzdares Sprint Series Handicap* didn't look to be the hottest class 3 sprint ever run at the course.

Arrangements for owners still carried restrictions which I communicated to the others a few days ago via our WhatsApp group:

Gents.

We have six allocated owners' badges for Monday. Unlike in normal circumstances, we can't buy extra badges that would give guests access to the owners' lounge, refreshments, the parade ring etc. Only Tim can't make it, and I'm going to snap up the sixth badge for Jennie, who retires tomorrow, and will be needed for driving duties on Monday as my heel is still no good. Hope everyone is OK with that. By the time we next run we'll hopefully be back to normal regarding buying additional badges at discounted prices. I'll allocate the tickets on Saturday afternoon and they'll be sent to you via email. You must have the ticket with you (printed or on your phone) as well as photo ID when you arrive at the course. You may also be required to do a bit of online Covid training in advance which most of you have done before. Think that's all for now. Fingers crossed FL remains sound and Mick doesn't start making noises about the ground being too quick!

My foot continued to be a cause of discomfort and frustration. It was now nearly seven months since the original tendon operation and the wound at the back of my heel still refused to close. I hadn't worn anything other than sandals and flip-flops during that period, which was ok for knocking about locally but not a great look with a suit. Matt was insistent that it was fine when we met at Sandown, assuring me that the sandals and socks combination, universally derided in the past, was now hipster chic. Fine if you were in your mid-twenties, sported a trendy beard, worked in marketing, and lived in Shoreditch or Stoke Newington. More difficult to pull off for a 63-year-old retired head teacher.

During the weekend just gone, I had subjected Tewkesbury Park Golf Course to another piece of cutting-edge fashion. The thought of missing out on our annual pilgrimage to Gloucestershire because of my ongoing foot problem was too painful to contemplate. I had to go, even if it meant I sank pints rather than putts. I took the view that I could drive around in a buggy and be part of the occasion, perhaps playing a few shots here and there, even if participation in the two-day competition wasn't possible. In the end, I played all 36 holes with a golf shoe on one foot and a sandal on the other.

I can't say it was the most comfortable sporting experience I've ever had. After the first round on Saturday, I retreated to my room and lay prostrate on the bed, smothering my grotesquely swollen foot with as much ice as the bar could spare. I watched Adayar power his way up the Epsom hill to land the Derby in impressive style, while the five-furlong Dash, a race I fancifully thought might be a target for Free Love one day, was won by the six-year-old Mokaatil who captured the £38k first prize off a rating of just 82.

Should Free Love win tonight's class 3 handicap off her mark of 81, she would capture £6k for her owners. The game is all about fine margins, especially for horses negotiating the dense jungle of the British handicapping system. Unless you're a rapidly improving creature – and Free Love was just that when she won three of her first five races as a three-year-old – you reach a settled mark and must wait until all the cards fall in the right place for your winning turn to come round again.

I can't say that Free Love looked to be holding a winning hand at Windsor. Her mark seemed fair enough, but no more than that. True, her last win was at the Berkshire track when she defied 86 to beat Dark Shadow by a neck in a pulsating finish. But the blanks she drew in seven attempts as a four-year-old resulted in a measly total drop of 2lbs. She paid the price for her own consistency, always trying her best and reaching the runner-up spot in three of those seven outings.

Positives included returning to the track where Free Love had put up two of the best performances of her life, one in victory the other in an agonisingly narrow defeat. Stall one was a welcome bonus. I had lost count of the number of poor draws our mare had been handed during her career. There would be no excuses on that count this evening. The going was also a plus. Although she had proved that she could handle soft ground, there is no doubt that Free Love's very best form was associated with quicker surfaces. However, we were now wary of running her on genuinely fast ground because of the ongoing problems with her feet.

The obvious negatives were the six-month absence from the track and a preparation interrupted by niggling problems. However, Free Love had managed four consecutive pieces of fast work within the last fortnight and, even if she was just short of full fitness, we were hopeful of a bold showing on ground described as good to firm following some welcome showers on Saturday evening.

Royal Windsor Racecourse was a sight to behold as we picked up our badges and walked onto the lawned area behind the grandstand. Food stalls and pop-up bars provided a takeaway service for the hundreds of racegoers who occupied the sea of picnic tables that filled the large space between the winner's enclosure and the parade ring. The evening air was full of animated chatter punctuated with bursts of laughter. It felt fabulous. As I walked around the course enclosures, I sensed that we were nearly there. It was a far cry from the dispiriting visit to the same racecourse in September when a limited number of owners were allowed restricted access to the racecourse and paying customers were still prohibited. Tonight, the place felt alive, and so did I.

Free Love looked in great shape as she paraded before the race. Theo was at pains to point out that she would probably need the run which was perfectly understandable. Trainers rarely, if ever, work their horses flat out at home. The acid test of fitness comes on the racecourse. But Free Love looked well enough and the recent pieces of fast work on the Langham gallops suggested she was unlikely to finish tailed off, huffing and puffing as she crossed the line in a state of near exhaustion.

The betting public seemed to agree and the 16/1 which was briefly available last night had vanished. 8/1 was now the top price on offer which made Free Love fourth pick behind the well supported 2/1 favourite, A Sure Welcome.

We all thought that anywhere in the frame would be a satisfactory return, but I felt we could do a bit better than that. Mick's stable appeared to be in good form and, with the track, going and draw in our favour, it wasn't inconceivable that our little sprinter could go very close, maybe even make a winning return.

But I always think like that. Whatever the size of the task and however challenging the conditions, I can always make a case for Free Love. But let's face it, surprises happen in racing, and it wouldn't be the biggest shock the sport had witnessed if the pride and joy of the North South Syndicate shrugged off the handicap of a six-month absence and hosed up, paving the way for a crack at the listed *Land O'Burns Stakes* at Ayr 15 days later. I kept that fanciful notion to myself.

Free Love went down calmly and entered the stalls in her usual unfussy way. When the gates opened, she popped out and settled in behind A Sure Welcome and Yimou who both made alert starts. Approaching halfway, Theo was just beginning to nudge away, asking his partner for her effort, when the race descended into carnage. Diligent Lady went crashing to the ground badly hampering Centurion Song who unseated his jockey in a high-speed crash that happened so quickly it was impossible to grasp what was going on.

I immediately glanced to the left where Theo had kept Free Love to the inside rail. They had been close to the catastrophe but managed to avoid it, and as the leaders approached the final furlong, Theo angled out towards the middle of the course, passed Yimou and went in pursuit of A Sure Welcome who had drifted over to the stands-side rail. For a moment it looked as if we might hunt down the leader but in the last hundred yards fitness told and our game mare's effort flattened out. A Sure Welcome was an emphatic winner, but Free Love was a clear second confirming that she had retained her ability and enthusiasm at the start of her fourth season as a racehorse.

I was buzzing as we hurried towards the winner's enclosure where only the first and second were allowed to return; a reminder that it wasn't quite business as usual just yet. I was particularly pleased for our two new partners, Kieran and Tim. Free Love's excellent reappearance must have made them feel that their investment would lead to plenty of enjoyable days at the races during a summer when large crowds returned to racecourses. Our sprinter had also shown enough to suggest that she had another win in her, maybe at class 3 level. The future looked rosy.

After an animated conversation with Theo, the patting of Free Love's warm and perspiring neck, and another round of memories captured on our mobile phones, it was time to move to the owners' and trainers' lounge to engage in excited talk about the future. It was only at this point that the seriousness of the incident triggered by Diligent Lady's fall became apparent to me as I looked down the straight and saw that ambulances were still on the track attending to the jockeys.

News filtered through that Diligent Lady had suffered a fatal injury which shocked me as I had seen both horses get to their feet. Immediately after the race I had spent an elated ten minutes in the winner's enclosure oblivious to what was going on elsewhere. One of Mick Appleby's longest-serving jockeys, Alistair Rawlinson, had sustained horrific injuries that would put him out of the game for months. While the medics treated Alistair, the veterinary team was euthanising poor Diligent Lady, one of seven racehorses bred by Mrs Monica Teversham from her own broodmare, Lady Filly. It must have been like losing a member of the family.

It's what every owner dreads. Fortunately, it doesn't happen that often on the flat but, when it does, the speed of events can be terrifying. I've done the maths. At the halfway point in a sprint, horses are often travelling at their fastest. The 10.5 seconds per furlong they hit equates to a shade over 42mph. Thank God that Free Love and Theo avoided the melee by virtue of racing a few yards to the right of where the incident took place. If they had been a bit closer to the ill-fated Diligent Lady, it would have been impossible to take evasive action given the high speeds involved. Free Love had run with great credit on her return but, more important than anything else, she lived to fight another day.

2 Road Trip

(Ayr, 22nd June 2021)

Tuesday 15th June 2021

Free Love came out of Windsor in good shape. She managed to lose her near-fore shoe during the race and was a little sore on that foot for a day or two afterwards, but there were no signs of the problems that had afflicted her in the spring and were responsible for such a belated seasonal reappearance.

Rather surprisingly, the handicapper eased Free Love's rating down a pound to 80. This looked lenient given that Yimou, who was a length behind us at Windsor, went down by only the same amount. I was sure Free Love would be left on 81 and, while I should have been delighted by the handicapper's generosity, part of me wanted her mark to remain as high as possible because of the kudos associated with a decent rating.

I knew that was a ridiculous notion. Most owners want their horses to have their handicap marks slashed to such a low level that winning a race or two becomes more likely. How does the saying go? Keep yourself in the best company, and your horses in the worst. Given that Free Love had put together a losing sequence of 17 since her last victory in July 2019, I should have been grateful for any help the handicapper was prepared to give. Winning a race of any description was surely the name of the game.

Not quite, though. There was still the allure of black type. There was only one realistic chance of having a go at that and it came up soon. I sent my thoughts to the others via an email.

Morning all,
How do you feel about taking a punt on an entry for the Land O'Burns Stakes

at Ayr on 22nd June?

I know we'd have to run it past Mick to make sure that Free Love would be ready following her Windsor exertions, but just for the moment let's assume that she is.

It would cost £220 to 'have a look' which is not a huge amount given that it's her last chance of nicking a bit of black type. There are only two five furlong listed races restricted to older fillies and mares in Europe. One has already gone, the Lansdown Stud Stakes at Bath in April.

The two races are invariably weakly contested, and it looks to be the same this year with five of the top female sprinters declared for tomorrow's King's Stands Stakes at Ascot. Ayr looks set to be a race for fillies and mares in the 80s and 90s.

Quite often something lowly rated pops up in the first three. Last year it was the thoroughly exposed 6yo handicapper Merry Banter who finished third off 82. She'd never been rated higher than 85 in her life but was only sent off at 25/1 which is an indicator of the weakness of the race.

In one of my anorak-moments, I analysed the history of the Bath and Ayr listed races (see attachment) and it looks like at least one in two renewals of the Ayr race throws up a filly rated in the eighties who makes the first three. Finishing third means £5k in prize money and maybe a £10k increase in the mare's value.

As I said, it's all about making an entry to see if the race looks weak enough to have a go at. Free Love would need to get the green light from Mick. If the race looked like cutting up and we had a real chance of hitting the frame, we could make a late decision to run.

What do you think? We're only talking about the principle of making an entry here. I won't bother to speak to Mick until I get your views.

Regards, Tony

It wasn't a huge amount of money to throw at our last chance to have a crack at black type. In any event, Free Love's exploits at

Windsor last week netted a welcome £3k in prize money. I always budgeted on the basis of not winning a bean all season, so any income, no matter how piffling, was viewed as a welcome bonus. Surely the boys wouldn't begrudge £220 for our one and only shot at a listed race?

Monday 21st June 2021
Today should have been 'Freedom Day', a moniker coined by the tabloids to hang on the date specified in the government's roadmap out of lockdown when all Covid restrictions would be removed. But last week the PM announced that people would have to wait another four weeks before limits on numbers at parties, weddings, funerals, and sports events were abandoned, and facemasks could be put in the bottom draw and kept safe for whenever the next pandemic arrived.

In the lead up to Boris Johnson's decision on whether to stick with 21st June or delay, the news was full of conflicting views. Case numbers were edging up again largely driven by the more transmissible Delta variant. (The scientific community opted for letters of the Greek alphabet rather than names of famous racehorses, but we were on the same page). The rising infection rates prompted many scientists to talk in sombre tones about the huge risks involved with rolling back restrictions. Others went further. It was madness, verging on irresponsible, to consider relaxations on social distancing.

But I sensed a growing weariness with what the nation had endured for the last 15 months. Most people in my friendship group couldn't wait for larger social gatherings, the theatre, big sports events and foreign travel to resume. Maybe it was our age. We'd spent decades doing lots of different things and were impatient for normal life to resume. We weren't interested in the 'new normals' espoused by twenty-something journalists in the magazines and feature sections of the Sunday broadsheets. Get jabbed and get on with it summed up my feelings on the subject.

Since my email, the WhatsApp group had been flooded with the agonised views of the other owners. Everyone saw the merit in having a crack at Ayr but, on the other hand, ending a long losing run by picking off a small handicap had equal appeal. Mick had made an entry for a fillies' and mares' sprint handicap at Haydock, but it looked to be a tough enough assignment giving weight away to some progressive three-year-olds on ground that would be plenty quick enough.

Everyone became more positive about having a crack at Ayr, especially when our trainer reported that Free Love was moving the best she had done for a while and we probably wouldn't have a better chance of grabbing a bit of black type.

It was our only chance as far as I could see. We were nowhere near good enough to take on the colts and geldings. It was the *Land O'Burns* or nothing. The entry was made and when we saw that only three of the opposition were rated over 90 – Wise Words, Dickiedooda and Keep Busy – we took the plunge and declared to run.

Tuesday 22nd June 2021

How could I get from Dartford to Ayr? I was desperate to be there, to see Free Love's heroic quest in the flesh, but there was no way I could drive that distance with my debilitating heel injury. I investigated trains and planes, but the schedules looked crazy and insanely expensive.

I was on the verge of giving up when Pete and Tim came to the rescue. Tim was keen to go and suggested me and Pete broke our journey and stayed with him in Cheshire the night before the race.

From there it was about a five-hour drive to Ayr. I booked two rooms at a Premier Inn close to Ayr racecourse, and at 7am me, Pete, Tim and his eldest son, Oliver, were on the road to the land of Rabbie Burns.

It was a beautiful morning and, once beyond Manchester, the traffic thinned and we were able to enjoy the magnificent and unspoilt landscapes of the Lake District as we cruised towards Penrith, Carlisle and the Scottish border.

The mood in the car was buoyant. We were surprised and disappointed that Keep Busy had been declared so soon after running an excellent fifth in Friday's Group 1 Kings Stands Stakes at Royal Ascot. She was rated 108 and forecast to be the odds-on favourite for this afternoon's contest. We couldn't beat her. I was also hoping for a no-show from Jessica Harrington's Irish raider, Dickiedooda, on account of the quickish ground. She had finished third in the *Lansdown Stud Stakes* at Bath in April and backed that up by grabbing some more black type in a Cork listed race which elevated her official rating to 101. Wise Words, just in front of Dickiedooda at Bath, and possibly underestimated on a mark of 94, was the other opponent that Free Love would struggle to finish in front of on all known form and ratings.

In a handicap we would receive a whopping two stones from Keep Busy, a stone-and-a-half from Dickiedooda, and a full stone from Wise Words. Meeting these opponents off level weights was a tall order and Free Love's 40/1 price was an indication of the scale of the task. But we'd all been in the game long enough to know that these races rarely pan out exactly in line with the ratings. We needed one of the big three to blow out, to run well below par for some reason. The race might come too soon after Ascot for Keep Busy. Maybe Dickiedooda wouldn't travel well from Ireland. Wise Words had been sparingly campaigned over the last two seasons suggesting

234

she might not be the most robust horse in training. Perhaps something would resurface at Ayr preventing her from running her race. We needed Free Love to run right up to her best, and one or two others to disappoint, if we were to have any chance of grabbing third place which was the ceiling of our ambition.

We arrived at the racecourse shortly after midday and went for an early lunch in the elegant surroundings of the Western House Hotel which adjoins the course and is used to provide race-day catering for owners and trainers. An hour or so later we were at the track, soaking up the west coast sunshine and getting a feel for the racecourse and its facilities.

Although things were gathering pace in England, there was a more cautious approach north of the border. There were no indoor bars open and no owners' and trainers' lounge to use as a base for the afternoon. The total attendance was limited to one thousand and that included all the jockeys, trainers, stable staff, and anyone else who was there in a professional capacity.

Despite the sparse crowd, it was difficult to find anywhere to sit down and have a drink. It was table service only but the pop-up bar by the parade ring only had half a dozen wooden picnic tables clustered around it and all of those were taken. It was just as well that the weather was good and there was no need to find comfort indoors. There was none to be had.

As is invariably the case when Free Love runs, I took little interest in the other races. In any event, the supporting card was strangely subdued. Apart from a four-runner class 3 handicap for three-year-olds over seven furlongs, everything else was humdrum class five and six fare. Rather than study the form for the uninspiring earlier contests, we circled the picnic tables in predatory style, pouncing when one became free.

It gave us an hour in the sun to sip a beer and finalise our predictions. 'Right, gun to head, where are we going to finish?' I demanded of Pete, Tim and Oliver. There was a broad consensus; one 5th, two 6ths and a 7th. As usual, I was the first one to talk up our case for exceeding these perfectly sensible predictions. I had voted for a 6th place finish, but I was fairly confident that the trio of top-rated fillies wouldn't fill the first three places. One of them would blow-out and something more moderately rated would sneak into the frame and spoil the party. That's just the way these races go. And why couldn't the party pooper be Free Love? She came here in good form and had her ground. Yes, the high draw was a niggling question mark, but she had plenty else in her favour.

As soon as the runners in the fourth race crossed the line, we were on our way to the pre-parade ring to get our first glance of Free Love. Mick had sent two runners to Ayr, which helped with the transport costs associated with the 630-mile round trip. Vicki was the box driver and senior member of staff with overall responsibility for the operation. Erika was her number two. Theo drove up separately this morning.

Yes, Theo. The jockey booking may have raised a few eyebrows. Why give the ride to a three-pound claimer in a race where apprentices aren't permitted to use their allowances? That's the rule. Apprentices are welcome to ride in listed and group races, but they're prohibited from using their claim. It's not until they have ridden 95 career winners that the allowance disappears altogether.

Owners rarely give apprentices opportunities in races like the *Land O'Burns*. Why should they? Free Love was set to carry 9st 4lbs in today's contest and, with Theo unable to reduce the burden by 3lbs, it made sense to replace him with a senior jockey who had plenty of experience at this exalted level. In a handicap, Theo's 3lbs claim was handy, and you could argue that Free Love's narrow wins at Catterick and Windsor would have been narrow defeats if journeyman riders had been in the saddle rather than Theo.

But there's a reason why young jockeys get a weight allowance at the start of their careers. They're not as good as the others. It's a trade-off. Owners and trainers use inexperienced riders, pitching them into battle against the likes of Ryan Moore, William Buick and Frankie Dettori knowing that the combat is unequal, but the weight allowance helps to bridge the gap.

Theo must have known that being given the heave-ho was on the cards. I was pretty sure he'd never had an opportunity at listed level before and there was no reason why we should favour him over someone like Tom Marquand or Hollie Doyle. This was our one and only shot at black type, and we could be forgiven a bit of ruthlessness.

There were two major obstacles to 'operation ruthless'. First, it was obvious that many of the top jockeys were giving Ayr a swerve. Most of them had rides lined up at Newbury for the big Lambourn and Newmarket trainers. William Buick is unfailingly professional and polite but I'm not sure how he'd respond to an invitation to jump off Sheikh Mohammed's blue-blooded mounts at Newbury and fly up to Ayr to ride a 40/1 no-hoper for the North South Syndicate. If we wanted to grab the services of a senior rider, it would have to be one of the pilots already committed to an afternoon in Scotland. And guess what? The small band of top jockeys riding at Ayr – Danny Tudhope, Ben Curtis, Paul Mulrennan - already had mounts in the *Land O'Burns*.

The second obstacle was my sentimentality. I wanted Theo to have the ride and was relieved that there were few attractive alternatives. It meant that I didn't need to argue my case, which was a relief, as I could only offer that it would be nice to stick with the young man who had ridden Free Love to all four of her victories - as well as 20 of her defeats, admittedly.

Theo adored the mare and as the story neared its conclusion, I wanted him to have a crack at listed race glory. Who knows, it might be his one and only opportunity as well. It would probably take him until next spring to ride the 25 winners he needed to hit the magic figure of 95. He would then have 'ridden out his claim' and be required to compete against Messrs Buick, Dettori, and Moore on level terms.

That's when it really gets tough, and many young jockeys don't make it beyond that point. The rides dry up, the finances of driving to Chepstow for one unfancied ride don't make sense, and the dream dies. If that happened to Theo and, in two- or three-years' time, he was a jockey's valet, trainee farrier, or double-glazing salesman, at least he could say that he gave it a shot and on one balmy June afternoon in 2021 he had sat at the top table. 'Yes, I rode plenty of winners, four of them on a filly called Free Love. She also gave me my only ride in a listed race.' The thought of Theo saying something like that to his grandchildren appealed to the romantic in me.

Free Love kept us waiting for about 10 minutes before she finally appeared in the small pre-parade ring. When she arrived, led in by Erika, she looked in fantastic shape. As you would expect, her summer coat was in full bloom and positively gleaming in the bright mid-afternoon sunshine. Stars and chevrons had been trace-clipped onto her hindquarters. The finishing touch of a neatly plaited mane made her look like a supermodel.

I was beginning to feel mildly optimistic. With a run under her belt, and a good one at that, Free Love looked ready to run up to her best which was maybe a mark of around 85. It probably wasn't good enough to snatch third place, but it might be. I even had fanciful thoughts of her pulling off a shock victory but kept those delusional fancies to myself.

Theo was in his usual upbeat mood when he entered the paddock. I suppose you have to exude confidence in this game. Owners don't want long-faced jockeys telling them about the impossibility of the task ahead. 'Don't know why you've come all the way to Ayr to run in this. You've got no chance' was unlikely to be our jockey's opening gambit. Instead, we all played the usual charade and heard ourselves talking about the excellent seasonal debut, the good work the mare had been producing on the Langham gallops, how well she looked, the suitability of the ground, getting a good tow into the race, blah, blah, blah.

But today wasn't about winning. It was all about third place, and Theo knew that. He talked about trying to keep up with the pace without getting the mare out of her comfort zone. Then kick for home two out. He knew we couldn't beat Keep Busy if she ran anywhere near her best form, but that wasn't the objective. It was all about picking up some crumbs.

I walked past the small group of bookmakers as the ten runners cantered down to the start. There were about half a dozen layers. Most were local firms for whom the last 15 months had been a complete disaster. Betting activity couldn't be described as brisk, but at least the small crowd generated a bit of business, however modest. I had my obligatory fiver each way on Free Love at 50/1 and made my way onto the sparsely populated grandstand steps. It would take less than 60 seconds to find out our fate.

I felt the usual buzz of excitement and frisson of nervous anticipation, but there was something else. It's hard to put my finger on it, but it felt like the type of serenity that comes with completion. Nearly four years ago, Pete and I went to the Tattersalls sales and, with the help of Tom and Jackie Clover, bought a cheap yearling filly. A season of fun was the aim. A little win would be the icing on the cake. It was all about fulfilling the dream of racehorse ownership and doing it on the cheap. The adventure exceeded all expectations. Free Love racked up four wins and twice appeared on the card at York's Ebor meeting. Now, in her valedictory season, she was taking aim at a listed race. It was as if everything, and more, had been achieved.

The stalls opened, and the field made a level break. Free Love was travelling well at halfway and was a handy fifth or sixth no more than three lengths off the pace, which was being set by two outsiders, Machree and Mid Winster. At the two-furlong pole, Theo asked his partner for her effort. Free Love responded generously but never looked like bridging the gap. She kept on gamely to finish sixth, only 3¼ lengths behind the odds-on winner, Keep Busy.

Three-and-a-quarter lengths. It's a game of fine margins. More importantly, we were just two lengths off the third-placed horse, Mid Winster. Yes, the 81-rated, five-year-old mare, Mid Winster. Dickiedooda filled the runner-up spot, but Wise Words found traffic problems mid-race and could only finish fourth, ensuring that the 'big three' didn't mop up all the black type.

It was all so irritating. Free Love's high draw meant that she raced towards the stands' side rail while Mid Winster bowled along in the centre of the track. We were about two lengths behind her at halfway, and the same distance adrift at the finishing line. If only we'd been drawn low…but it was pointless indulging in such 'what ifs?'. And I was just kidding myself, anyway. Free Love broke well, had a clear passage, and ran her race hitting the line hard. Maybe it would have helped if they had gone a bit faster and we were drawn nearer to where the pace was. But here's the truth. The apple of my eye was 7-10lbs below what was needed to be competitive in this type of race. Yes, it was close, and you could run the same contest ten times on ten different days, and, on one occasion, Free Love might hit the frame. But we didn't have ten chances, just one, and we came up short.

With only the first-placed horse and her connections allowed in the winner's enclosure (a good example of the First Minister's determination to impose perfunctory, performative and pointless measures to tackle Covid) the race debrief was a bit of a rugby scrum with nine horses milling around on a small patch of turf beyond the paddock and close to the stables. The irony wasn't lost on me. Theo was pleased with the mare's effort. He said she gave him the best feel since her three-year-old days. To be beaten just over three lengths in such company was clearly a source of pride for our young jockey who departed by thanking us for keeping the faith and giving him the opportunity of riding in such a prestigious race.

We walked back to our table but, to nobody's surprise, saw that it had been snapped up by another group. There was nothing to do other than mill around aimlessly next to the small band of bookmakers who were pricing up the next race, an event in which I had no interest whatsoever. Tim sensed that I was disappointed.

'Cheer up mate. We've just been beaten three lengths in a listed race. It's a cracking effort that shows Free Love is in great form, and she's come back safe and well suggesting there will be plenty more days in the sun. You can't ask for much more than that.'

Tim was right, of course. It was a great effort, possibly even more creditable as Free Love had managed to lose a shoe again, this time her off-fore. However, as Theo was oblivious to the loss, I don't suppose it had any impact on the outcome. No, I wasn't disappointed. I felt proud that our ten-thousand guinea purchase had, not for the first time, punched above her weight, but the day was tinged with an inexplicable sadness. Maybe it was the realisation that things were coming to an end, or perhaps it was the final confirmation that any dream of success in top handicaps and black type races was at last extinguished. We'd given £50k class 2 handicaps a go and now we'd had our pop at a listed race. All the evidence, and there was enough of it, pointed in only one direction; however hard little Free Love tried, she was what she was, a genuine sprint handicapper rated somewhere in the low 80s. It had taken me a long time to accept that truth.

3 Here Comes the Summer

(Doncaster, 2ⁿᵈ July 2021)

Tuesday 29th June 2021

Ayr felt like an experience from another era as I booted up my laptop in readiness to see how the handicapper had assessed last week's *Land O'Burns Stakes*. Keep Busy was left on 108 with the runner-up, Dickiedooda, also untouched on 101. But there was no great movement elsewhere either. Mid Winster was moved up only four to 85 despite finishing within touching distance of two much more highly rated opponents, and Free Love was left alone on 80.

The assessor's message was, that in a relatively slowly run race, the form couldn't be taken that literally. You could make a good case for Free Love going up two or three, but that would be both flattering *and* unfair. Being left on 80 was what I had expected.

Mid Winster's heroics still stuck in the craw. She had an incredibly similar profile to Free Love. She had won three from 24 before Ayr racing off marks mostly in the low 80s. She briefly reached the dizzy height of 90 and ran off that rating when six places behind Free Love in the big apprentice handicap at York on Ebor day 2019. Free Love was on 89. Who would have thought that two years later the fillies would cross swords again at listed level?

Before I composed my update to the others, I glanced at last week's photos from Ayr. The images would scream 'summer 2021' for many years to come. The masks confirmed the ongoing pandemic, and wearing sandals with my linen summer suit was a reminder of my achilles tendon problem which showed no sign of improvement. Other pictures captured our night out in Ayr. Like all good tourists, I had taken snaps of some of the town's more interesting features – the seafront and its sweeping esplanade, the soaring spire of the town hall, and the remnants of Oliver Cromwell's fortifications.

I like Ayr. It has a remote, old-world charm but, like many large British towns and cities, there is an air of optimism about the place. The streets are dotted with growing numbers of independent shops, modern bars, and restaurants with cosmopolitan menus. It feels like a place that is confident about its future. Having said that, our night in the town was a strange one. A curfew was still in place which meant last orders were at 9.30pm and all bars and restaurants were expected to be empty and locked up by 10pm. It was just late enough for small groups of Saltire-waving locals to watch Scotland's crucial group stage game against Croatia in the handful of pubs that chose to show it. We avoided those watering holes and kept tabs on progress via our phones. It was another gallant but unsuccessful effort from the Scots whose 3-1 defeat sent them crashing out of the European Championships.

I picked a few photos to send to the boys along with an update about our money. The assault on Ayr wasn't the financial disaster it could have been. Free Love picked up over £600 for finishing sixth which paid for the transport. She was a nose away from the £1,250 fifth prize which would have covered everything.

As I sorted out the pictures, I realised that, in a funny way, *The Land O'Burns* was one of the best racing experiences I've ever had. Sure, there had been obstacles to overcome, the trip for one. But Tim and Pete shared the driving and without them it would have been impossible for me to get there. There was the small crowd, the limited on-course facilities, the unsatisfactory paddock arrangements, and the 10pm curfew in town, but what a trip. I'd got over the pitiful handwringing about Free Love being 7-10lbs short of listed class. I had a share in a horse good enough to have a shot at the *Land O'Burns,* and I was lucky enough to be there with friends I had known for more than four decades. What was there to moan about?

One image I had already shared was the photo Theo took of Free Love (or Clover as she is known in the yard) the day after her Ayr exploits. The mare was spreadeagled on a bed of straw, enjoying a deserved lie-in. I knew how she felt. I was exhausted after our odyssey and, for that reason, the two sprint handicap entries for Doncaster on 2nd July took me by surprise.

Perhaps Mick thought it was a case of striking while the iron was hot. After all, he's the one who sees the mare every day and is best placed to make a judgement about her wellbeing. Nevertheless, we all thought that our next run was likely to be in 3-4 weeks' time. The gap between Ayr and Doncaster was 10 days.

Friday 2nd July 2021

During the last few days, the WhatsApp group fizzed with lively opinions about the rights and wrongs of going to Doncaster. In the end we decided to leave it to Mick. If he felt Free Love was in good shape, we'd run. It was then a case of expressing a preference for which race. All came down in favour of the class 2 handicap which had attracted a small initial entry and looked like ending up as a single-figure field. The other race was a class 4 event restricted to fillies and mares, but it looked competitive, and the likely favourite was Mid Winster who would be able to run off her old mark of 81 as the weights were framed before Tuesday's reassessments were made.

A couple of days ago, Mick worked Free Love with the 86-rated Nigel Nott. The video clip sent by Louise showed the pair breezing up the all-weather gallop. Mick felt our mare remained in good shape and was happy to aim at the class 2 race as it meant a low weight in what was likely to be a small field. By 10.30am on

Wednesday, we knew that the *Sky Sports Racing Sky 415 Handicap* had a field of seven. Free Love was allotted 8st 8lbs, receiving weight from all.

It was a rare miss for me. For months Jennie and I had tried to pin down our three children on a date when we could get together for a long weekend to celebrate a return to normality. Even though 'freedom day' had been pushed back to 19th July, we went ahead with the first weekend in the month as it seemed to be the only date everyone could do this side of Christmas. As the runners for the *Sky Sports Racing Sky 415 Handicap* cantered down to the start, I was unhitching our caravan at Kelling Heath campsite, a beautiful expanse of woodland perched above Sheringham on the North Norfolk coast.

I temporarily abandoned our ageing two-berth Sterling Europa and found a patch of shade under a line of shrubs that marked the border of our pitch. I'd made it, but only just. I knew our holiday itinerary left no room for me to make a diversion to Doncaster, but I was determined to watch the race live even if it meant pulling over into a lay-by with the caravan. I'm sure it's not something that Sheikh Mohammed or Sir Andrew Lloyd Webber have ever been forced to do.

The opposition was talented and battle-hardened. Two of the older horses were serial class 2 performers with winning form at that level, and a couple of the three-year-olds boasted placed efforts in listed and group races when juveniles. But in handicaps, weight is the leveller, and the public came for the lightly weighted Free Love snapping up the early 12/1 and forcing her price down to 6/1 at the off.

I was confident of a decent run. We were drawn bang in the middle of the seven runners so Theo could go whichever way he wanted. The run at Ayr and subsequent gallop at Langham suggested Free Love was in good shape and, racing off a mark of 80, which was six below her last winning mark achieved at Windsor on similarly quick ground, what wasn't there to like about her chances? There was just the nagging thought that this was coming soon enough after a hard race at Ayr. I kept seeing the image of Free Love, the morning after the *Land O'Burns,* sprawled on her bed of straw, one eye half-open looking at Theo taking a picture of her on his mobile phone. 'Leave me alone. I'm knackered after all those hours in the horsebox. Carrying you on my back while trying to keep up with those ridiculously fast friends was hardly relaxation therapy either.' If only they could talk.

Jennie, Joe and I were crouched in the shadow of the laurels, eyes glued to the screen of my mobile phone as Free Love pinged the lid and quickly established a lead. The three-year-old, Nomadic Way, went with her but after a furlong the pair were over a length clear of the others and Theo was able to shift right and bag the nearside rail. It was looking good. Theo was dictating matters and his partner was travelling comfortably. This was no break-neck early pace. We looked to be controlling the race from the front.

At halfway, Free Love was bowling along a neck ahead of Nomadic Way with Muker making a move on the outside. The others were keeping their powder dry, but I was happy. In a relatively slowly run race the best place to be is near the front. Free Love should have gallons of petrol left in the tank given the even early pace and I was hopeful that when Theo kicked for home, our little sprinter would find plenty.

The two-furlong pole came into view and Theo asked the mare for her effort. But instead of shooting a length clear, there was no immediate response. Free Love didn't weaken, she just plodded on at the same pace, gradually losing places as she dropped back through the field to finish last behind the facile winner, Jawwaal.

We were only beaten four lengths in total so you couldn't say it was a terrible effort, but it was devastatingly disappointing as far as I was concerned. This was way below how she had performed at Ayr. We had been closer to Keep Busy (108) and Dickiedooda (101) off level weights than we were to the 94-rated Jawwaal who conceded a whole stone into the bargain. I know it's dangerous to compare a listed race for fillies and mares with a class 2 handicap for experienced speedsters (the other six runners at Doncaster were all strapping geldings), but the two performances looked poles apart.

Mick Appleby called within minutes of the race's conclusion. He felt the ground was too quick for the mare. It may have been her preferred surface when she was younger and free of the foot problems that had recently emerged, but Mick advised that we looked for easier going in future. He also conceded that the race may have come too soon after Ayr even though Free Love looked in good order at home and ready to race. You never know for sure until you run them. If only they could talk.

Theo's call was hot on the heels of Mick's. He echoed our trainer's thoughts about the going. He didn't think the mare let herself down on the ground as she did on slightly easier going at Ayr. When pressed, he conceded that Free Love may have needed a bit more time to recover from her arduous trip to Scotland. But his main point was that Free Love's best chance to get back in the winner's enclosure was down in her own class and on ground with a little cut.

'In her own class.' What did that mean? Class 4 handicaps at Yarmouth and Leicester? The evidence was stacking up. Although Free Love had won a class 3 and gone close in a couple of others – most noticeably when losing by a pixel to Glamorous Anna at Windsor – she had been well beaten in all her attempts at a higher level. You couldn't argue with the facts. She'd held her form for a couple of years, neither improving nor regressing in any significant way. As a result, she'd become hard to win with. The losing run had steadily mounted and now hit 19. Sure, she's been in the first four on nine of those 19 occasions, but we needed a win, so perhaps it was time to abandon lofty ambitions and focus on winning a race of any description.

Saturday 24th July 2021

It was time for a visit to Langham to finalise plans for our next race. Mick reported Free Love was a little jarred after Doncaster, a term used in horseracing to describe a bit of temporary soreness usually caused by firm ground. He gave the mare an easy time for a bit and didn't put her back on the gallops until a fortnight later. In the meantime, the handicapper had at last shown a sliver of compassion by dropping Free Love 3lbs to 77. It was the biggest single downward adjustment made during the mare's 19-race losing sequence and was surely a winning mark.

It was a dull, nondescript morning when Trevor and I set off for Mick's at 7am sharp, but we were grateful for a break in the weather which had produced blistering heat all over the country from the second week in July onwards. The soaring temperatures weren't evident during our long weekend in Norfolk, but it was warm enough to be out and about and swimming in the sea. The following week was lift-off with most of the UK experiencing thermometer readings in the high twenties. That even included the Forest of Bowland in rural Lancashire.

We were there to see the son of two of our closest friends marry his fiancé in the church next to the Whitewell Inn, an old hunting lodge at the very heart of the forest. Not in their wildest dreams could the bride and groom have anticipated the unrelenting sunshine and dry Mediterranean heat that marked their special day.

I don't suppose there are many occasions when you can sip champagne on the banks of the river Hodder without the need of an umbrella, but this was one of them.

Given the stress involved in organising their big day, the new Mr and Mrs Tuohy thoroughly deserved their slice of luck with the weather. At various points in the lead-up to the wedding, the event was going to be postponed, restricted to 30 guests, or allowed to go ahead without stipulations. As the occasion fell two days before the new date for the removal of all restrictions (19th July), the wedding breakfast was limited to 30 guests, but the church was more accommodating allowing double that number to attend the service. The half-masked congregation was even allowed to sing a few hymns. Afterwards, everyone gathered on the lawned area between the hotel and the river for speeches and toasts, turning what looked like a difficult day a few weeks ago into a perfect one.

After the nuptial celebrations, Jennie and I moved on to Arnside in Cumbria for a couple of days. If anything, it became even hotter, and trying to find a patch of shade at Cartmel races on the Monday was as difficult as unearthing winners. It was my first visit to the picturesque jumps track which nestles on the southern edge of the Lake District, but it didn't disappoint. It was 'freedom day' take two and a large crowd of local old hands turned up ready to picnic and party in their pre-booked grass parking bays.

We finished our northern jaunt with a swim in Lake Windermere and a flying visit to my brother and his family in Altrincham. Jennie had waved goodbye to work when she left her part-time job with Link Age Southwark at the beginning of June and her feet hadn't touched the ground in the seven weeks since. Her retirement coincided with significant easing of Covid restrictions, so we were out and about a lot catching up with family and friends and just pleasing ourselves.

By contrast, Trevor was still hard at it. Unsurprisingly, he had plenty to tell me about the continuing impact of the pandemic on the life of his church. Things were getting easier, but it had been a long and exhausting haul, and it was hard to know if the end was in sight. Despite rising infections rates and dire warnings from some parts of the scientific community, the Government decided to press on with its policy of opening everything up in England. It was as if Boris Johnson was a punter who had decided to put every last penny of his available cash on a horse called Fully Vaccinated.

The journey passed quickly and we arrived at Langham in good time to see Free Love gallop up the all-weather strip with the 91-rated Zim Baby, a four-year-old filly with a profile not dissimilar to Free Love's except in one crucial respect – she had managed to snatch some black type when out-running her 40/1 odds in a listed race at Doncaster last November. Mind you, that earned her a 10lbs hike to 90 and since then her losing streak was mounting. Be careful what you wish for.

Free Love appeared to work well, but all you get from these pieces of exercise are indications of well-being. I remember watching the first horse in which I had a tiny share, Clear Daylight, gallop with Rising Cross, a filly who had been placed in the 2006 Epsom Oaks. It was the summer of 2007 and Clear Daylight was an unraced two-year-old trained by John Best at his base near the sleepy village of Hucking in Kent. Our Daylami colt was a month or two away from making his seasonal debut and Heart of the South had organised a stable visit for any of the 20 owners who were able to make it. It was the first time I had been in a racing stable, and I remember my child-like excitement as I watched Clear Daylight match strides with a filly who had been placed in an English Classic.

I am sure it was all good PR as far as John Best and Heart of the South were concerned. I now know that most thoroughbreds have enough natural pace to keep up with each other if they're asked to gallop below full-tilt and for a limited distance. The wheat is sorted from the chaff on the racecourse which is the only place where horses are asked for maximum effort. With the benefit of hindsight, it was no surprise that Clear Daylight was able to keep pace with his illustrious work companion, who was probably doing no more than helping the youngster with his education, but at the time I thought it was evidence of the coming of the second Pegasus. It didn't take long for Clear Daylight to prove to the world that he was useless, a fifth-placed effort in a class 6 nursery handicap at Kempton being the closest he managed to sprouting wings.

It's the negatives that arise from early morning gallops that are likely to be more informative. The work riders know their horses and they can tell if they're not moving with their usual verve and elan. I guess that's what trainers mean when they say that such-and-such a star 'failed to sparkle' in a recent piece of work and will miss his big race target. As far as Erika was concerned, Free Love felt great and she couldn't wait for the chance to ride her in a fortnight's time.

About a week ago, I sounded out Mick about an apprentice handicap at Haydock which was part of the new Sky Bet Sunday Series aimed at widening racing's appeal. The three meetings were late afternoon starts covered live by ITV. All sorts of initiatives and novelties were planned in the hope of attracting new customers on course and in front of goggleboxes at home. It was a worthy venture, but the feature that seemed most laudable to me was the stumping up of decent prize money for ordinary horses. All the races were class 4 0-85 handicaps with a minimum of £25k total prize money. That's three times the average for such contests. The conditions of the Haydock race meant that Theo couldn't take the ride. It was part of an apprentice series in which only jockeys who had ridden fewer than 20 winners were eligible to participate.

It was clear that Mick already had this target in mind when we spoke to him as the horses from the last exercise lot were washed down watched by a smattering of doting owners. Apparently, Erika was the series leader and a good showing on Free Love would seal the title for her. It was perfect. Clover's regular work rider would get the chance to ride her favourite horse in public in what would surely be a decent chance for us to end that long losing run.

Trevor and I returned home via a low-key meeting at Newmarket. It was King George day and nearly every racegoer paused at 3.35pm to gaze at the big screens and witness the Derby winner, Adayar, repel the challenges of Mishriff and Love in the manner of a top-class racehorse. Trevor won a packet on a lucky 15, the few remaining diaphanous clouds disappeared leaving the July course bathed in sunshine, and everything seemed good with the world.

4 False Step

(Windsor, 16ᵗʰ August 2021)

Wednesday 4th August 2021

July finished in a blaze of optimism. Jennie and I celebrated our 31st wedding anniversary with a trip to Glorious Goodwood and a flying visit the following day to Hastings where we took in an exhibition of British seaside art at the new Hastings Contemporary gallery.

It felt that the good times were rolling again as we wandered through the champagne bars dotted around the lawned area behind the paddock of the elegant Sussex racecourse. A freshening breeze had chased away the threat of rain and a large crowd was enjoying fabulous sport at one of the most spectacularly beautiful racecourses on the planet. There was little or no evidence of what we had all endured for the last 16 months.

Hastings felt nearly there, but not quite. The gallery insisted on masks for everyone, which was an inconvenience rather than an outrage and I was happy to go along with any local rules that made people feel safe and more relaxed about restarting their lives.

There were other signs that we still had a way to go. Trying to book a table at a decent restaurant for our anniversary dinner proved to be more difficult than I had anticipated. The pent-up demand to do something as simple as enjoy a meal out meant that most of the good eateries were fully booked. Walking through the old town after we had seen enough of Ravilious, Lowry and Hepworth, we discovered another reason why there was so much pressure on restaurant covers. Pubs and bistros displayed notices explaining that their kitchens were shut or operating limited opening hours due to staff shortages. The hospitality industry, which had been shut down or severely restricted for the duration of the pandemic, was clearly struggling to recruit now that establishments were allowed to offer a full service again.

Although infection rates remained relatively high, they weren't matched by a sharp rise in hospital admissions which was proof that the vaccination programme was having a significant impact. There were still those who seemed stubbornly resistant about getting a jab, many of them young and confident that the virus didn't pose a threat to their own health. I had gained some interesting first-hand insights into the thinking of young men when I made my visit to the prison last week to perform my voluntary duties.

It was my turn to do the rounds for the Independent Monitoring Board at the unfortunately named HMP Isis, a prison for 18–25-year-olds. I began visiting again in April when I was able to drive again following my tendon operation, but it was hard work collecting evidence for the weekly report which IMB members composed on a rota basis. The prisoners were still spending long periods of time in their cells, so it was difficult to strike up the type of informal conversations which are so useful for finding out how things are really going. As you can imagine, their views were often at odds with the official line presented by the prison's governor.

There wasn't a great deal going on as I wandered over from the houseblocks to the multi-faith centre. Before I had a chance to talk to the chaplains about how they were supporting their incarcerated flocks, I bumped into two young men who were busily engaged in their cleaning orderly roles. It was a chance to pick their brains about the vaccination rates in the prison which were depressingly low. They needed little persuasion to lean on their brooms for five minutes to give me their thoughts.

One had already been jabbed. In calm and measured tones, he set out the case in favour of vaccination, touching on themes of personal safety and social responsibility. He was articulate and engaging. Although I never ask, my curiosity was almost getting the better of me. What had this impressive young man done to earn a custodial sentence? It seemed crazy that somebody like this was in a prison.

His work companion offered a contrary view. He had no intention of being vaccinated. He was young and felt in no personal danger from the virus. In any event, he was sure he had already caught it last year. It was a plausible enough stance, but I wasn't expecting what followed. He went on to explain that the whole vaccination programme was designed by the government to inject citizens with controlling drugs that could alter their DNA. I was taken aback by somebody espousing this conspiracy theory to my face. I knew it was doing the rounds on Twitter, but I didn't think for one moment that I'd meet anyone who seriously believed such far-fetched drivel. In any event, what did he think the government wanted to change him into? A law-abiding citizen, perhaps?

That was last week. Today I was more interested in what everyone thought about the entries for Haydock on Sunday and who intended to go. Free Love was certainly on track. This morning's video showed her working enthusiastically with Case Key, one of Mick's run-of-the-mill sprint handicappers. The going at Haydock was currently good but the forecast was unsettled. The consensus was that we should run, whatever the weather threw at us. It was too good an opportunity to miss.

Sunday 8th August 2021

My alarm sounded at 7am but I resisted the temptation to hit the snooze button and, seconds later, I was sat upright in bed perusing the Racing Post app on my phone. The weather had been dreadful in the north-west for the last couple of days, and yesterday's televised racing from Haydock looked like hard work; tired horses and mud-flecked jockeys fighting out slow motion finishes. The official going description was soft, but before the end of the meeting it was heavy, and more downpours were on the way. I checked every weather website last night desperately seeking favourable forecasts, but they were all sure that there would be further rain. They just disagreed about how much.

The ground would be terrible, but at least it would be loose and Free Love would be able to get through it with a bit of luck. It wouldn't be dissimilar to what she encountered last October at Nottingham when she chased home Wrenthorpe in a competitive class 3 handicap. The betting public seemed to share my optimism. Last night, Free Love was a 14/1 shot to lead the field of 15 home. This morning she was no more than half that price.

There was no news on the RP app about an early morning inspection at Haydock, but I was sure the clerk of the course would be out in his wellies taking a good look at conditions. If his going stick and dog disappeared into the squelching mud never to return, then I guess it would be game over.

It was 7.37am when my phone buzzed. It was a text from Mick. 'Morning Tony. Haydock has been abandoned.' The course had phoned the trainers first to make sure that nobody started to travel unnecessarily. The bad news cascaded down to owners and within an hour the Racing Post put punters in the picture.

I usually talk myself out of the prospect of bad news and this was no exception. Even though I had seen the Met Office's satellite images of banks of rain sweeping over Liverpool and Manchester, I somehow thought that we might get lucky. It was a ridiculous notion. Who needed weather apps anyway? Tim was no more than an hour's drive from Haydock, and he messaged me last night to say that it hadn't stopped tipping down for 24 hours. That was the clue.

It was the side of global warming and climate change that nobody wanted to talk about – the impact on owners of 0-85 handicappers with delicate feet. A fortnight ago it was 30 degrees, and the ground was rock hard. Now it was ark building weather.

I spent the next hour swapping messages with the boys and talking to the Kirkland Hotel to see if they could do anything about the pre-paid rooms that four of us and our partners had booked. We had also reserved a dinner table for eight and, for the last week, I had fancifully imagined a scene of carefree conviviality where a bottle or two of champagne oiled the celebrations or eased the pain. In a year when so much had been cancelled, banned or severely restricted, the disappointment of not meeting up with old friends was even greater than the loss of a good opportunity for our horse.

Tuesday 10th August 2021

We needed a run for Free Love. The flat turf season was nearly five months old, and our sprinter had managed just three appearances. This was meant to be the year that we put the nightmare of the pandemic behind us and enjoyed our modest ownership experience in the company of our family and friends on racecourses bustling with crowds. 2020 had been a write-off. Free Love had managed just eight runs (two of them backend appearances on Southwell's fibresand) and, on all occasions, the paying public was absent, and owners restricted in the numbers allowed to attend. It was miserable.

It was hard to believe that there had been a weekend deluge as I walked across the allotments in brilliant sunshine on my way to pick up a few bits and pieces from the Tesco Express on Dartford Road. I sauntered through a cavalcade of late summer colours and scents. My senses were almost overwhelmed by fragrant rosemary and lavender, vibrant sunflowers, ripening tomatoes, hedgerows drooping under the weight of blackberries, and poppies dancing in the gentlest of summer breezes.

This bucolic bliss didn't stop me from fiddling with my phone as I made my way through the plots. The entries for a class 4 handicap at Windsor on Monday evening closed at noon and we were unanimous that we should go for it. Although the Racing Post reported on Monday that discussions had already began about rescheduling Haydock's abandoned card, which was an integral part of the Sky Bet Sunday Series, the tentative new date was 12th September. If we waited for that it would be more than two months between runs, which was preposterous. Free Love was a class 4 sprint handicapper, not Stradivarius.

It was nearly midday when I returned from my errand. Half an hour ago, Free Love was one of just six entries for Windsor. As the seconds ticked down to closing, the BHA website confirmed that the total had only reached ten. It looked like quick compensation could be near at hand.

Monday 16th August 2021

There were six declared runners for the *Visit @ edengrovelondon-road.co.uk Handicap*. Two of them were three-year-olds – The Princes Poet and Country Carnival – which was a little disconcerting as at this time of year younger, improving horses often seem to have the edge on thoroughly exposed campaigners which, I suppose, is how Free Love could now be described. Nevertheless, we looked to have a decent chance off our current mark which was the lowest for well over two years.

Only yesterday it was confirmed that the abandoned Haydock meeting would be moved to Sunday 12th September to preserve the Sky Bet races that were lost. That meant an ideal gap of nearly four weeks between Windsor and Haydock. Even if we won tonight, we'd still get into the Sunday Series race as it was hard to imagine the handicapper raising Free Love above 85 even if she bolted up throwing handsprings.

Things were looking up. Last week, I was downcast about missed opportunities. Haydock had gone down the drain and the big sprint handicap for fillies and mares on the first day of York's Ebor meeting had attracted only 20 entries. The highest rated was Caroline Dale on a modest mark of 94 which was way short of what Free Love was up against last year when she was sixth behind listed and group race performers Lady In France and Keep Busy. This year's renewal looked no more competitive than a decent class 3 handicap.

If Haydock had gone ahead and Free Love had won or run well, I was going to suggest a speculative entry for York which would have only cost us £75. Considering the total prize money for the race had been elevated to pre-pandemic levels and now stood at £70k, it would surely have been worth a look. After last Sunday's abandonment, I didn't even mention the York race. It would have meant choosing between that and Windsor and, given Free Love's dismal record on the Knavesmire, I thought there was little point floating the idea. In any event, I reminded myself that after four unsuccessful attempts, I had taken an oath, signed in blood, that Free Love would never again set hoof on Yorkshire's premier track. Unless the prize money looked good.

There was also the Racing League card at Windsor in another week's time, but we were excluded from that strange initiative which tried to foist the razzamatazz of a team competition onto a sport which is so obviously all about individuals. I couldn't see punters clamouring to buy scarves and replica tops in the colours of Team Swish, Newmarket Red or Goat Racing. The idea of supporting a racing team in the same way that loyal fans follow their favourite football club didn't make sense to me. To be fair to the organisers, they attracted new sponsors which helped guarantee that Racing

League contests had prize money pots of £50k. Given that they were all 0-90 class 3 handicaps, owners could hardly pull faces at the new initiative or, if they did, they made sure it was behind the sponsors' backs.

But I knew from our last stable visit that we weren't in the frame. Around 20 trainers had signed up for the Racing League including Mick Appleby who was one of four trainers in Team Arena. The three jockeys were Paul Mulrennan, Danny Tudhope and Cam Hardie, and the joint managers, who were responsible for selecting the horses, were Racing TV presenter Chris Dixon and his brother Martin, two of Mick's biggest owners. Free Love didn't even make the subs' bench.

Unsurprisingly, those sitting snugly within the new Racing League community urged everyone to get behind this exciting and innovative project. However, those jockeys, trainers and owners who had not been picked saw a brave new world that was elitist and exclusive. I had mixed feelings about it all, but when I learned from Mick that Free Love hadn't been put forward for the team, I became committed to making sure the organisers were the first ones up against the wall after the revolution.

Ok, so even if the £25k Sky Bet race at Haydock had been postponed, the £70k York handicap bypassed, and the £50k Racing League wasn't accessible to our caste, there was still tonight's *Visit @ edengrove-londonroad.co.uk Handicap* which was worth four-and-a-half grand to the winner with £300 appearance money on offer for the sixth and final finisher. More importantly, it was the first time in ages that I would be attending a racecourse completely free of the restrictions that had become a way of life nearly 18 months ago. Shishkin's demolition of the opposition in Huntingdon's Sidney Banks memorial Novices' Hurdle in February 2020 was the last time I had experienced carefree, pre-pandemic racing.

And that was the whole point of this evening. I had two main priorities when we decided to keep Free Love in training for one final season. One was to have a crack at black type, but I knew that was ambitious and it wouldn't be the end of the world if we gave it a swerve. The other was all about putting the fun back into the ownership experience and, as this was our first run since the government removed all restrictions and social distancing requirements on 19th July, it was mission accomplished. Hopefully, this was the beginning of uninhibited late summer visits to racecourses up and down the country to see our pocket rocket in action.

The early morning market had difficulty in identifying a favourite, but I didn't hang around waiting to see how the prices were fluctuating. I kept it simple and had £30 on the nose at 7/1. I was sure Free Love would be shorter than that, but I wasn't bothered if she wasn't. My interest in betting was waning and my attitude now was to have a bet early and get it out of the way or not bother punting at all.

Erika was in the saddle. We decided that it would make up for the disappointment she must have felt for missing out at Haydock. Sticking with Erika would be just reward for all the work she had done with the mare at Langham.

Free Love looked relaxed and a picture of good health as she ambled around the parade ring led by Mick's travelling head lad, Nigel. The money continued to come for our mare and as post time neared, she was a well-supported 3/1 shot with only Hans Solo Berger preferred in the betting. We all agreed that this was our chance. The going was described as good to firm but the horses in earlier races were leaving clear prints on the turf, and the race times suggested that conditions were no faster than good. There could be no excuses on account of the ground, and we even had a plum inside draw. Surely, on a track where Free Love had won, and with plenty of other cards falling in the right place, we had been dealt a winning hand that would eradicate that long losing sequence.

When the starter's flag fell and Free Love broke smartly to dispute the lead with Hans Solo Berger, things looked to be going to plan. Erika was travelling ominously well at halfway and although it was only a small field, the action seemed to be on the nearside where Free Love had bagged the rail. Approaching the final furlong, Erika gave her partner a tap behind the saddle and, with her head set low, it looked like Free Love was about to put the race to bed. But there was no immediate increase in the neck advantage she still held and, with 100 yards to run, she drifted off the rail allowing The Princes Poet to come with a late run to land the spoils. Even more alarming was our mare's weak finish which saw her surrender two further places in that draining final half furlong. We went from likely winner to well beaten fourth in less than ten seconds.

I couldn't conceal my disappointment as I went to get the debrief from Erika. All the earlier nonsense about restricting numbers in the winner's enclosure had been swept away, so at least the chat with our jockey would take place in the area designated for horses who had made the frame, or so I thought. When Free Love was no more than 20 yards away, Erika hopped off. I walked over to her and asked if there was a problem, but we all know what it means when a jockey dismounts at the end of a race. It's invariably because they think the horse isn't sound.

Erika confirmed that Free Love didn't feel quite right. The huddle of concerned owners was soon joined by a smartly dressed official sporting a BHA lanyard.

'Are you the owners?' she enquired. We nodded in sombre unison. 'We're going to ask the racecourse vet to examine your mare. It's just routine, but we feel she was rather disappointing.'

'*You're* disappointed,' I replied. 'That's well below what we expected. Our jockey felt something was amiss after the race, but she didn't mention anything about feeling a problem during it.'

Erika had gone to weigh-in so wasn't on hand to provide any further information. The travelling head lad, Nigel, had taken over and was holding on to Free Love when the vet joined the party. He explained that he'd conduct an examination and arrange for a sample to be taken. If we were happy to hang on for ten minutes, he'd report back to us with his findings.

Patrick, Pete, Tim, Trevor and I exchanged thoughts while we waited for the vet to do his stuff. We were all down in the dumps about the outcome. Maybe something had gone wrong during the final stages of the race and Free Love was in pain, which would account for her tame finish. She went from travelling like the winner to a struggling also-ran in a matter of a few strides. In some ways it would be a relief to have an explanation other than she simply wasn't good enough to land a blow in in a class 4 handicap.

While we were still conducting our bleak discussions the vet returned with news. Free Love was lame. It was her near-fore. It was difficult to tell how bad it was but, in terms of how much pain she appeared to be in, the vet said that on a sliding scale of one to ten, he'd plump for something no higher than two. He told us he'd give Free Love a painkiller and apply a bandage to the affected fetlock joint to make sure that our mare was comfortable for her journey home. We thanked him for his efforts and wandered back to the owners' and trainers' lounge where there was a subdued mood during our complimentary meal. It wasn't the joyous return of 'normal' racing that I had spent 18 months anticipating.

Wednesday 18th August 2021
Two days after Windsor, I was at York for the first day of the Ebor

meeting. Twelve months ago, I witnessed the International Stakes from an eerily empty and silent grandstand before watching Free Love finish a disappointing seventh in the class 2 fillies' and mares' sprint handicap. What a difference a year had made. Today it was business as usual with around 25,000 ebullient, smartly attired spectators thronging the bars, concourses and viewing areas. Pandemic? What pandemic?

I love York. I've always found it appallingly difficult to find winners there, but the sport is invariably top-drawer. When I first started going to the Ebor meeting in the early 1980s, the bookmakers displayed their prices in chalk, and after striking a bet I would walk away from the bookie's pitch clutching a small, numbered ticket no bigger than a business card. I remember squeezing a stamp and a short message onto a losing one and sending it to Jennie as a makeshift postcard. It got there and must have been one of the most expensive 'wish you were here' messages ever dispatched.

As I stared at the electronic boards displaying the odds for the first race, I was aware that although the technology had changed, the scale of the task remained reassuringly familiar. The opener was a red-hot 22-runner sprint handicap for horses rated 0-105. It was impossible, but I somehow managed to get my each-way punt into the frame and, thanks to a solitary winner in the two-mile handicap (I managed to talk myself out of backing the impressive International Stakes winner, Mishriff), I kept my head above water on day one.

After the racing finished, I was making my way to the Winning Post pub when Mick called. I wasn't expecting good news, so it was no surprise when I didn't get it. He told me that the vet had examined Free Love and taken a scan and X-ray. Someone from the Oakham Veterinary Hospital would call me tomorrow to give a full diagnosis. All Mick could say at this stage was that the problem appeared to be with the sesamoid bone, but only close examination of the scans would reveal the extent of the damage.

It didn't sound like Free Love would be racing again any time soon. In my heart, I knew it was almost certainly the end of her racing career. I had hoped that a banged joint or tweaked muscle was the culprit which would have meant a few weeks on the easy list, but Mick's call confirmed my worst fears.

The news was in line with the observations of one of my eagle-eyed racing friends, Paul Davis, who noticed Free Love stumble as she approached the furlong pole on Monday night. Paul watched the race on television from his Gloucestershire home and sent a text urging me to have a closer look at the race replay. I didn't see it at the time but when I watched the recording of the race at home later that evening, I could clearly see the false step Free Love took just at the point where Erika asked for her final effort. That had to be it. The mare's falter was almost imperceptible but the more I played the replay the clearer it became. That's where the damage was done, and Free Love's weak finish could only be attributed to the pain and discomfort she must have felt immediately after she injured herself.

Thursday 19th August 2021

Jennie and I were up and sipping our first mug of tea in the cosy warmth of our touring caravan when my mobile phone disturbed our peace. As was the case two years ago, we were using Moor End Farm camping site in Acaster Malbis as a base for a short holiday in 'God's Own County'. It was Emily from the Oakham Veterinary Hospital. Fortunately, I'd done my homework and now knew where sesamoid bones were located on racehorses. Apparently, they are at the back of the fetlock which is the joint immediately above the foot; the human equivalent of the ankle, I guess.

Emily's prognosis was crystal clear. Free Love had fractured her near-fore sesamoid. She didn't think that an operation to screw the detached piece of bone back in place was viable due to its small, wafer-thin nature. Instead, she recommended a more conservative management of the injury: bandaging the joint and restricting the patient to box rest for 6-8 weeks. That should be enough time for the fracture to naturally fuse. Once fully recovered, Free Love would be able to walk and trot free of pain. It would allow her to have a new career as a broodmare, but her riding and racing days were over.

I didn't message the others straight away as I would be seeing a couple of them later this afternoon. We had arranged a bit of a gathering for ladies' day. Yesterday it was just the boys doing battle with the Knavesmire bookies but today was a more social affair with partners joining in the fun. The chance to dress up and sip champagne in York's County enclosure wasn't hard to sell. Patrick and Kieran were attending, so it would be a chance to break the bad news to them in person before calling or messaging the others.

Nobody was surprised by the news. Mick's feedback during the two days after the race had been gloomy, and the vet was only confirming what he and everybody else feared. Even Theo's chirpy optimism deserted him during a sombre telephone call on Tuesday evening. Theo had seen Free Love at the stable on the morning after the race and thought it looked like the end of the road. Now I knew for certain that he was right.

5 Bolt from the Blue

Friday 3rd September 2021

Nearly ten months after my achilles tendon operation, I was under the knife again. In June I was referred to the Plastics team at St Thomas's Hospital. The recommendation was that I should go back to square one and have the sutures from the original procedure removed because they were almost certainly harbouring a bacterial infection. Everything needed to be taken out and a skin graft would be required as well.

I limped through the whole of the summer waiting for my date. As it was an operation that had gone critically wrong, I was told that I would be seen quickly and that the impact of the pandemic shouldn't hold things up too much. It wasn't a case of being thrown onto the ever-growing waiting list for elective surgery.

When I saw the consultant in June, he told me that he was confident that I would be seen before the end of the summer. He had one very urgent case to deal with – described as a man with two black feet – but after that he thought he could get through his caseload in 6-8 weeks and that included me. I was grateful for small mercies. My corrective surgery was seen as routine rather than urgent and I wasn't being lumped together with the double amputee.

As far as Free Love's health was concerned, nothing much had happened during the last fortnight. The mare stayed with Mick at Langham for the first part of her period of box rest but, at the end of August, she was moved to a small nearby recovery yard where she would be free of the hustle and bustle of a busy training complex.

Everyone made their £400 monthly contribution at the end of August, and I calculated that one more would be needed at the end of September to cover all costs until the Tattersalls December breeding stock sale. Trevor floated the idea of a private sale, but it was hard to see who would want to buy a potential broodmare when she still had a lot of healing to do. But I understood his point. It would cost us around £4k in keep, vet's fees, and costs associated with the sale if we went all the way to Tattersalls in early December.

Money wasn't the main consideration now. In the past, there were times when Free Love's value was temptingly high. It was only eight months ago that we had a firm offer of £13k from Sami, the Israeli bloodstock agent. Our mare looked to have dodged a bullet when we decided to hang onto her, as a few months later, bombs rained down on Beersheba in the latest tit-for-tat violence in that troubled part of the world. Prior to that, I suppose her value was north of £50k when she racked up those three wins at the start of her three-year-old campaign. And now? Maybe £5k when she was fit. She would be pushing six by the time of the sale and the absence of black type in her race record and pedigree would count against her.

But we were never in the game for money. It was all about the exhilaration of being part of the absurd and addictive sporting theatre where owners of all means and backgrounds throw their hats in the ring and roar, 'My horse can run faster than your horse!' I loved being part of it, but now it was time to make a bow and leave. The focus was on Free Love's welfare. It was now a case of spending the cash to get her to full fitness. Beyond that, a good home with a small breeder was the best we could hope for.

In the early evening I was discharged from hospital, the gaping wound at the back of my right heel covered by a large, air-tight dressing which was connected by plastic tubes to an ActiVAC machine, a box about the size of a small biscuit tin that produced a constant sucking action which drained away blood and lymph fluid while also accelerating cell growth and healing. I was in agony.

Thursday 9th September 2021

I've never taken myself to an A&E department. I needed eight stitches to my right thumb joint following an accident with a glass lemonade bottle when I was about seven. I have a vague memory of my dad driving me to a hospital somewhere in the Glasgow suburbs, but I can't recall anything else about the incident. A large scar on my right hand is a permanent reminder of the distant trauma.

The only other times I've visited A&E have been for the usual things that happen to children. My daughter, Celia, suffered a greenstick fracture to her arm in a fall from a skateboard when she was about ten. And my eldest son, Matthew, knocked himself out cold in a collision with a wooden dresser when he was a toddler, and his running skills were at a rudimentary stage of development. Joseph completed the hat-trick with a hastily arranged operation to remove his appendix when he was fifteen.

At 7am this morning, following a night of agonising abdominal pain, I decided against waiting for my GP surgery to open, knowing full well that I wouldn't get an appointment and would only be told to go to A&E if I was that concerned about how I was feeling. That's how it still was during these strange Covid times.

I wasn't looking forward to going. I wanted the excruciating pain to end and knew I needed some sort of treatment, but I find hospitals dispiriting. I should be more used to them considering how many tedious hours I've spent in outpatient waiting rooms during the last nine months because of my heel but, as soon as I'm inside a hospital, all I can think about is how quickly I can get out.

The entrance to the A&E Department at Darent Valley Hospital was depressingly Covid-compliant. Punters queued at two-metre intervals before approaching a Perspex screen behind which stood visored members of staff who were on hand to make a note of the basics – name, date of birth, GP, nature of illness or injury – before directing visitors to take a seat in the functional and cheerless waiting area.

It was just before 8am and there were only about half a dozen morose-looking souls dotted around the large room. To pass the time, I looked at each fellow sufferer and tried to work out why they were there. One tall, middle-aged man in a yellow high-vis jacket and building site attire was holding a bloodied handkerchief to his forehead, suggesting he had been caught by a piece of scaffold or a wayward lump of masonry. A clean up and a few stitches would probably sort him out. A much younger bloke, wearing designer jeans and trainers, sported a fat lip and a t-shirt splattered in blood suggesting involvement in a brawl rather than anything to do with the construction industry. He was the only one not wearing a mask. Perhaps he lost it in the fight, along with his sunflower lanyard, no doubt.

It was harder to work out why my other waiting room companions were there. Apart from the street-fighting man who was up and down like a jack-in-the-box, nearly everyone else exuded a quiet stoicism indicating that they knew they were in it for the long haul.

It was just as well that Covid rules prohibited Jennie from keeping me company. It turned out to be a protracted and uncomfortable day. In between long waits, I was seen by the triage nurse, sent for blood and urine tests, examined by a doctor, and eventually sent for a CT scan.

At around 3pm, over seven hours after I checked in, I found myself in a small holding bay with two or three other patients who were awaiting some form of feedback following whatever had been done to them earlier in the day. I had been given stronger painkillers to help with the draining discomfort I was still experiencing, but it was difficult to find any meaningful relief. When my phone died, I couldn't even use the Racing Post app to keep tabs on the second day of Doncaster's St Leger meeting as a distraction from the debilitating pain.

I had a feeling that things weren't going my way when a frowning doctor approached me and pulled the curtain around my cubicle to create the illusion of privacy. In hushed and sombre tones, he told me that the CT scan had revealed a growth around my right kidney that could be cancer.

It's funny, but the news didn't shock me. I had been struggling all day moving around the hospital with my aching heel attached to a machine by a spaghetti tree of plastic tubing. The stabbing, cramping pains in my abdomen and side were only marginally less severe than they had been in the early hours of the morning. I felt like shit, and I accepted the latest piece of bad news with resignation rather than consternation and distress. I was told that somebody from the Urology Department would see me as soon as they were free. In the meantime, keep taking the pills.

An hour later, I was sat in a small room staring at a screen displaying images of my earlier scan. The urologist directed my attention to what he told me was my right kidney.

'What can you see?', he asked in an attempt to give me some sort of ownership of the situation. After a pause, I ventured that the grainy blob on the right looked considerably bigger than the one on the left. There were no prizes for my correct response.

'What is it likely to be?', I asked, knowing full well what answer would follow. The doctor gently dismissed my desperate suggestion that it might be fatty tissue and confirmed that it was almost certainly a cancer tumour. He wanted me to have a contrast dye scan before I left. This would make organs, blood vessels and tissue more noticeable during imaging and would detect if I had any rogue cells elsewhere in my body. I was exhausted and desperate to go home, but I was persuaded that it was far better for the scan to be done now rather than later. It would hasten an accurate diagnosis, and the quicker these things were sorted out the better.

It was just after 5pm when I left the hospital. I went outside and sat on a bench taking in the autumn sunshine and the distant view of the Queen Elizabeth II Bridge. A nurse had let me use a phone to call Jennie and she would be here in ten minutes. I wondered how I would break the news. Poor Jennie had been worried sick by my heel for the best part of ten months and now I was about to tell her that I had cancer.

Looking on the bright side, the urologist had told me that kidney cancer is often restricted to one organ and is not responsible for aggressively spreading the disease elsewhere, although nothing could be said with certainty until all the scans and tests were analysed. It looked like a three-horse race to me with the betting something like this: 1/5 Right Kidney, 9/2 Problems Elsewhere, 33/1 Fatty Tissue.

I spared Jennie the racing analogy when she arrived. I told her the most likely outcome was cancer restricted to the right kidney which would mean an operation to remove the offending organ. However, we wouldn't know for a week and in the meantime, we agreed to tell curious family members and friends that kidney stones were suspected but I wouldn't know for sure until all the tests had been analysed. There were no tears, just palpable shock. We embraced before driving out of the hospital grounds while contemplating a future which was now full of new uncertainties.

Friday 17th September 2021

The last week had been filled with pain and dread anticipation. My heel was calming down despite still being attached to the ActiVAC box, but I was experiencing high levels of discomfort on the right-hand side of my abdomen where the troublesome kidney was located. The distraction of Free Love was a welcome one.

Kieran, Patrick, Pete and Tim were happy with the proposals sent to them at the end of August, but Trevor was dogged in his pursuit of a private sale. Over the years, he's had small shares in horses trained by the Kent-based handler Linda Jewell. He picked Linda's brains but was told that nobody would be in a rush to take Free Love off our hands until the veterinary treatment was completed and the mare was completely sound. Why buy a lame duck now and take on the cost of rehabilitation? I suppose you might do it if the creature was being given away. Hence the derisory offer of a grand I received about a fortnight ago from Free Love's breeder, Brendan Boyle.

The majority vote was for sitting tight, looking after Free Love, and hopefully finding her a decent home with a small breeder via the December sale. Entries closed today, and we went ahead with the £450 entry fee for the last, cheapest and least prestigious day of the auction. I knew it would cost about £4k to get us to Tattersalls and took Trevor's point that a sale tag of £5k would make us no better off financially than accepting a grand now. But there was always the chance that we might get a bit more. If we didn't, there was also the fanciful prospect of my buying her back and setting up a small breeding syndicate myself.

That may have been how I was thinking at the back end of August when it was confirmed that Free Love wouldn't race again, but now it felt that all bets were off. Maybe I was being a bit melodramatic, but it was hard to think about the pros and cons of a breeding project that wouldn't produce a young horse ready to race until summer 2025 when there was no guarantee that I'd be around to see it happen.

I'd be wiser before darkness fell. I was due to get my diagnosis today. Earlier in the week I phoned the hospital to see if there was any news and was told that my case was scheduled for the weekly review meeting held on Friday. Somebody would call me late in the afternoon to tell me about the proposed 'treatment plan'. Fatty Tissue eased out to 66/1.

I had been in limbo since my initial visit to A&E. For more than a week, I chewed over what the final diagnosis might be, but feeling terrible somehow made the prospect of bad news easier to bear. I was taking plenty of morphine sulphate to tackle the pain, and the ActiVAC contraption was still rigged up to the back of my right foot making movement and sleep difficult. The prospect of lying flat on my back and drifting into endless sleep under the influence of a strong opiate didn't seem as terrifying as it should be.

At least I had been around to see my children grow into adulthood and I knew Jennie would be financially secure. True, Joe was only 19, but the family wouldn't be fractured by my early departure in the way that Jennie's had been when her mum died leaving behind three young daughters of school-age and a husband lacking the means of looking after them on his own.

I put aside these morbid and self-pitying thoughts as the day wore on and, by the time the landline telephone rang at around 6pm, I had wagered every last penny on the long odds-on shot romping home. It was going to be good news. Surely the cancer would be restricted to the right kidney which would be swiftly removed?

I nearly ignored the call, but something told me that this landline call wasn't going to be a voice from the other side of the globe telling me that they could help with my workplace injury claim. I was right. It was Alan, the urology team nurse with whom I had spoken earlier in the week. He had warned me that his call might come quite late in the day.

After the briefest of pleasantries had been exchanged, Alan

calmly relayed the news in a direct but compassionate manner. Experience has taught him to avoid distracting flannel.

'It's not good news, I'm afraid. All the tests confirm that the growth on your right kidney is cancerous. The kidney will have to be removed, but the good news is that the cancer appears to be restricted to the right organ and wasn't found elsewhere.' I listened without interrupting as Alan continued in the same measured vein. 'There's a tiny nodule showing on one of your lungs, but the doctors are pretty sure that it's benign and not of significant concern.'

'That's good news, Alan. It really is,' I replied, my upbeat manner maybe taking him by surprise. 'I knew it was cancer, I just wanted to hear that it was almost certainly restricted to one area and could be dealt with by fairly straightforward surgery.' Like a trainer responsible for a winning odds-on shot in a big race, I was more relieved than elated by the outcome.

6 A Leap in the Dark

Wednesday 20th October 2021

Today was spent at a windswept Newmarket watching an end of season card full of races for backward two-year-olds who were getting a bit of experience before being put away for the winter, in readiness for careers that would start in earnest next spring. Some would have another go or two on all-weather tracks between now and then, but most were well-bred and from big stables where a patient approach was often preferred.

Over a fortnight ago, the day after Germany's Torquator Tasso stunned the racing world with a shock win in a well-contested Prix de l'Arc de Triomphe, I was told that my operation would take place on Monday 25th October. This prompted a frenzy of activity ahead of my pre-op assessment and Covid test which were scheduled for the Friday before the procedure, or nephrectomy as I was now getting used to calling it.

My first port of call was Free Love. As soon as I got news of my date, I was on the phone to Tara Derry, who ran the recovery stable, to organise a visit. Although I finally got rid of the ActiVAC box at the beginning of the month and could manage a little local driving, a return trip to Belton-in-Rutland was beyond me. Fortunately, Jennie was happy to take on all chauffeuring duties and we spent a restorative half an hour feeding carrots to our injured heroine and generally making a fuss of her.

Poor Free Love. Her near fore was still heavily bandaged, and she seemed reluctant to put much weight on it. It was now nine weeks since she sustained the injury and I had hoped to see a bit more progress, but that assumption was based on ignorance. I had no idea how long it would take for the bone to fuse and at what point she would feel comfortable and confident enough to have a gentle walk

277

in one of Tara's small paddocks. One thing was for sure – we could just about manage four good legs between us.

We left Greenacres Farm wondering whether the sale in early December would come too soon. Tara was sceptical about Free Love being able to do herself justice when asked to walk and trot for prospective buyers, given her appointment with Tattersalls was only six weeks away. A day or two later I had a conversation with Alex, the senior partner at the Oakham Veterinary Hospital, who confirmed that Free Love's return to soundness had been a little slower than anticipated. There was another sale in early February and Alex thought it would be wiser to aim at that. I let the others know and received a collective shrug of shoulders in reply. There was little else we could do.

The week before our visit to Greenacres, we were in Northumberland staying in a cottage close to Bamburgh. It was a short break to celebrate my older brother's 65th birthday but it had been deferred for a year due to the pandemic. Paul was now sixty-six, but we still had an excuse to raise a glass; he was now able to draw his state pension.

The coastline in that part of the world is sublime. I don't think I've ever walked on a beach as breathtakingly beautiful as Cocklawburn or as picturesque as the expanse of white sand overlooked by the imposing Bamburgh Castle, which is built on a rocky outcrop and a landmark that can be seen for miles.

My younger brother, Peter, and his wife, Siobhan, know the area well and they organised the cottage and had plenty of suggestions about places to visit. Seahouses, Berwick-upon-Tweed, Dunstan-burgh Castle and Craster all featured on the itinerary. The weather even allowed for a boat trip to see the seal pups on Inner Farne Island, the inhospitable home of Grace Darling whose heroic exploits are celebrated in an excellent little museum in Bamburgh.

But it was Lindisfarne, that captured Jennie's imagination.

The Holy Island of Lindisfarne is a magical place, made even more alluring by access which is limited by the sea. It's reached by a causeway which is periodically submerged by the surges of high tides. If visitors lose track of time when wandering around the ruins of the abbey and mistime their departure, they have a six-hour wait until it's safe enough to drive back to the mainland.

The tarmac causeway for cars and coaches was not constructed until the mid-1950s, and more adventurous pilgrims who want to travel in the footsteps of ancient visitors to the place where Saint Aidan and Saint Cuthbert brought Christianity to the north east, can walk across the wet, muddy sands at low tide. If they get their calculations wrong and feel the cold incoming sea washing around their shins, they must scramble into small, wooden refuge boxes which stand on stilts, and wait for five or six hours until the waters subside and it's safe to continue their journey on foot.

Jennie was captivated by the place. I had been before, once quite recently and on another occasion when I was very young and the family lived in Newcastle-upon-Tyne, the place of my birth. I have no memory of my first encounter, but I could see why my parents took me there. As devoted Catholics, it was a place of pilgrimage for them, but it was also a place of wild, majestic beauty. It's somewhere where you can stare out to sea and lose yourself in private thought; a sanctuary where you feel the presence of the quick and the dead, the living and those who lie sleeping in the dust of the earth.

That was last week. Today's final fling was on the Rowley Mile, a last outing before another period of confinement. Although I was getting about much better and beginning to drive with more confidence, my old teaching pal, Colin Turtle, offered me a lift. He isn't really a racing fan but likes a day out at the races and he and his wife, Emma, had an outrageously good time when they joined us at

York for ladies' day in August. Fellow North South Syndicate member, Pete, made up the small but select field of three.

I love those backend flat meetings when the season is fading as quickly as the light, and last races are run in autumnal gloom. They provide a sense of passing, of things coming to a natural conclusion. Yet they also give a glimpse of what's to come. That was no more evident than when Claymore, a bargain-basement £10k purchase from a breeze-up sale at Newmarket in June, hung left, ran green, and cocked his jaw at an ungainly angle when making a winning debut in the third race on the card. He ran away from more regally bred youngsters, putting four lengths between himself and his nearest pursuer. His value went from £10k to £500k in the space of seven furlongs. Claymore's owners had a whole winter of dreaming ahead of them. He could be anything.

Monday 25th October 2021

A third general anaesthetic in less than a year. I wasn't looking forward to this morning's procedure - a non-threatening way to describe four hours on a slab during which a large incision, the length of a missable putt, is made in the muscle wall of the abdomen before an organ is ripped out.

In the week leading up to the operation I became pre-occupied with the prospect of not waking up after the anaesthetic. I knew it was an absurd fear, but my little nephrectomy information booklet, given to me at the pre-op assessment on Friday, laid out the probabilities of various side effects in the manner of odds chalked up by a bookmaker. The risk of 'bulging of the abdominal wall below the wound' (not the snappiest name for a horse) was expressed as between 1 in 2 and 1 in 10, making the average price 5/1. 'Chest infection' (much better) was a 25/1 shot. Those looking for each-way value might be attracted by 'cardiovascular problems requiring intensive care – including stroke, heart attack, pulmonary embolus, and death' (way in excess of the 18 characters, including spaces, permitted for a racehorse name) at 250/1.

F**k me! That couldn't be right! I read in one of the other jolly leaflets supplied by the local urology team that deaths under general anaesthetic were extremely rare. The incidence was reported as approximately five in a million. It seemed to me that patients needed to shop around for the best value. Who in their right mind would take 250/1 on 'Death' with William Hill when 200,000/1 was available elsewhere?

I knew that given my relatively young age (is 63 still young?) and general level of fitness, it was irrational to think that I wouldn't regain consciousness after crashing out halfway through the first couple of sentences of whatever banal conversation the anaesthetist chose to instigate after administering the sedative that would send me into a deep, dreamless sleep. It was ridiculous to think that my last earthly thoughts might centre on a chat about what I did for a living before I retired. Even worse, prove that I could count to ten. It depressed me that my last mortal thought could be 'four'.

At about 3pm, seven hours after I arrived at the imposing Medway Maritime Hospital and following radical surgery that kept me in theatre for over four hours, I opened my eyes, blinked, and observed the reassuring sight of a solitary nurse sat at a desk studying a computer screen. Five, six, seven, eight, nine, ten. Made it.

Saturday 27th November 2021

Hennessy day. For those with more years behind them than ahead, the big handicap steeplechase on the last Saturday of November will always be known by that name. The brandy producer's sponsorship ended after the 60th running of the Hennessy Cognac Gold Cup in 2016, thus ending British racing's longest running commercial sponsorship. Ever since, it has been known as The Ladbrokes Trophy Chase, but I'm too long in the tooth to refer to it as anything other than 'The Hennessy' although I admit to some stubborn unwillingness to embrace the change.

There have been some wonderful winners of the contest. I was only six, and totally oblivious to the world of horseracing when Arkle won the Newbury showcase for the first time in 1964. Yet well before I took an interest in the sport, I knew all about 'Himself'. Arkle was one of those equine superstars who became a household name. Others to seep into the wider public's consciousness have included the likes of Red Rum, Nijinsky and Frankel. Even the most po-faced, anti-gambling campaigners have heard of them.

The winner of today's race was unlikely to achieve such immortality. The talented but inconsistent Cloudy Glen pulled off a 33/1 surprise, toppling several lofty reputations in the process. I watched his triumph in disbelief from the comfort of my sofa, a piece of furniture I had used a lot since my operation.

It had been a tough month. The large, swirling wound on my abdomen, shaped like the type of line graph used to illustrate a wave of Covid infection, was beginning to heal, but that first fortnight was agonising. It was ok while I was still, but any movement was painfully difficult, and morphine became my new bedmate. Things weren't helped by yesterday's news at St Thomas's that I would need a **third** operation on my heel as there was still something in there that was causing irritation and infection. Liaison between medical teams was needed to determine when this could be done. I was due to start taking some serious medication in the early new year to tackle any remaining cancer cells that the surgeon couldn't remove during his epic four-hour operation, making the timing of another procedure on my heel far from straightforward.

Another potential barrier to progress had emerged earlier in the week when the World Health Organisation declared a new coronavirus mutation to be 'of concern'. Thought to be more transmissible than Delta and with the ability to reinfect previous Covid sufferers, the newly named Omicron variant was first reported to the WHO from South Africa on 24th November. In the immediate panic that ensued, 3.5% was wiped off the value of the FTSE in one day. Travel bans and hastily arranged new quarantine rules were put in place by many different countries as a sickening sense of déjà vu emerged.

At around 6pm today, Boris Johnson addressed the nation via a televised press conference from Downing Street. He drew short at implementing 'Plan B', something that had been doing the rounds in the press for the last month or so. Instead, he opted for compulsory mask wearing in shops and on public transport as well as the need for testing and isolating when entering the country. He was 'confident' that Christmas wasn't at risk, but it didn't feel like that.

Mind you, if you read around the subject, instead of garnering your evidence from tabloid headlines which were keen to highlight the worst-case figures uttered by scientific advisers, it was possible to remain cautiously optimistic. Omicron may be more transmissible, but early data suggested it was a milder form of disease and, as one health official put it, it was bad news but 'not Doomsday'. Maybe the pubs would stay open, and racing wouldn't be forced behind closed doors. The next few weeks would be critical.

Saturday 4th December 2021

By 8.30am Jennie and I were on the road for the short journey from The Royal Oak in Duddington to Langham. We had spent yesterday ambling around Stamford's Georgian streets taking in the history of a town we had always wanted to visit but somehow managed to avoid as we whizzed up and down the A1 on various trips. Having promised ourselves on numerous occasions that one day we would 'do' Stamford, we finally found an occasion to take in the town's period elegance. Rather than leave at the crack of dawn from Dartford to get to Mick's yard, we decided to stay overnight in the Stamford area following our day in the town, making the drive to Mick's the following morning short and free from the stresses of the M25 and M11.

Free Love had left Mick's at the beginning of September, and the reason for the visit was to see Mops Gem in action. Following an encouraging debut at Yarmouth last September, I took a 5% lease share in the filly. At the time, Free Love's racing career seemed likely to end within a couple of months and I was desperate to have some sort of stake in a horse that would allow me to attend racecourses as an owner.

'Owner' isn't really the right word. 'Leaseholder' is more accurate. Mick had bred Mops Gem himself. He won a couple of races with the dam, Mops Angel, who was no great shakes and finished her racing career languishing on a rating of 49. Nevertheless, she had shown a bit of speed and ability which was enough for Mick to take a chance on her as a broodmare. Mick retained ownership of her offspring and he syndicated Mops Gem as a Mick Appleby Racing Club horse. Twenty shares were up for grabs with no initial outlay and just £60 a month asked to cover training fees. Mick was barely covering expenses at these rates.

Mops Gem managed to win a small class 6 claiming race at Wolverhampton in February and recorded a couple of decent placed efforts in lowly handicap company afterwards, but by June Mick decided that the filly had been busy enough (13 runs since her debut last September) and gave her a decent break. She was now back cantering, and this morning's stable visit was designed to get all the Mick Appleby Racing Club members together ahead of signing up for another twelve months at the beginning of the new year.

The main event, however, took place twenty minutes' drive away at Belton-in-Rutland. As soon as Louise announced, via the Racing Club Facebook group, that a stable visit was being organised to see Mops Gem on the gallops, I knew I could double up and use it as an excuse to see Free Love. It also gave me a chance to talk to Mick's racing secretary, Jane Hales, about what I'd need to do to enter Free Love for the February sale now that I'd cancelled Mick's authority to act on our behalf. I was relieved to hear that she could help if I found dealing directly with Tattersalls all a bit bewildering.

We left Langham without seeing Mops Gem work. She was in the very last lot and if we stayed for that we would have been way behind schedule for our visit to Greenacres. It didn't feel like a sacrilege. I just didn't have the same emotional attachment to Mops Gem. Sure, we patted and petted her in her box before she was saddled up for exercise and took loads of photos, but I knew that watching her canter up the all-weather gallop wouldn't be the same as seeing Free Love breeze by.

I had quick chats with Mick and Theo before leaving and at about 11.30am, half an hour later than planned, we arrived in Belton-in-Rutland where Tara was busy in her small yard looking after the five convalescing racehorses in her care.

Free Love appeared pleased to see me. Or maybe it was Jennie's carrots that induced the show of affection. She looked in good shape and had gained a bit of condition around the girth since we last saw her. Tara said that she had started a controlled walking regime and Free Love was much more confident about putting weight on her near fore. The mare was still spending plenty of time in her box, which she didn't seem to mind, but with the sale still two months away there was time to step up the exercise programme and get her into decent physical shape for potential buyers.

We left Greenacres shortly after midday. The wound on my abdomen was healing well enough to allow me to do bits of driving, but Jennie cheerfully volunteered to take charge for the home leg which allowed me to sit contentedly in the passenger seat and turn over various options in my mind. The sensible thing was to sell, take what little money came our way and see who wanted to go again in the autumn when all the big yearling sales took place. But it was the prospect of Free Love being snapped up for a pittance that kept haunting me. Could I really allow that to happen? It occurred to me that I needed to register as an authorised buyer with Tattersalls. I couldn't bear the idea of the bidding stalling with the electronic display board stuck on 1,500 guineas, with me powerless to do anything about it.

It was crucial that I was able to bid. If Free Love looked like fetching no more than two or three grand, I could buy her back and breed from her myself. I'd need help. My original calculations suggested I'd spend around £25k over a three-year period by which time I'd be the proud owner of a yearling and a pregnant mare. My west country racing pal, Paul Davis, shared his more detailed financial projections with me which put the figure nearer to £35k. Paul was one step ahead of me and had already given serious thought about putting together a breeding syndicate using one of Martin Keighley's mares. On Paul's more realistic figures, the first three years would cost about a grand a month.

So, what did I need? Maybe about five or six brave souls to put down two grand each and commit to a further £100 a month for three years. And then what? We could either sell the yearling to recoup some money or keep the creature and shell out even more on training fees. The sums made no sense at all. It was clear that becoming a breeder could only be viewed as a hobby, and an expensive one at that. A few get lucky, I suppose. Free Love's unraced half-sister by Gregorian might turn out to be a world beater which would dramatically increase the value of the family's stock, but I'm almost sure that most owner-breeders cheerfully lose money pursuing something that they love.

Despite the financial pitfalls, the allure of the adventure was strong. Wouldn't it be great to choose a stallion, visit Free Love when she was in foal, and be there for the birth of a gangly-legged baby thoroughbred?

I put my dreaming to one side when we were home in Dartford. Instead, I busied myself writing a short report to accompany the photos I intended to send to the others. Apart from news of Free Love's health, I was able to tell my fellow owners that our finances looked solid. Since the bandages came off Free Love's fetlock, veterinary costs were much reduced. She was checked when the vet came to Greenacres to look at the other inmates, but the treatment of the injury had now finished. The farrier hadn't been sighted since August. When exercising and racing, Free Love's plates were changed monthly. Tara thought the mare might need a new front pair of shoes quite soon, but there was no hurry. Our monthly insurance premium was also reduced now that Free Love was officially out of training and was being prepared for a new life as a broodmare.

All these savings added up, and our total monthly expenses had been squeezed down to around £600 which was a far cry from some of the bills we received when Free Love was racing. By the time transport, entry and riding fees were added to the total, it wasn't uncommon to shell out two-and-a-half grand in any given month. It still looked like we could cover all expenses - including those associated with the sale - out of our existing funds, which was a bit of a triumph considering our last contribution to the syndicate's bank account was made at the beginning of October. It would be tight, but I thought we could settle all our bills and still have a couple of hundred left in the bank by the time Free Love entered the sales ring at Tattersalls.

Friday 17th December 2021
The sun made a valiant but short-lived effort to pierce the dense cloud that shrouded Ascot racecourse, but the brilliant afternoon forecast failed to materialise. Trevor and I spent a fair bit of time in the warmth and comfort of the Queen Anne enclosure's smart bars, venturing outside to the paddock on only two or three occasions. One of them was to see Jonbon, racing in the colours of legendary National Hunt enthusiast, JP McManus, and trained by Nicky Henderson.

The Walk In The Park gelding looked magnificent. I know next to nothing about horse conformation, but Jonbon strutted around the parade ring as if he owned it. He was athletic, alert and exuded star quality. That assessment may lack the forensic detail an expert judge of horseflesh could provide, but what a handsome beast he was – and he knew it. 'So that's what half a million quid looks like,' I said to Trevor as the warm favourite for the Grade 2 Kennel Gate Novices' Hurdle left the paddock and cantered down to the start.

I couldn't help thinking about the different ends of the equine financial spectrum represented by Free Love and Jonbon. The latter was a full brother to the top-class Cheltenham Festival winner, Douvan. It was therefore no surprise that he made €140,000 as an unraced three-year-old when sold in Ireland in June 2019. At the beginning of November 2020, he made his racing debut in a point-to-point race at Dromohane winning by a wide margin. Four days later, he turned up in the UK for the Goffs Yorton Farm Sale and

'JP' had to go to £570,000 to seal the deal.

Jonbon gave every indication that he would be joining racing's top table when he sauntered to an easy win. It's great to be on a racecourse when you think you may have seen something a bit special and that's the feeling that Nicky Henderson's spring-heeled gelding evoked during a drab afternoon in Berkshire.

It wasn't a bad crowd, despite the meeting's closeness to Christmas and the added layer of bureaucracy which required all racegoers to show proof of vaccination before they were granted entry to the course. On 8th December, Boris Johnson had announced new measures to tackle the rapid increase in Omicron. It meant mandatory mask-wearing in shops and on public transport, and attendance at outdoor sports events with crowds of more than 4,000 was only allowed if punters could demonstrate proof of two Covid vaccine doses, preferably via the NHS app.

The rising tide of Omicron was producing much higher levels of infection – the seven-day average was nearing 100,000 – and I suppose some old or frail racegoers may have been wary about attending their favourite sport. For that reason, I was surprised to see a bookstall set up on the bottom floor of the grandstand manned by an elderly gentleman who could only be Sir Rupert Mackeson. He was wearing a mask which covered a lockdown beard making it difficult for me to identify him with certainty, but a quick enquiry confirmed that it was indeed the one and only Sir Rupert.

We had a brief and civilised chat about how he was faring, and I brought him up to date with the Free Love story. Tongue in cheek, I apologised in advance for inflicting a third and final book on him, probably in the summer, by which time the adventure was odds-on to be concluded. We were back on good terms following a barrage of emails which were critical of the approximate costs of racehorse ownership which I set out towards the end of my second book,

Another Year of Free Love.

Rupert thought the figures were inaccurate and misleading and he didn't pull any punches in one email sent last summer. He insisted that my costings were presented in a 'fraudulent' way and all copies of the book should be pulped by 9.30am on Monday 13th July otherwise he would feel obliged to take the matter further.

The message wasn't signed off 'with kindest regards' or something similar, but it didn't stop me from sending a chatty and conciliatory reply about a month later by which time I thought Rupert may have cooled down:

Dear Rupert,

I hope this finds you in good health.

No, I haven't pulped the books. I think we're talking at cross purposes though, and it may be my fault for not making the figures clear in the table towards the end of the book. The £41,500 which represents the cash that the five co-owners put into the project is correct - £8,300 each. However, the prize money (less deductions) went straight into our racing account and was used to fund ongoing training fees, meaning the true cost of the project was much nearer to the £70k figure that you have calculated. However, it is also factually correct that the £8,300 each of us has invested is the amount we were out of pocket by the end of 2019. It's a little bit more now.

....The book tries to capture the personal experience of small-scale ownership by a lifelong racing enthusiast. It's not pretending to be any grander than that. I know both books don't have a wide appeal, but I've received positive feedback from people who have dabbled in racing clubs, syndicates and small partnerships, and who recognise the journey I've taken. In the end it's a very amateur project which I took on during retirement for pleasure and not profit. Just as well I hear you say!

My email also contained an update on how Free Love was doing and where we thought she might run next following a disappointing effort at York. I knew Rupert was a volatile character – his Zimbabwean exploits suggested nothing less - so I wasn't upset by his diatribe. I was happy to pour oil over troubled waters and move on. We occasionally swapped emails thereafter and I was genuinely pleased to see him today at Ascot. Without doubt, Sir Rupert Mackeson is one of the great characters of British horse racing.

On the way home, Trevor and I mused over the state of the nation. Despite neither of us being a fan of our current Prime Minister, we felt the government was on the right track with its 'learning to live with Covid' approach. Although highly transmissible, there were early signs that the illness caused by the Omicron variant was milder than Delta. If infection rates were high but hospital admissions remained low, the UK's approach, which was out of step with most other Western European countries, might prove to be a winning one.

Away from the world of current affairs, we talked about the extraordinary case of national hunt jockeys Bryony Frost and Robbie Dunne. Frost's accusations of bullying and threatening behaviour were upheld during an independent disciplinary hearing which delivered its verdict just over a week ago. Dunne was banned for 15 months for the prolonged and sinister vendetta he conducted against one of racing's most popular jump jockeys, but he wasn't the only loser. It was a catastrophic piece of bad publicity for the sport.

There was also the Freddie Tylicki case to discuss. Tylicki had made a high-court claim against Graham Gibbons for negligent riding which had resulted in a fall at Kempton in 2016 that left the German-born rider partially paralysed and a wheelchair user ever since. Again, the papers were full of it, relishing the unsavoury description of Gibbons as a jockey with a drink problem. The verdict was expected early next week. The good news story of Rachael Blackmore winning the Grand National seemed to belong to another era.

At least it made the journey home fly by. We weren't short of other topics of conversation either. Trevor faced a busy fortnight, and this was likely to be his only day off between now and the Feast of the Epiphany. At a stroke, Plan B had thrown his church's Christmas services into disarray. What they were able to do now was very different to what had been planned a few weeks ago. But it was the same all over. It looked like Christmas was going to be that bit smaller and lower-key for nearly everyone.

Wednesday 22nd December 2021
Although the closing date for the Tattersalls February sale was not until 4th January, I made the entry yesterday as I wanted to deal with the matter before the Christmas break. It had become apparent that I would be responsible for all aspects of sale administration as Free Love was no longer in the care of a licenced trainer. In the past, Mick's racing secretary, Jane Hales, had sorted out everything. There was a lot to do but I could leave most of it until the new year and seek help from Jane if needed. The first and most important job was to register an account with Tattersalls and make the entry. Once that had been done, I could relax for a couple of weeks.

Today I was due to see the oncologist at Maidstone Hospital – another good reason for getting the sale entry and all other distractions out of the way. We left early for a 9.30am appointment anticipating the usual queues for a parking place but, when we arrived, we were greeted by a sprawling 1980s complex that resembled a featureless retail park with a generous allocation of parking bays. It was in stark contrast to the Medway Maritime Hospital which, although built in 1905 on the site of a much smaller naval hospital close to the historic Chatham Dockyard, has parts which wouldn't look out of place in a Sunday night TV costume drama about the Napoleonic Wars.

Jennie and I faced hand sanitisers, temperature checks and questions about our current state of health before we were allowed to sit down in the waiting room ahead of my appointment with Doctor Clarke. As this was the part of the hospital that treated cancer patients, the additional precautions came as no surprise.

We chatted through our masks about the questions we must remember to ask. I was keen to know how long my treatment would go on for. About a month ago, a member of the urology nursing team caught me off guard during a routine check to see how I was recovering from my kidney operation when she floated the idea of me being on medication for the rest of my life. I wasn't expecting that. I thought three months of drugs to make sure the cancer was suppressed would be followed by six-monthly scans to check that everything was clear. I suppose I didn't mind the idea of popping a daily pill until I went to meet my maker, but I hoped it wouldn't be anything more than that.

The consultation was with Doctor Clarke's Registrar who confirmed, much to my relief, that she had access to last Tuesday's CT scan. I presumed we couldn't proceed with any treatment until the images had been studied and was dreading being told that this was a preliminary meeting to see how I was getting on and I would need to return a month later when the team had had a chance to peruse the scan.

I needn't have worried. Doctor Kviat had everything on her computer screen and a well-rehearsed script to accompany the diagnosis. In calm and even tones she informed me that the cancer had spread to my lungs and, although it could be treated, it couldn't be cured.

Silence.

Jennie squeezed my hand tight as she tried to suppress her tears.

I had the presence of mind to ask for a timescale and was told that two years was typical. Some patients limped on for longer and five years wasn't out of the question. I didn't ask for prices though. I was already reeling from the defeat of the odds-on favourite.

Doctor Kviat fielded some questions, most of which I can't remember asking, before explaining what sort of treatment I would be having to try to keep the cancer at bay. Without medication the spread of the disease could be rapid. I did lots of nodding as the immunotherapy treatment and its possible side effects were explained to me.

'Ticking this first box often frightens people, but you shouldn't think it means an imminent end.'

I saw the doctor pass over the 'curative' box and place a black biro tick in the 'palliative' one instead. She explained that the aim wasn't to cure, it was to control and slow the spread of the disease improving both my quality of life and length of survival.

She then proceeded to make me aware of what side effects I might experience when I started my course of Ipilimumab and Nivolumab. I was on autopilot when she read out the list, nodding as she ticked each box. Nausea, nod. Diarrhoea, nod. Inflammation of the liver, nod. Joint pain, nod. Blurred vision, nod.

There were over 30 boxes to tick and as many nods of understanding to accompany every mark of her pen. I couldn't fault Doctor Kviat's sympathetic manner and professional approach. It can't be easy conveying news like this. When she finished going through the extensive list of side effects, she left us to see if Doctor Clarke was free. It was an opportunity for Jennie to cry without restraint. She was still holding my hand tightly, refusing to let go as she hugged me and told me she didn't know what she was going to do because I was 'the love of her life'.

It dawned on me that I had been dealt the better hand. In some strange way, I felt I was letting her down. We held our embrace, and I offered no resistance to tears of my own as we sat in a small room in Maidstone trying to make sense of it all.

7 The End of the Affair

Thursday 6th January 2022

'The tree with the garden waste in bay 8 and the bottles in the container marked 'bottles', mate.'

This time I didn't reflect on the passing of years as we hurled the seven-foot Nordic Spruce into its grave. Now it was a case of trying to look forward into a future that was short and uncertain. It wasn't a two-man job, but Jennie and I both went to the recycling centre to complete this annual ritual. We tend to do most things together and I knew that would continue to be the case for whatever time we had left.

During early new year, Jennie and I took advantage of some gloriously sunny winter weather to make impromptu visits to the likes of Rochester Castle and the imposing Naval War Memorial in Chatham. The latter, a towering obelisk, stands on the top of a hill overlooking the Medway and the former glory of its now redundant dockyards. I've lived in Kent for more than fifty years but didn't know of the memorial's existence until I saw it featured in a film adaptation of Graham Swift's *Last Orders*. Erected in 1924 to commemorate those lost at sea in the First World War, it was expanded and updated after the second global conflict and displays the names of all 16,654 men and women who perished during active service with the Royal Navy. It was a poignant reminder of the transitory nature of life.

It was the same everywhere I went. It was hard to find a beating second of any day when my thoughts weren't consumed by death. I couldn't escape it, even during our magical visit to Margate on New Year's Eve. It was a spur of the moment thing. I announced mid-morning that I wanted to go to the seaside and Margate old town was my first pick. It wasn't a great day but at least it was dry and, if we couldn't get into the Buoy and Oyster restaurant for lunch, we'd find somewhere else for a bite to eat. It was only a flying visit, a bit of a whim.

You know how it is when all the cards fall unexpectedly into place. It heightens the experience and deepens the memory of the event. That's what happened to us on the last day of 2021 when the clouds scuttled away leaving Margate bathed in dazzling sunshine, and the restaurant had a cancellation and was able to squeeze us in for a light lunch of oysters and mussels washed down with a crisp white wine from Biddenden. It was a day that would never be forgotten, and we had the selfies to prove it. The photos were beautiful but tinged with sadness. As we snapped them on our mobile phones, every single one felt like a memento in the making, something for Jennie to stare at when I was no longer there.

Tuesday 11th January 2022

Today I received my first dose of immunotherapy. By mid-morning I was sitting in a red, faux leather recliner attached to a drip through which the two unpronounceable drugs trickled into my bloodstream. It was a painless enough two-and-a-half hours, and the Pine Therapy Unit at Darent Valley Hospital was pleasantly informal. But the realisation that this would be a regular event for the rest of my life – however long, or short, that might be – wasn't an uplifting thought. Fifteen months ago, I was swimming, going for long yomps, playing golf and anticipating a return to veterans' football once my achilles tendon was sorted. Now look at me. I had to pinch myself to take in the transformation.

The staff in the unit were friendly, empathetic and professional. One of the nurses, a Ghanaian mountain of a man, fancied himself as a stand-up comedian. As I'm a fan of lame jokes, and tell enough of them myself, I appreciated his humorous approach which helped me feel that I was merely there for a cup of tea and a biscuit. You can't knock our front-line NHS staff. They are drawn from the four corners of the earth, and it is surely a source of national pride, whatever the shortcomings of the management and administration of the service, that the UK has created something special, something unique; health provision for all delivered by a highly skilled and dedicated workforce made up of all nations and races, bonded together by a desire to improve the lives of ordinary people.

Friday 14th January 2022

It was early days but, as I wasn't experiencing any adverse reactions to my first session of immunotherapy, Jennie gave the green light for a final visit to Free Love. We arranged with Tara to arrive mid-morning to take some photos and video footage which I could upload to the Tattersalls website. There were the transport arrangements to thrash out as well. The vet was booked for Monday to undertake all the pre-sale tests that were stipulated by the auctioneers. Most of them were for things I'd never heard of. The veterinary checks, sale entry fee and transport costs would come to about a grand and I calculated that once everything had been settled, including Tara's last invoice for keep, we were still on track to have about two-hundred quid left in our account.

The first part of the journey was the usual slow chug, but we were soon in the clear. It was a magnificent morning. The early frost had surrendered to a low, iridescent winter sun and the only mist we encountered was a thick bank on the A47 due south of Rutland Water. At that point it didn't look that it was going to be ideal weather for photos and videos but, just as I was cursing our luck, the mist cleared and minutes later we arrived at Belton-in-Rutland, once again drenched in sunlight.

I will remember the visit for as long as I live, which I hope is a bit more than the two-year estimate I was given when my terminal diagnosis was disclosed before Christmas. Free Love was taken out of her box to do a little walking and trotting. The camera adored her, and we took the best set of pictures I've ever assembled at a stable visit. It was a fitting way to say goodbye.

After the photo-shoot and the finalisation of transport arrangements, Jennie and I gave Free Love one last affectionate stroke before heading to the Exeter Arms in the small village of Barrowden. It wasn't even our first-choice pub which was closed for a refurbishment, but as soon as we entered the substitute hostelry, we knew our winning streak hadn't ended. It was perfect. The smart leather chairs and bar stools were upholstered in sea-green and royal-blue Mackenzie tartan. The tables were for both drinkers and diners with no sense that you were grudgingly welcome if you only wanted a pint. To cap it all, the local belly pork baguette and JHB Oakham bitter were outstanding.

We had a wander around the village, which was bigger than we thought, and popped into the community shop which sold an impressive array of local produce. We left with a pork pie, a bottle of barley wine and a small, potted wintergreen bulging with blood-red berries. It was a perfect day, marred only by the unspoken sadness we both felt. At least from tomorrow we would be able to share the burden.

Saturday 15th January 2022

It wasn't a family gathering I was looking forward to, but it would be unfair to say that we bottled it with our children. The original plan was to tell them when we were all together on Christmas Eve. It seemed a good idea at the time, but on the morning of the 24th Jennie and I agreed that the revelation about my health would ruin everyone's Christmas so we decided to wait until the early new year before breaking the news.

This weekend was the earliest that we were able to get Matthew, Celia and Joseph together. I told them that it was important to hear it from the horse's mouth about the implications of my ongoing immunotherapy treatment, which was true, but although they may have had their suspicions about the type of update they were about to receive, they clearly weren't prepared for news of the cancer spreading elsewhere and a revised life expectancy of around two years.

I had had three weeks to prepare how I was going to break the news which in some ways helped. I'd been through the 'why me' stage. I was nearing my sixty-fourth birthday. I'd experienced good health nearly all my life, found deep and enduring love in marriage, and lived to see my three children grow into impressive adulthood. Jennie was fifteen and the oldest of three sisters when her mum died suddenly, fracturing her family beyond repair. We had been spared that type of tragedy.

But there were only so many blessings to count and although my three children accepted that things could have been worse and, yes, I would be spared the indignity and distress of a senile old age, all they wanted to do was cry and hug. So that's what we did. We all agreed that we had to make the most of what we had left, and we started straight away with a meal, a good few drinks, and there was even a bit of dancing as the evening edged towards midnight.

Saturday 22nd January 2022
Omicron infection rates looked to be on the wane and, on this occasion, the UK government's light-touch tactics looked spot on. The current wave peaked at nearly 220,000 cases on 3rd January, but numbers were now less than half of that and falling steadily. The health service appeared to be coping as well. Elsewhere in Europe,

where governments had been more draconian with their restrictions, infection rates remained high and disgruntled citizens took to the streets to protest about their loss of freedoms.

The falling rates didn't stop me from testing positive and being sent home on Wednesday morning from St Thomas's Hospital where I was about to have my third, and hopefully final, operation on my troublesome achilles tendon. My oncologist knew that the quality of my life would be greatly enhanced if I could get my heel sorted – I told her that myself – and she was happy for the procedure to go ahead even if it coincided with the immunotherapy treatment.

Being sent home on the day of the operation was a bit like seeing the final leg of your Tote Jackpot fall when five lengths clear at the last. I was so nearly there, fourteen months after the original procedure which had kept me out of the swimming pool and off the golf course ever since.

For the last four days, I had been at home in isolation feeling sorry for myself but at least it meant I could devote my full attention to Free Love's sale entry. There was so much to do.

The results of the various health checks and blood tests carried out by the vet earlier in the week had already been emailed to me and, with the help of an extremely understanding member of the Tattersalls team, I uploaded everything apart from evidence of a recent equine flu jab. I knew Free Love had been given a booster last month, but I needed to contact Weatherbys early next week to find out how I could provide proof of the vaccination on the Tattersalls website.

Tuesday 25th January 2022
Yesterday I put the final bits of sale administration to bed. I even had time to upload a video clip taken on my mobile of Free Love

walking and trotting at Tara's. I was feeling quite pleased with the way I had negotiated all the sale requirements, admittedly with more than a little help from Liz Wood, the member of staff at Tattersalls who had guided me through everything with the patience of a latter-day saint.

. My smugness was short lived. At around midday, I took a call from Matt Prior, one of the Tattersalls sales team. He wasn't getting in touch to congratulate me on the myriad of health certificates which I had successfully uploaded. He came straight to the point. Free Love looked lame. He'd scrutinised my video clip taken at Tara's and thought that the mare didn't look sound at the walk. As far as Matt was concerned, Tattersalls couldn't offer her for sale in that condition and he suggested aiming at the Ascot sale in March instead.

It was a disaster. As soon as I finished speaking with Matt, I watched the video several times over. I was struggling to see it. Free Love may have looked to be moving a little bit gingerly as she walked back towards the camera, but she was travelling downhill on a mettled surface and was without front shoes. The farrier fitted them the day after the video was taken.

Just how lame was she? Tara always maintained that Free Love might never again walk 100% sound. Within two days of her Windsor injury, the Oakham veterinary team told me that not only was the mare's racing career over, but it was also recommended that she wasn't ridden again. It was all about giving time to recover in the hope that she would be sound enough to become a broodmare.

Thursday 27th January 2022

I had been busy since Matt Prior's gloomy telephone call. I'd registered a non-racing agreement for Free Love on the BHA website. That meant the auctioneer would make prospective buyers aware that they were not allowed to put the mare back into training. I'd also arranged for our vet to visit Tara's yard next Monday to inspect Free Love and write a short report which would be shared with Tattersalls. I made it clear that I wasn't angling for a vet's certificate to dodge a penalty for withdrawing from the sale at this late stage. I just wanted an honest assessment of her condition.

I also outlined the options for the boys to consider. It was all dependent on what the vet thought, but if we couldn't go to Tattersalls next week there were other routes to consider. First up was the March sale at Ascot. We had been offered a free entry by Matt, but it was hardly the type of sale that would be thronging with prospective broodmare buyers. The breeding season finished in early July, and I imagine most breeders wanted their mares covered much earlier than that. It didn't leave much time to get everything organised, especially if you wanted a foal born in March rather than May. Late foals are the equivalent of summer-born school children who often struggle to catch up with their autumn-born peers. If I wanted to buy a broodmare, I don't think I'd head to Ascot on the last day of March.

More ambitious plans included giving Free Love a bit more time and having her covered in April or early May before presenting her as a mare in foal at either the July sale or the breeding stock sale in November. But this required more patience and cash and, although Patrick saw the merits of this option, most of the others thought it was a non-starter. Tim even suggested giving the mare away to a good home if the vet didn't pass her fit on Monday. It's not as if we had a fortune to lose. It was hard to put a value on Free Love, but I thought if we got her to Tattersalls on Thursday, we'd do well to get five grand for her.

Monday 31st January 2022

The vet was due to make an early visit to Tara's yard and by mid-morning we'd know our fate. During the weekend I once again chewed over the options and made my decision. If Free Love wasn't fit to go to the sale, I would ask the boys to give the mare to me. There would be no cash compensation as I was effectively saving them further upkeep costs.

I'd arrange for Free Love to be covered and give myself until November to put a small breeding syndicate together. Tara had fallen in love with the mare – it was easy to do given her attractive looks and friendly nature – and had already hinted that she may be able to help with stabling costs if I found myself as the sole owner. If I couldn't put a little syndicate together, Free Love would go to the breeding stock sale as a mare-in-foal. At worst, I'd lose a few grand, but it wouldn't have an impact on Jennie's long-term financial security which was now my main consideration.

By mid-morning, the decision was taken out of my hands. Oakham Veterinary Hospital's senior partner, Alex Knott, telephoned to confirm that he had seen Free Love and, although his report would not say that she was 100% sound, it would confirm that she was fit enough for a new career as a broodmare. Within an hour of our conversation the report was emailed to me, and I immediately pinged it to Matt Prior who promptly replied giving the go ahead for Free Love to be presented at next Thursday's sale.

Thursday 3rd February 2022

It was damp and overcast as we drove into the Tattersalls car park at 8.30am. This is where the story started more than four years ago What was meant to be a one-year fling had turned into a passionate and absorbing relationship, the end of which was now only a few hours away, perhaps.

Free Love was Lot 40 and was due through the ring at about midday. I was determined to be there early to talk to prospective buyers, but I needn't have bothered. Tara had everything under control. By the time we met her at the Highflyer Paddock where Free Love was stabled, she had already taken the mare out of her box for a couple of potential bidders to inspect. While I was there, a smartly dressed gent carrying an annotated sales catalogue asked to see Free Love. I was on him like a shot, talking up Free Love's racing career and her virtues of speed and honesty. It was only towards the end of the conversation that I realised he wasn't an agent working on behalf of Godolphin or some other wealthy owner, he was one of the auctioneers. Still, at least I had given him a few titbits to throw at the crowd when it was Lot 40's turn to come under the hammer.

The Tattersalls site is built on a substantial mound and after the auctioneer moved on, Pete, Jennie and I left Tara to it and made our way to the summit which is the hub of the operation. It's an extraordinary set-up. There must be over a thousand boxes to accommodate the horses and everywhere you walk, there are thoroughbreds being groomed, inspected, or just ambling to and fro. The sales ring sits on the top of the hill and is surrounded by various offices and a couple of places to eat and drink. It's quite extraordinary that such a vast development is entirely devoted to the ancient pursuit of determining whether my horse can run a bit faster than yours.

As midday approached, the place was filling up. Plan B restrictions had been ditched a week ago and a large, relaxed crowd milled around the paddock outside the sales ring to watch a parade of stallions from Whitsbury Manor Stud. Only the occasional, voluntary mask wearer provided a reminder that we were still in the shadow of a pandemic.

I leant up against the white plastic rail and watched the likes of Showcasing, Due Diligence and Sergei Prokofiev parade their testosterone for admiring onlookers. The last-named was one of the sires on my shortlist for Free Love. A little while ago, when I mentioned the possibility of becoming a breeder, Brendan Boyle intimated that he had a nomination for Sergei Prokofiev which he could let me have for a bit less than the six grand asking price.

It boiled down to this: I was prepared to buy back Free Love for a maximum of 3,000 guineas. I'd never forgive myself if she was sold for a grand, but my limit was necessarily modest. At three grand to buy her back, a discounted four grand for Sergei Prokofiev's services, and another three grand for veterinary fees, transport costs and sundries, I'd be waving goodbye to ten big ones just to get the project off the ground.

I really didn't know what our mare would fetch, but it was hard to be optimistic given that it was only prospective breeders who would take an interest in her. Plenty of buyers were looking for something that could race. I thought she'd make four, and seven or eight would be a real result.

The stallion parade progressed at a leisurely pace, delaying the start of the sale, so we retreated to the restaurant for a warming cup of tea with Patrick and Sally, who had travelled down from York to witness the final chapter of the Free Love story. The last time I had seen the couple was on Ladies' Day at the Ebor meeting in August when my only health concern was my achilles tendon. Less than six months later I had a terminal cancer diagnosis.

I greeted my northern friends warmly and dealt with their enquiry about my health with a shrug of the shoulders and a reply that intimated that I had known better times. After that, I quickly moved the conversation on to horses. I knew that when I disappeared to the toilet or went outside to the parade ring, poor Jennie would be left to provide a detailed medical update. I found it easier to avoid the subject and concentrate instead on the job in hand.

The first lots were ready to be presented and I wandered into the sales ring which is housed in a large, enclosed, octagonal amphitheatre. I found a spot in the banked seating with ease; it was far from a bumper crowd. I watched the early lots enter from the left in one ownership and depart to the right in new hands. First up was Warmhearted, a reasonably well-bred mare who had won on the flat and was being sold as a broodmare. She had been covered by a minor sire, Portamento, but was not believed to be in foal. The seven-year-old daughter of Invincible Spirit made a paltry 2,500 guineas.

The early exchanges suggested that there was money for horses who were still in training – the admirably named Trouser The Cash attracted a top bid of 6,500 guineas despite a lowly rating of 59 – but it was harder work for potential broodmares. I tried to convince myself that there would surely be money for a four-time winner who had reached a career-high rating of 90. But, although Free Love's racing record looked well ahead of most of the horses in the catalogue, it was the absence of black type in her immediate family that was the sticking point. Her long absence from the racecourse didn't help either.

I returned to the others who were still in the restaurant and gave them the sobering news about how the first lots had fared. I had a brief conversation with Eloise Penny and her father, John, the founders of Heart of the South Racing, the organisation that introduced me to small scale ownership fifteen years ago via the hopeless Clear Daylight, a horse who avoided the frame on seven occasions before retiring to a farm in Kent. Fifth place in a class 6 nursery handicap at Kempton was the best the creature could manage, but I had been bitten. I wanted more, and over the next ten years had tiny shares in several more Heart of the South horses.

Bumping into Eloise and John made me feel that the wheel had turned full circle.

Time passed, and from the vantage point of the restaurant, which is adjacent to the outside paddock, I could see the horses parading; the small, numbered white stickers on their hindquarters indicating that Lots 20 to 30 were already being walked around. It was time.

We all made our way outside and waited for Free Love to appear. The sky was brighter, and here and there the cloud cover was punctuated with a patch of blue. Tara had recruited Danni, one of Mick Appleby's staff who was looking after two horses from Langham, to parade our mare. It turned out to be a wise move as when the pride of The North South Syndicate arrived, she was as fresh as paint, a picture of good health and vivacity. She looked magnificent as she jig-jogged around the paddock, compelling Danni to use all her experience to keep a lid on the mare's exuberance.

Lot 35 was called forward, so I decided to enter the sales ring building and secure a good pitch directly opposite the auctioneer's rostrum. If I was required to bid, I wanted to make sure that I was clearly visible to the man with the gavel. Patrick, Sally, Jennie and Pete soon appeared, and took up a position near the auctioneer. I gave them a wave as Lot 38 departed, sold for a respectable 10,000 guineas.

There was just enough time for a final stock-take, to turn over the figures in my head, and mentally reiterate my strategy. I knew I should just let go. Even if I was able to secure Free Love for buttons and put together a little breeding syndicate to offset the considerable costs involved, it would be more than three years before the mare's first offspring was ready to race. That might be longer than I had left. But I was unwilling to let her go for a pittance and, in the final seconds before Lot 40 entered the ring, I promised myself that I'd go to 3,000 guineas but not a penny more.

Free Love entered the ring and started to parade. She was still quite fresh, playfully throwing her head about as she walked around the perfect oval of straw in the middle of the ring. She looked great. I just needed two other people to share that view; a pair of bidders to do battle with each other.

The auctioneer's preamble included some of the things we had discussed a couple of hours earlier. 'Next up is Lot 40, Free Love, a four-time winning daughter of Equiano from a family of winners. Tough and genuine, she'll make a wonderful broodmare. Who'll start me at ten? Five? Two?'

It is normal for auctioneers to start by asking for ten knowing full well that the opening bid will be a thousand, and this was no exception. It wasn't long before the electronic display board showed 1,000 guineas. We had lift-off. I waited until Free Love had completed half a circuit of the ring to see how things progressed. The auctioneer was rattling out his lines, exhorting those present to get involved, but despite his best efforts to start a bidding war, nothing was happening.

It was time to intervene. I raised a hand and the auctioneer announced that 1,500 guineas were now the bid. It didn't take long for two thousand to be registered. Although there were two people taking a serious interest in the mare, one of them was me. I made a second and final bid. The display board showed 2,500 guineas and at that price Free Love was mine. A few seconds later, 3,000 guineas was on display and my four-year love affair with the bay daughter of Equiano and Peace And Love was over.

The auctioneer tried valiantly to drum up more business, but the gavel came down without a further bid and, after taking one more turn, Free Love disappeared through the side exit and vanished from my life forever.

Free Love cools down following her disappointing workout while being prepared for her final season. March 2021.

Theo Ladd and the North South Syndicate ahead of Free Love's seasonal debut at Windsor, June 2021

The author with Peter Smith at Ayr Harbour following Free Love's tilt at the Land O'Burns Stakes, June 2021.

Free Love parades before entering the sales ring at tattersalls, February 2022

8 Last Word

Two days after the sale I was in hospital with acute kidney injury. I didn't feel great at Newmarket, so it came as no surprise when I received a phone call from the Pine Cancer Unit at Darent Valley Hospital telling me that my Saturday morning blood test had flagged up some serious concerns about my one remaining kidney and I needed to be admitted immediately.

I delayed my departure by 20 minutes and stayed glued to the telly to catch L'Homme Presse's impressive victory in the Grade 1 Scilly Isles Novices' Chase at Sandown. My procrastination turned out to be far from life-threatening as there was little sense of urgency when I arrived at the hospital. The route to a bed in a ward was via A&E where I languished for 12 hours before I was wheeled into the Poplar Unit at about four o'clock in the morning. It seemed a crazy way to manage an 'urgent' admission.

The next two months were miserable. I got over the kidney problem, but a few weeks later more blood tests revealed a struggling liver and in early March I was back in hospital. I lost 21lbs during a 20-day period when everything I ate came back up three hours later. You could set your watch by my vomiting routine. The doctors weren't sure what was going on but, after various scans and tests, they concluded that an adverse reaction to the immunotherapy drugs which I started in mid-January was the only plausible explanation.

During that second period in hospital I'd never felt more ill in my life. Before it was ruled out, I thought the most likely explanation for my problems was the spread of cancer to other parts of my body. I was bracing myself for the worst. I fretted about all the things I had left undone. I worried about the afterlife. Was there one? I don't think many bookmakers were offering odds on that eternal question. But more than anything, I was overwhelmed with a deep sadness for the love and friendship I would be unable to give to Jennie because of my absence from her life.

I had time to mull over all sorts of morbid stuff, which was understandable as, at one point, when every part of my body seemed to be failing me, I really thought I was dying.

Thankfully, things began to turn around and by the end of March I was back home celebrating my 64th birthday, albeit in suitably low-key style. By mid-April I was put on a different immunotherapy treatment and days later I was at Newmarket's Craven meeting to see Native Trail consolidate his position as favourite for the 2,000 Guineas when he won the season's first important Classic trial in emphatic style.

Although my terminal cancer diagnosis hung heavily over me, life gradually returned to some sort of normality. There's only so much time you can spend thinking about your mortality when the grass is crying out to be cut and the dishwasher needs emptying.

Amidst all my health preoccupations, which included a third and final operation on my heel, I didn't forget about Free Love. When the gavel fell and she left my ownership, I was numb and in no state to hear what the auctioneer said about the buyer. Tara thought she heard 'Whitby Stud', a name that wasn't familiar to me, but on the way home Paul Davis, who was watching the sale online, sent me a message telling me that he was sure Ed Harper, the Director of Whitsbury Manor Stud had made the final bid.

During the early part of my first stay in hospital, I emailed Ed who confirmed that he had bought Free Love for somebody who wanted to have a go at breeding and the plan was to have her covered by Sergei Prokofiev. It was either a case of great minds thinking alike, or fools seldom differing. On the one hand I was pleased that Free Love had found a good home and I could keep tabs on her progress. But there was also regret about what could have been had I been a bit bolder, a bit more determined to pursue the adventure of breeding. Maybe that was unfair as time, rather than money, was the commodity in shortest supply.

Come Epsom Derby Day in early June, I felt in pretty good shape. I had made tentative returns to the golf course and swimming pool and was looking forward to a summer of being out and about and doing things. On the day of the race, we invited about 15 close friends to help us christen our new garden. The popping of champagne corks paused at 4.30pm to allow everybody to watch Desert Crown waltz home in the 'Blue Riband' of the turf.

The garden refurbishment had cost a small fortune, but it was all paid for out of the Range Rover money. I didn't tell you about that bizarre windfall. During the pandemic, when all football was played behind closed doors and matches were live- streamed, I regularly paid my tenner to watch Charlton Athletic's dour progress in League One. The club was in new ownership following a period when a bunch of shady characters took charge of affairs. East Street Investments appeared to specialise in profligacy and corruption, and one unedifying stunt was the purchase of a fleet of brand-new Range Rovers which were given to company cronies for their personal use.

In September 2020, Thomas Sangaard, a reputable Danish businessman, became Charlton Athletic's new owner and was quick to start the Herculean task of sweeping clean the mess left behind by his dodgy predecessors. Sangaard promptly sold six of the seven Range Rovers but kept one back as a lavish raffle prize. Every time a Charlton fan bought a live-stream match they were entered into the draw.

I thought nothing of it until on Boxing Day 2020 my mobile phone buzzed and I found myself talking to Scott Minto, Charlton

TV's anchorman, who told me that my name had been drawn out of the electronic hat and I was now the proud owner of a top-of-the-range car whose bodywork was covered in garish CAFC decals.

I never got to drive the thing. When Jennie and I went to collect our prize at The Valley, my right foot was in a surgical boot following my first achilles tendon op. It was a nervous drive home given the size and value of the car, and although we appreciated its luxury (Jennie felt she could get used to tootling around in it) we quickly agreed that we would sell it and use the windfall to fund various projects that were already in the pipeline - our garden makeover, help for Joe at university, replacing the car, and a host of improvements to the house. There might even be a bit left for a share in a horse. More important than all of that was the additional help it would provide for Jennie when the time came for her to cope on her own.

That day seemed to edge even nearer when by mid-July my latest scan results indicated a lesion on the brain which was almost certainly cancerous. The following day, when a barely believable and record breaking 40.3 degrees centigrade was recorded in rural Lincolnshire, I found myself in the cool and serene setting of the multifaith room at Darent Valley Hospital. It's a short walk from the Pine Cancer Therapy Unit to this small room devoted to prayer and contemplation and I've been a frequent visitor of late. There's not much there, just a wooden altar, a shelf of sacred texts, a tabernacle and a couple of chairs, but on the way out I was drawn to the prayer tree, a forked branch stripped of bark and sanded to a smooth finish. On it hung entreaties written on the cards provided. One read, 'Please God, help me through my loss and give me comfort'. The thought of Jennie writing something similar one day was unbearable.

And what can I tell you about Jennie Linnett? You won't find a more unassuming, vivacious and generous spirit on God's earth and I have been lucky enough to be loved by her for more than forty years. It's been my privilege to return that love as we've negotiated life's ups and downs together. It was a big down we were now experiencing, and I could put up with any amount of morale draining hospital visits if it meant that the active time we had left together could be extended, if only by a bit. We both knew that the vision of a long, idyllic retirement had faded, but we were committed to making the most of what we had. That's how it's always been.

It would be impossible for me to pick out the highlights of my life with Jennie and our three children, Matthew, Celia and Joseph. I have so many wonderful memories of holidays in Normandy, the celebration of family milestones and, of course, trips to the races.

Which brings me to racehorses and what these books are all about. It's taken me nearly a quarter of a million words to write a love letter to the sport of racing and it all started nearly 50 years ago when I was sixteen and had a summer holiday job on a construction site. I took an interest in an older workmate's daily attempts to pick a few winners. I became intrigued and joined the lunchtime ritual of studying the form in The Daily Mirror so I could make my own selections, even if I was too young to bet.

That was the start, but it doesn't explain why I became so caught up in the world of horseracing; why I developed such an intense, almost obsessive interest in the sport. But I have an answer of sorts: I fell in love with the thoroughbred racehorse. I was mesmerised by its grace, power and speed. I have no words to describe the exhilaration I experienced when witnessing Sea Pigeon surge to victory in the 1981 Champion Hurdle or Dancing Brave swoop late in the 1986 Arc de Triomphe. Having a few quid on wasn't essential, but it certainly heightened the thrill of it all and reinforced the feeling that these equine superstars belonged to me, in some way.

I've had many equine heroes, but the dream was always to own a racehorse, or part of one, when I managed to cobble together enough money to give it a go. I didn't know if I would ever be able to afford it, but I eventually achieved my lifetime ambition through Free Love and The North South Syndicate.

A single minute at Catterick Bridge Racecourse on Saturday 22nd September 2018 sums up what it all meant to me. It was as if decades of passionate engagement were distilled into the 60.08 seconds it took to run a modest class 5 nursery handicap. Fifty yards from the finish, Free Love stormed into the lead, and I knew she was about to win her first race. It was a magical moment as she crossed the line with half a length to spare. All had been accomplished and although the bay Equiano mare has left me now, she will never be forgotten. I will carry vivid memories of the adventure with me to the grave, which may be nearer than I would like. But there's no initial bitterness, no sense of injustice. That's not to say that I'm ready to leave.

I know in those last few days and hours I'll experience pain and fear, and I'm sure my phlegmatic approach to my trials will be abandoned. But I've enjoyed every glorious moment of being alive. Yes, there have been lows, but they only serve to sharpen the appreciation of the highs. It's been a fabulous ride during which I've loved and been loved, and who can ask for more than that?

Before tendon operations, global pandemics and a terminal diagnosis. Jennie and Tony Linnett posing in front of the statue of Special Cargo at Sandown Park, July 2019